other titles in the

irreverent guide

series

Frommer's®

irreverent guide to Walt Disney World

3rd Edition

By
Diane Bair
and
Pamela Wright

A BALLIETT & FITZGERALD BOOK
IDG BOOKS WORLDWIDE, INC.

a disclaimer

Prices fluctuate in the course of time, and travel information changes under the impact of the varied and volatile factors that influence the travel industry. Neither the author nor the publisher can be held responsible for the experiences of readers while traveling. Readers are invited to write to the publisher with ideas, comments, and suggestions for future editions.

about the author

Diane Bair and Pamela Wright are authors of more than a dozen travel books. They also write about travel and the outdoors for several magazines, including *Family Fun, Parenting, Better Homes & Gardens,* and *Backpacker.*

Balliett & Fitzgerald, Inc.

Creative Director: Lynne Arany/Production Manager: Maria Fernandez/Production Editor: Michael Walters/Project Editor: Kristen Couse/Line Editor: Royce Flippin/Copyeditor: Rick Willett/Proofreaders: Jodi Brandon and Donna Stonecipher/Editorial Interns: Jen Pass, Adam Mazel, and Graham Meyer

IDG Books Worldwide, Inc.

An International Data Group Company
909 Third Avenue
New York, NY 10022

Copyright © 2001 by IDG Books Worldwide, Inc.
Maps © by IDG Books Worldwide, Inc.

ISBN 0-7645-6229-0
ISSN 1520-4316

Interior design contributed to by Tsang Seymour Design Studio

special sales

For general information on IDG Books Worldwide's books in the U.S., please call our Consumer Customer Service department at 1-800-762-2974. For reseller information, including discounts, bulk sales, customized editions, and premium sales, please call our Reseller Customer Service department at 1-800-434-3422.

Manufactured in the United States of America

what's so irreverent?

It's up to you.

You can buy a traditional guidebook with its fluff, its promotional hype, its let's-find-something-nice-to-say-about-everything point of view. Or you can buy an Irreverent guide.

What the Irreverents give you is the lowdown, the inside story. They have nothing to sell but the truth, which includes a balance of good and bad. They praise, they trash, they weigh, and leave the final decisions up to you. No tourist board, no chamber of commerce will ever recommend them.

Our writers are insiders who feel passionate about the cities they live in, and have strong opinions they want to share with you. They take a special pleasure leading you where other guides fear to tread.

How irreverent are they? One of our authors insisted on writing under a pseudonym. "I couldn't show my face in town again if I used my own name," she told me. "My friends would never speak to me." Such is the price of honesty. She, like you, should know she'll always have a friend at Frommer's.

Warm regards,

Michael Spring

Michael Spring
Publisher

contents

introduction

Love it or loathe it, the Walt Disney Company has become a giant, mouse-eared symbol of American culture. Last year, Disney attractions logged more than 65 million visitors from around the globe. Of course, there are still a few holdouts: Like people who brag that they don't own a television set, some snobbier-than-thou types enjoy snorting that they've never, ever done Disney. "It's so *fake*, so…*happy*," shuddered one colleague, when asked why he'd never set foot in the theme parks. Another (decidedly anti-Mickey) chum summed up the Walt Disney World experience with three words: "Grotesque and appalling." You betcha. And those are just two of the many things we love about the place.

Indeed, what's *not* to love? Orlando is faux, it's fun, it's blissfully over-the-top. Think Vegas, without the sleaze: Instead of battling with one-armed bandits, you're kept busy dodging dinosaurs and evading attacking aliens; here, the unreal becomes completely real, if only for a few seconds. The big trend in theme parks nowadays is "total immersion" adventures, where the line between the Real World and virtual reality becomes disconcertingly blurred. (Isn't that why everyone took drugs in the '60s? Sounds like the perfect prescription for family fun to us.) The newest, most cutting-edge rides, just launched at

Orlando's theme parks, take this concept to dizzying heights. Universal's Spider-Man Adventure, considered the most technically complex of the park's attractions, aims to give riders the illusion that they're flying through the air, as they leap from the tops of skyscrapers, narrowly escaping destruction at every turn. Bring the seasickness bag or, if the grandparents are in tow, the nitroglycerin; during the death-defying ride, guests are rolled, jerked, pitched forward, and tilted in their seats like so many human pinballs.

Once you've stopped hyperventilating, still more adventure awaits at the Triceratops Encounter, where you'll be shoved in the face of a dinosaur so lifelike, it moves, breathes, bellows, blinks, reacts to light, and even shows emotion. To bring their dinos to life, Universal employed the same company that built the robotic arm for NASA's space shuttle. Over at Disney's Animal Kingdom, meanwhile, they've re-created an African safari experience so real, all it lacks is malarial mosquitoes. Talk for a few minutes to the ride-engineering types who build these attractions, and you'll hear high-flying phrases like "simulation technology," "roving base simulator," "hydraulic physics," and "space-age robotics." Child's play, it ain't. All this, and giant, pants-wearing rodents, too.

Of course, kids go along with this concept from the get-go. Adults, on the other hand, can't help but feel a tad cynical about a place that, after all, is designed chiefly to separate them from large sums of hard-earned cash. It's all intensely, crassly commercial—where else can you buy pasta shaped like Mickey Mouse ears?—and the presentation is all so slick and seamless that it's a little scary. It's hard to get past the fact that these theme parks are shrewdly calibrated utopias where every thrill is manufactured, every lawsuit anticipated, every cost subjected to yield-management analysis. Long lines may be the only problem they haven't solved yet. Then again, perhaps to a park pro with a movie mentality, a long line may just be proof that you've got a hit on your hands.

But hey, you're going to Disney World—so lighten up, already. It's time to suspend your politically correct outrage at the homogenization of American culture, and your ecologically based horror at the fact that, since your last visit, a few more of Florida's last remaining undeveloped acres have disappeared. Look at the bright side: The park is wholesome, it's clean, and it's highly unlikely that you'll be massacred by machete-wielding locals on *this* vacation. How petty to complain about a place where Mickey Mouse and Cinderella get to live happily ever after! Take a cue from the kids, and let the magic do its number on you. No matter what their parents' attitude, for youngsters, the Disney Magic is just that: magic. Disney's imagineers know that the kids are still a primary engine that drives the parks, and they cater to this audience with expert abandon. Many youngsters remember their first Magic Kingdom vacation with the same reverence reserved for their first two-wheel bike and visit from the tooth fairy. Whatever you think of the Disney mystique, it's hard not to feel good watching your children's eyes widen as they crane their necks up at Space Mountain, or whirl, thrilled, on the flying Dumbos. Disney counts on this kid appeal to keep pulling in the families year after year, but who cares, when the kids are having this much fun?

The fact that Walt Disney World built a wild animal park carries a certain irony, considering that the company is largely responsible for altering Orlando's natural landscape. Surrounded now by high-maintenance foliage shaped like Mickey, it's hard to imagine this area when it was all mangrove swamp, orange groves, and grasslands. Those vistas are long gone by now, gobbled up not only by manicured resorts but by strip malls, restaurants, motels, gator shows, water parks, and go-cart tracks. Kissimmee, the town closest to Disney World, was once populated with cattlemen and their herds. Today, the closest you'll get to a cow in these parts will be at the Ponderosa Steakhouse All-U-Can-Eat buffet.

So bring your sense of humor with you, and accept the fact that you may feel ambivalent about this theme park version of virtual reality. Just three pieces of practical advice: (1) Once you do make your peace and dive in, don't, as sometimes happens, get overly ambitious and get sucked into the we-gotta-do-everything compulsion that can prevail around here. Concentrate on your must-sees, and take in the rest only if you have the time and energy. Skip the lines if they look too long, damn it. Unless you've allotted a good five days just for theme parks, you won't see everything anyway. (2) Don't confuse fun with free-spirited spontaneity. (After all, Disney certainly doesn't.) Take a fairly organized approach, or else you'll end up wandering around, eyes glazed over, by mid-morning. (3) Don't let a thwarted itinerary ruin your mood. One of our best trips to Disney was with our then three-year-old girl who wanted to ride the Mad Hatter's Tea Party teacups over and over again. That was pretty much all we did—but she was the picture of joy.

Disney won again....And so did we.

Orlando/Walt Disney World Area Orientation

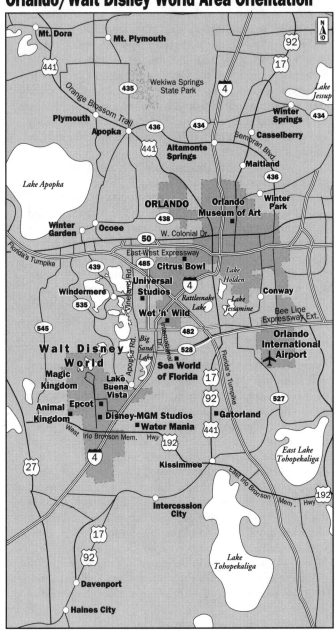

you probably didn't know

What do Viagra and Walt Disney World have in common?... Answer: Both require you to wait an hour for a two-minute ride. Unless you take a VIP tour (see Diversions) or you just won the Super Bowl, you can't avoid waiting in lines around here. During the busiest week of the year (Christmas till New Year's), the Disney parks can suffer gridlock so severe it would shock even Manhattanites. There are times when the searing Florida heat and the endless tank-topped crowds can seem like a preview of hell itself—not, certainly, "The Happiest Place on Earth," as Disney calls itself. The lines are especially hideous at Disney's most popular park, the Magic Kingdom, or maybe it just seems that way because you're dodging double strollers at every turn. And it's not just Disney, either: When Universal Studios' newest park, Islands of Adventure, is busy—which it nearly always is—waits of 90 minutes to get into rides are not uncommon. (Could relief be on the horizon? See p. 8.) Long lines are also a fact of life at Disney-MGM Studios, though the process seems to run a tad more efficiently there. On the other hand, you'll spend very little time waiting in lines at Sea World compared to the other theme parks, a big plus for those who'd rather avoid this particular stress inducer while on vacation. The action at Sea World centers around the scheduled shows; you plan your itinerary around them, and spend the rest of your time touring walk-through exhibits like *Penguin Encounter* and *Manatees: The Last Generation?* Most likely, you'll only have to queue up at two places: the Kraken roller coaster and the Atlantis thrill rides. The big Sea World shows are held in outdoor stadiums, too, so you can see how big the crowds are as you walk up to enter. Elsewhere, seemingly short lines can be deceiving. You'll soon discover that for most shows, getting in the door is only the first step— once inside, you're herded into three more rooms before hitting the main theater. In each "staging area," as they call them, there are attractions (or, more accurately, distractions) to keep you amused while you wait for the main event. If all this hurry-up-and-wait causes you to burn out mid-day, here's our advice: Take an afternoon break (for a late lunch, a swim, or a nap) and then return to the park around 5 or 6pm. You'll feel refreshed, perky, and ready for action—just when most everyone else is heading home.

How far in advance should I plan my trip?...

Planning a Disney/Orlando vacation entails about as much spontaneity as throwing a Martha Stewart Christmas party. Rental cars are often booked up six months in advance, while reservations at the best-deal resorts must be made a year ahead of time (and sometimes more); Disney takes restaurant reservations 60 days in advance (though it really isn't necessary to call that far ahead); and if you simply want to receive information from Orlando's Official Visitor Center (tel 407/363–5872 or 800/551–0181), you'll have to give them 4 to 6 weeks just to mail it to you. Of course, if you're web-savvy, you can accomplish all of this with a few clicks of the mouse. Visit www.disneyworld.com and make reservations on line; for Orlando info and links, go to www.Go2orlando.com. If you're the adventurous type, wait until the last minute and take your chances. With 99,000 hotel rooms (and counting), you'll find *someplace* to stay, provided you're not too picky.

Is it possible to do Disney on the cheap?...

We have a couple of, um, "friends" who manage to pare down

the cost of their Orlando getaways to a few dollars a day, but this requires mooching off family and friends, and walking a very fine line between what's legal and illegal. Aside from shady maneuvers, there are several ways to see Cinderella's Castle for less than a princely sum. Here are our best tips: 1. Be flexible and a bit adventurous. If you absolutely must stay in a specific hotel or resort, you'll most likely pay through the nose. Instead, look around and negotiate. Better yet, when you pull into town, head straight for the Orlando Visitor Center on International Drive and ask for their "little black book." This book is a list of hotels that have dumped vacant rooms for the night, often at discounts of up to 50 percent or more off regular rates. 2. Time your vacation for off-peak value seasons (for the best times to go, see below). 3. Look for hotels that offer extras, like free breakfast (at some hotels, such as Holiday Inn, kids eat free all day), free shuttles to the major parks and attractions (this will save on parking fees), and free shuttles to and from the airport. 4. If you're planning on a night out, check for OTIX!. These half-price, same-day tickets to more than 90 cultural, music, and theater events throughout the Orlando area can be obtained at the Visitor Center. 5. You can also save big by packing drinks, snacks—even lunch—for the day. (Freeze juice/water bottles ahead of time to keep them cold.) Technically, this is against the rules, but nobody's ever frisked us—yet. 6. Finally, whatever you do, avoid buying souveniers at the park. We know, we know, every ride dumps you smack into the gift shop, but you can pick up your Mickey hats and Goofy ears at any one of the gazillion discount shops in Orlando.

When is the best time to visit Disney World?...

Picking the best time to visit Disney World is becoming more and more of a crap shoot. It's always crowded, and you can invariably count on lines. If you can travel off-season (any time school is in session), you can save big bucks and enjoy the parks when they're not choked with little guests. The downside to off-season visits? The parks close earlier, and some of the evening pageants are suspended. If you're really crowd-phobic, go the week after Labor Day (or right after any major holiday) or during the period between Thanksgiving weekend and the week before Christmas—that's the slowest time at Disney

World. At all costs, no matter what you have to do, DO NOT plan your trip for the Christmas holiday week. This is Disney's busiest week of the year—a time when you don't want to be anywhere near this place. Summers (yes, when central Florida turns into a sweltering sweat-box) are also busy, since the kids are out of school and family vacations are under way. In January and February, the international crowd rolls into town, and the prices are lower ("super-value season," in Disney parlance), but once you start getting into those February, March, and April school breaks, look out. Easter? Forget about it. May is better than most months, although Florida school kids arrive in droves on their end-of-year field trips. September through early December is value season again. If there's a big convention in town, though, all bets are off. The convention high season runs from January through June.

Am I hallucinating, or does that corn flake have mouse ears?... Call it cute, or call it subliminal seduction, but we're told Disney's Imagineers subtly hide Mickey Mouse silhouettes in plain sight all over Disney World. Way Hitchcockian, no? These "Hidden Mickeys" are an inside joke among pranksterish Disney cast members (i.e., employees). You'll catch them lurking about where you'd least expect them: There's a plush Mickey tucked away in the Tower of Terror, a broccoli Mickey in the Body Wars mural in Epcot, a Viking sporting mouse ears in Epcot's Maelstrom, and so on. So, if you're sharp-eyed, Mickey-obsessed, or just bored silly, see if you can ferret out a Hidden Mickey or two along the way. You can even post your sighting on the official Hidden Mickey website (www.hiddenmickeys.org); they'll tell you if it's the real thing, or just wishful thinking on your part.

What's this I hear about no waiting at Disney attractions?... Credit Disney for trying to do something about the horrendous lines at their theme parks. They've installed something called Fastpass, which is currently available at a dozen or so of their most popular rides and shows. Here's how it works: Early in the day, you go to the Fastpass turnstile (located at the ride or show's entrance), insert your park ticket into a slot, and out comes a free Fastpass ticket, telling you what time to return. Sort of a ride by appointment. At the appointed time, simply return to the attraction and head for the Fastpass entrance, leaving the poor chumps in the regular line staring at your dust. Instead of waiting, say, an hour to board Test Track, you only have to wait about 15 minutes. Not bad…until everybody catches on to the scheme. Even now, your Fastpass may well instruct you to come back in 5 hours, if all the earlier Fastpass times are filled. On the plus side, using the Fastpass gives some structure to your day—it's perfect for type-A families, and those prone to Line Rage. On the negative side, your fun day at the theme park will take on all the spontaneity of Marine boot camp. And, wow, what a coincidence! Universal has recently introduced its own version of a fast-track ticket, called "Express Pass." Express Pass is free with the purchase of Universal's two- or three-day Escape Pass, and it promises faster access to selected rides between 7 and 10am daily, with a maximum wait of 15 minutes. Current Escape Pass prices are: two-day pass, $84.95 adult/$69.96 child; three-day pass, $99.95 adult/$79.95 child. Unused days have no expiration date, but are not transferable to other visitors. Call it whatever you want; anything that reduces that cattle-drive feeling is okay by us.

Where can I get a room with an ocean view?…

Don't laugh—this is reportedly the most frequently asked question at the Orlando Visitor Center. Apparently lots of folks don't realize that Orlando is inland. Sorry, folks, the closest oceanfront room is about 90 miles away, in the Cocoa Beach area near Spaceport U.S.A. The Big Red Boat does not drop you off at the docks of Disney World. Still, if waterfront digs are what you crave, those you can have. (We just can't guarantee that the water is a natural feature of the landscape.) There are lakes and waterways everywhere in the Orlando area: There are more than 125 lakes inside the city limits, while the surrounding region boasts a couple thousand more. And that doesn't even count the innumerable water parks, fountains, and pools. Disney resorts that offer rooms with water views include the Wilderness Lodge, the Yacht and Beach Club Resorts, Port Orleans, Dixie Landings, Caribbean Beach, Fort Wilderness Campground, the BoardWalk inn and villas, the Polynesian, the Contemporary, and the Grand Floridian. The Dolphin and Swan resorts face a lagoon and share a sliver of beach between them. Take a peek behind some of the budget-priced lodgings on U.S. 192 in

Kissimmee (Golden Link Motel, Hosteling International Orlando Resort) and you'll see bustling Lake Cecile. And at Westgate Lakes in Orlando, guests have a large lakefront beach with waterskiing, paddle boats, and fishing at their doorstep.

I wanna live here. I'm huggable. How do I get to be Mickey?... Yeah, and it's always been our dream to be Snow White. Sad to say, even if you can tolerate being hugged by 10,000 children per day, and can sign autographs wearing oversized rubber gloves—never mind wearing a huge head and a prickly costume in sweltering heat—you can't be Mickey. Or Minnie, or Goofy, or any of the other big cheeses at WDW, for that matter. As a Disney PR person explained it, "You can't be Mickey. Mickey just…is." She stuck to this story, and we're convinced she believes it. However, if your ambitions are a bit more realistic—say, you want to pick up trash at Epcot, or work at one of the resort's restaurants—give a call to Disney's Casting Center (tel 407/828–1000). You can listen to a tape-recording of WDW's job opportunities, which are updated weekly, and arrange for an interview. Or—here's a real tip—you can walk right into the Casting Center (near the main entrance of the park). You'll find postings with job offerings (some not available over the phone) and you might even be able to arrange an on-the-spot interview.

Where can I get discounted tickets to the attractions?... The first rule of Orlando is, never, ever pay full price. The one exception—and it's a biggie—is Disney World. But there are scads of deals to be had on admission tickets to Sea World, Universal Studios and Islands of Adventure, Gatorland, dinner theaters, clubs, golf courses, water parks, and more. Check with your hotel first; often the concierge or front desk will have discount coupons for guests. The Orlando Visitor Center always offers 10 to 25 percent off on Sea World and Universal Studios admissions, and on a handful of other local attractions as well. Pick up one of the many travel guidebooks and flyers you'll see lying around everywhere—they're full of offers. An even better idea is to call the Visitor Center ahead of time (tel 800/551–0181), and they'll mail you a slew of their latest coupon books. Inquire about the free Orlando Magicard, which entitles you to a variety of savings at more than 80 attractions, stores, restaurants, and accommodations. You can also purchase Disney World tickets at the Visitor Center, hotels, and shops, but remember, the big boys don't play ball in the discount field.

We're thinking about getting married at Disney...

You and the rest of the starry-eyed world, it seems. *Modern Bride* magazine recently ranked Orlando as the number-one honeymoon destination in the world. (We won't even get into why newlyweds would choose to stand in line for an alien encounter rather than, well, do other things.) So why not have the whole ceremony here? For those who love prefab romance, Disney offers "fairy-tale" wedding packages: The ceremony takes place in a multimillion-dollar wedding pavilion built on an island in the Seven Seas Lagoon, with Cinderella's Castle as the backdrop. Brides select all the various elements needed to make it the day of their dreams. A variety of fantasy receptions are available, too, including ones with *Beauty and the Beast* or *Aladdin* themes. The ultimate (perhaps in insanity) is Cinderella's Ball: The bride arrives in a glass carriage drawn by six white ponies, a costumed fairy godmother and stepsisters mingle with the guests at the reception, and dessert is served in a white chocolate slipper. Kind of makes your teeth hurt, huh? If your tastes—and budget—are a *little* more real, but you still have to get hitched before leaving Orlando, in order to fulfill that weird clause in Uncle Fred's will and come into the big inheritance, there are a number of local wedding chapels and services. Try Crownline Wedding Services (tel 407/354–0985) or Just Marry! Inc. (tel 407/629–2747, 800/986–2779). Orlando's Official Visitor Center (tel 407/363-5872, 800/551–0181) is also ready to assist.

Is it worth getting up at the crack of dawn?...

You betcha. Here's why: If you're staying at a Disney resort, you get a special incentive to rise and shine, in the form of the "Surprise Morning," where they open a Disney theme park an hour early (on a rotating schedule) as a perk for Disney resort guests only. Universal does the same thing, offering early admission and "Front of the Line" privileges (until 10am) to *their* hotel guests. (Plus, 7 to 10am is when their Express Pass program kicks in; see above.) In spite of this, *everybody* rolls into the parks in mid-morning. So if you're hell-bent on doing the hottest rides without spending all day waiting in line, pass up your morning shower (thanks to the special effects, you'll wind up smelling like propane anyway), skip the 'do (you'll get soaking wet several times during the day on the river raft and "splash" attractions), and plan to arrive at the park a half hour before its scheduled opening time. Hit the road at the crack of dawn, scarf down that bagel in the car, and sprint to those turnstiles. Immediately go to the hottest rides (Aerosmith's Rock 'n' Roller Coaster, Space Mountain, Spider-Man, The Hulk, Dr. Doom) and have at it, while everybody else is still navigating the parking lots. We once got to the Magic Kingdom more than an hour before the official opening time on the day after Christmas (mega-high season), parked in the first row, and arrived with the maintenance crew. We did all the major rides, without waiting, by 11am, just as the park was filling up. Doing Disney is always great, but beating the system is sublime.

Which is better, Universal Studios Florida or Disney-MGM?... This is the question on everyone's lips. We like 'em both, being thrilled that there's something fun and escapist for adults to experience in Theme Park Land. The magic of the movies is an easy sell, of course, but the two parks are surprisingly different—you could do both in the same trip and not be bored. Universal is more of a working movie and TV studio than is Disney-MGM; you'll see more real production work going on in the back-lot sets, should you wish to pay attention. (With Universal's new Islands of Adventure right next door, there's more going on in one location here, too.) Universal also strikes us as a bit hipper than Disney-MGM, with more of an edge. (Example: Islands of Adventure calls one dinosaur attraction "You Bet Jurassic." Walt would be turning over in his grave.) Both parks put on funny, engrossing shows. But—and this is big—Universal has wilder rides, packing an amazing amount of excitement into a few short minutes. Twister, Back to the Future, Jaws, King Kong, the San Francisco earthquake cable-car ride, and Terminator 2 3-D all feature special effects that are simply unparalleled. However, since there's so much to see at Universal Studios (it's bigger and more spread out than Disney-MGM), it's difficult to do it all in one day unless you power-tour. Given the time spent waiting in line for the hottest rides, and the amount of acreage you have to cover to get around the park, it can take a good 10 hours to see everything at Universal Studios. In contrast, Disney-MGM is smaller and more compact, so you can see it all in a mere 8 hours or so. But with the exception of the Twilight Zone Tower of Terror and Aerosmith's Rock 'n' Roller Coaster, Disney-MGM's rides aren't as intense or over-the-top thrilling as Universal's. Overall, we'd give higher marks to Universal, both for pioneering this art form (at Universal Studios Hollywood) and for being a bit more out there.

What happens when the sign says "full" at the theme park?... You mean *after* your five-year-old throws the tantrum and you start panicking? This happens a lot more often than the Disney folk would like to admit: It's Saturday, 10am, and the Magic Kingdom gate attendant tells you there's no more room in the parking lot. Disney water parks, too, are often closed to new arrivals just minutes after the doors open, due to full-capacity crowds. Go before opening and wait in line; finally get in, and wait in more lines. Yikes! Several things can be done, however. You could lie to the attendant: "Uhh, I'm just dropping off someone/picking up someone/meeting someone...." Sometimes it works. Or you can park at a Disney resort and try to sneak onto the boat/bus/monorail, even though you're not a Disney resort guest. Sometimes *that* works. (Of course, if you're staying at a Disney resort, it's no problem to simply take internal transportation into the park.) But by far the smartest move, whether you're a Disney resort guest or not, is simply to adjust your plans: Go back to the hotel and spend a lovely day at the pool. While everyone else is waiting 2 hours for a 5-minute ride on the teacups, you'll be sipping daiquiris and watching little Melinda splash around in the water. Then go back to the park later in the afternoon; often the parking lot opens as the early crowds thin. Or you could just pick another theme park to go to; hell, with nearly 100 attractions and amusements in the area, you certainly won't be left (God forbid!) with nothing to do.

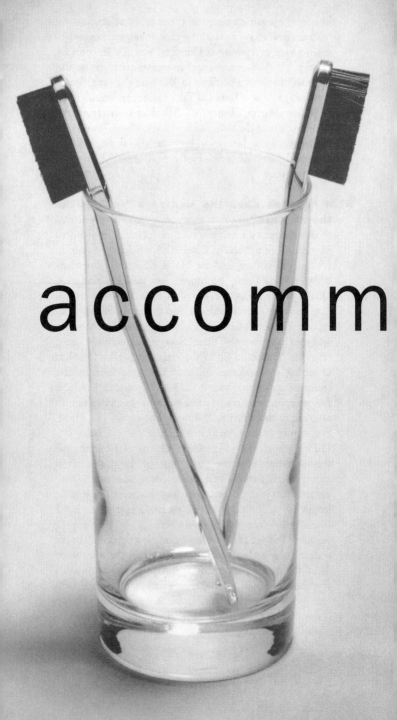

accomm

1
odations

"Deciding where
you're going to stay
during your Disney
World vacation is
probably the single
toughest decision
you'll make."

We've seen perfectly calm, sane friends go absolutely mad after hours—no, days—spent looking over literature, talking to the Disney folk, listening to friends, and searching the web, all to one purpose: Where to stay? The range of options is truly dizzying. Orlando boasts 99,000 hotel/motel rooms, the highest concentration per square mile in the entire country, and by the time you finish reading this paragraph, there'll be more. Disney alone offers 18 full-scale themed hotel properties, with a total of more than 25,000 guest rooms. Universal Studios has entered the accomodations market, too, with its own destination resorts. Universal Studios Escape will eventually include not only Universal's two theme parks (Universal Studios and Islands of Adventure) and CityWalk, its entertainment/restaurant area, but will also feature five brand new on-site hotels (two of them already up and running). No doubt about it, folks, deciding where to bed down can suck the F-word (F stands for fun, okay?) right out of your vacation planning.

In Orlando, you don't merely look for a room. No, no, no....(Of course, if you're so inclined, that would make life easy. You'll find plenty of reasonable, ordinary options around town; think **Red Roof, Comfort Inn, Holiday Inn, Howard Johnson, Hilton, DoubleTree, Days Inn, Marriott, Embassy Suites, Ramada, Radisson, Best Western....** Pick any one—you know what to expect; they're all the same.) To do the Disney experience right, on the other hand, you must first decide what theme you can live with, if only for a few days, and how much it's worth to you. Never mind that there are no mountains in Florida; you can still have a Rocky Mountain–high room at the Wilderness Lodge, a retreat overlooking bubbling hot springs and an erupting geyser. Or soak up Southern-style hospitality at Dixie Landings, a spread of elegant manor homes complete with a Mississippi-style river, banjos strumming, and magnolias blossoming. At Marriott's Orlando World Center or the 1,500-acre Hyatt Regency Grand Cypress resort, you can swim in grottoes and under waterfalls; check into the Port Orleans resort and you can zip down a water slide that drops you out of the mouth of a sea serpent. Sleep in a purple jester's bed studded with jewels at The Castle, or in a tree house tucked in the woods at the Villas at The Disney Institute.

If you want to spend a fortune, the penthouse suite of Disney's Grand Floridian (at a mere $1,500 a night) delivers two very nice bedrooms, a baby grand piano, surround-sound stereo, a full bar, a Jacuzzi tub, turndown service, high tea, hors d'oeuvres and dessert—and there's a view of Cinderella's Castle, too. (Oooh…restless heart, be still.) How about being surrounded by a giant circus tent, with pineapple headboards, parrot lamps, and sea horses (not real) dangling from chandeliers? You'll find it all at the side-by-side Walt Disney World Dolphin and Swan resorts, designed by world-famous architect Michael Graves. If you're looking for quiet elegance instead of hit-you-over-the-head decor, check into the Peabody Hotel, where the atrium lobby soothes the soul with exotic plants, gentle waterfalls, and an eye-catching art collection. Alas, even the Peabody has a gimmick: the ducks (they're real). Each morning and evening, a 75-foot red carpet is rolled out, and the fabled Peabody Ducks—descendants of ducks that once graced the fountain of Memphis's original Peabody in the 1930s—waddle to the Orlando lobby's marble fountain, where they spend the day before heading back to the Royal Duck Palace for bed. (Turndown service at the Peabody also includes filling your bathtub and floating a yellow rubber ducky in it.) Here's where to start: Request the free *Official Accommodations Guide* from the Orlando/Orange County Convention and Visitors Bureau by calling 800/551–0181.

Let's Make a Deal

Middle Eastern oil moguls could take lessons from Orlando hoteliers. The $60 you paid for a room during "value season" will surely double—or more—in price when the kids are out of school. Location may be everything in the rest of the world, but here, it's timing, timing, timing. Go off-season and you can name your price; but plan to go when everyone else does and you'd better make reservations at least six months ahead of time. Some of the more popular resorts book rooms up to a year in advance. That said, you can nearly always negotiate the price, whatever the time of year. Ask for a better deal, and chances are you'll get it. (This is generally not true, however, with Disney properties; they're sticklers when it comes to room rates.) If you're really feeling adventurous, roll into town without a room reservation and head to Orlando's **Official Visitor Center** at 8723 International Drive (at the corner of Austrian Row). Then, ask if there are any rooms currently available. Orlando hotels phone the center each day, looking for folks to fill their properties. The Visitor Center's **"little black book"** lists available hotel rooms, with prices often slashed 50 percent or more. On a recent visit during peak spring break time, we snatched a two-bedroom, full-kitchen condo (nice digs), just minutes from Disney World, for $79 a night. The regular rate would have been double that. Web-savvy surfers can get the latest prices and book airfare, lodging, even theme park tickets on-line. Start with Disney's official website, www.disney world.com. You might check out hotel brokers, too, who snatch unsold rooms and offer them at deeply discounted rates. Some to try: **Discount Hotels America** (407/294–9600, www.discounthotelsamerica.com); **Accommodations USA** (407/931–0003); and **Orlando Magic Vacations** (888/399–2665). If you don't mind doing a bit of calculation, check into the various Disney World/Universal Studios/Orlando package deals. Several airline companies offer Orlando/Disney World packages complete with airfare and lodging, including **US Airways Vacations** (800/451–6767; www.usairwaysvaca tions.com) and **Delta Dream Vacations** (800/221–6666; www.deltaairlines.com).

For people who just can't get enough of the Mouse, the Disney experience extends beyond the Orlando area with the **Disney Cruise Line.** Two ships, *Disney Magic* and *Disney Wonder,* both docked at Port Canaveral, Florida, offer three- and four-day cruises to the Bahamas, as well as seven-day land and sea vacations. Also new is a seven-day Caribbean cruise (can you picture Minnie in a sarong?) with a stop at Castaway Cay, Disney's private Bahamian island. For information, call 800/769–7918.

Is There a Right Address?

There are five major lodging areas in Orlando to choose from: the **U.S. 192 strip,** situated southeast of Disney World along the road to Kissimmee; the **International Drive area,** which lies east of the World; the **Downtown Disney Village Resort area,** just outside of Disney World; the **Disney resorts area** inside Disney World itself, which includes 18 on-site hotels, and **Universal Studios' new resort area.** The U.S. 192 strip offers the most economical choices—including not only all the major chain hotels, but also a selection of local mom-and-pop motels. You can find many rooms on the strip for $50 or less per night, and "high-end" here usually means under $150. Accommodations in this area are often referred to as "Main Gate" residences, touted as being the closest to Disney attractions. Well, technically speaking, the hotels at the Disney end of U.S. 192 are probably a few minutes closer than the lodgings on International Drive; stay here and you may be even closer than the guests at some of the more remote Disney resorts. But don't read this as convenient—

you still have to fight the inevitable traffic in this neighborhood. And even though you might save 10 minutes or so in the car getting to the Magic Kingdom, you'll make up for it trying to find a decent restaurant at the end of the day. There are more fast-food joints on this stretch of highway than in the entire states of Montana, Wyoming, and Idaho combined. Living smack dab in the midst of tourist-gouging shops and cheap amusements (how 'bout a spin around the go-cart track after that All-U-Can-Eat buffet at Ponderosa?), you have to have a high tolerance for tack to spend much time on U.S. 192. Still, if you're traveling *en famille,* who can argue with the convenience of an IHOP next door to your hotel and a Pizza Hut down the street? And besides, after a long day of fighting crowds, and blowing your budget on admission tickets and not-so-good lunch at Disney, maybe all you need is a clean, cheap room and a clean, cool pool. **Downtown Disney resort** hotels command higher prices for their convenient location. Downtown Disney resorts include seven independently owned hotels: the **Wyndham Palace Resort & Spa**, **Courtyard by Marriott**, **DoubleTree Guest Suites**, **Grosvenor Resort**, **Hilton, Hotel Royal Plaza**, and **Best Western Lake Buena Vista**. WDW parks and the restaurants and attractions on International Drive are all nearby and easily accessible. Shuttle service is provided to WDW areas. Beware of what you book in this area, however; it's a mixed bag when it comes to value. You can pay up to $200 a night at cookie-cutter high-rise hotels, just for the Disney affiliation. But make a reservation at the new **Holiday Inn Family Fun Suites,** just down the road and only a half mile or so off Disney property, and you'll get a two-bedroom suite, free breakfast, free meals for kids all day long, a fab pool, free shuttles to parking, and more, all for about $155 a night. **International Drive** (I Drive to those in the know) lodgings offer some of the best values, with rooms ranging from $50 to $200 a night. In case you're wondering, by the way, there's nothing international about International Drive: It's pure Americana, with hundreds of restaurants, shops, amusements, and hotels. But you'll find some great places to stay—and generally they'll have a much smaller price tag than their Disney resort counterparts. Two additional advantages of staying on International Drive: You'll have access to tons of high-quality, reasonably priced restaurants, and you'll be closer to other top non-Disney attractions, like Sea World and Universal Studios. Most hotels on International Drive provide free shuttle service to these attractions. If you stay outside the World, expect to spend some grueling time in the car trying to

ACCOMMODATIONS | INTRODUCTION

get anywhere else. L.A. commuters don't have it any worse than this—it's not uncommon to spend about 45 minutes going less than 10 miles (are we having fun yet?).

When it comes to staying at **Disney World resorts,** you have to decide not only how much you're willing to pay, but also what theme you can tolerate best. Get ready for virtual vacationing. Why travel to the New England coast when you can book a room at the Yacht Club? Yearning for that easy island feeling? Pack your sarong and head to the Caribbean Beach resort. Longing for the romance of the Wild, Wild West? Disney's answer is the Wilderness Lodge. Disney does a magnificent job of capturing everything in cliché, and nowhere is their mastery of illusion and attention to detail more pronounced than at their resorts. Walk up to the Wilderness Lodge and you'll see towering pine trees and western wildflowers. At Dixie Landings, magnolia trees line the river. At the Port Orleans resort, you can stroll cobblestoned, lantern-lit streets, weaving through courtyards and gardens. (You won't, however, find dreadlocked locals selling ganga and good times on Disney's Caribbean Beach.) You may feel compelled to explain to your children, at least once during your stay, that, no, the West/East/South/Caribbean (fill in the blank) isn't exactly like this. But if you want to be totally immersed in Disney fantasy day and night, then go for it (and get your wallet out). Universal Studios has now jumped into the game, too. Their plans call for five on-site, themed resorts to begin operations in the near future (the Portofino Bay hotel was the first to open, with the Hard Rock hot on its heels). If you plan to spend a good deal of time at the Universal theme parks (and we think it's a good idea, especially if you have older children in tow), then consider staying on site and saving yourself a bunch of time on the road, waiting in traffic. Guests staying at Universal Studios resorts receive some nice privileges, too, such as early theme park admission (one hour before the gates open to the general public), front-of-the-line access to selected attractions for the first hour after the parks open to the public, and priority seating at restaurants throughout the parks and CityWalk venues. There's also complimentary transportation to and from all parks and on-site hotels.

To Disney or Not to Disney

Disney offers room rates ranging all the way from $79 to over $1,500 a night. In general, you'll pay more for Disney resort accommodations than for comparable rooms off site (although they *do* offer the very real added advantage of early admission to one of their parks each day you're with them—see below). For example, a standard room (two queen-size beds and a daybed) at Disney's **Grand Floridian** runs $299 a night, while a similarly-sized room at Disney's **Yacht and Beach Club Resorts** runs about $260. Ouch. Compare that to a standard room at International Drive's **DoubleTree Castle,** replete with jeweled chairs, pointy headboards, and its own cast of castle characters, for about $99 to $199. Small studio villas at Disney's new **BoardWalk** feature a scant 359 square feet (not a lot of room, especially with rambunctious kids), a microwave oven, mini-refrigerator, coffeemaker, and wet bar, and will cost you about $250 a night; compare that to the **Summerfield Suites** on I Drive—a 738-square-foot, two-bedroom suite with full kitchen and living area, for about $179 a night. A better deal are Disney's "moderate" or "value-priced" options, like the **All-Star resorts, Port Orleans, Caribbean Beach, Coronado Springs,** and **Dixie Landings,** all of which range from $79 to $154 per night. For about $175 a night, the **Wilderness Lodge,** a faux mountain retreat, is one of Disney's best theme presentations. An economical option for campers is Disney's **Fort Wilderness Campground.** It's a help to know that Disney's resorts are clustered around each of its theme parks. If you plan on spending most of your time at one particular park, you'll save commuting time if you stay at a resort nearby. Here's how they're bunched: **Magic Kingdom** area resorts are the **Contemporary, Grand Floridian Resort & Spa, Polynesian, Wilderness Lodge, Fort Wilderness,** and **Shades of Green** (open to military members and their families only). **Epcot** area resorts are **Caribbean Beach, BoardWalk, Yacht and Beach Club,** and **Swan and Dolphin.** Area resorts for the **Animal Kingdom** are **Coronado Springs, All-Star Sports, All-Star Music, All-Star Movies,** and the new **Animal Kingdom Lodge. Downtown Disney** resorts include **Villas at Disney Institute, Port Orleans, Dixie Landings, Old Key West,** and the independently operated **Wyndham Palace Resort & Spa, Grosvenor, DoubleTree Guest Suites, Hilton, Courtyard by Marriott, Hotel Royal Plaza,** and **Travelodge.**

Let's take a look at the Disney resorts' list of privileges/enticements. Service? Yes, you can count on that. Convenience? Not always. Getting around Disney quickly and efficiently requires the savvy maneuvering of a New York cabbie in rush hour. Depending on where you stay in the World, your return trip could take up to a half hour—even longer—on crowded buses, boats, and monorails. After standing in line all day at the park, plan on standing in line again to catch your ride home. You'll hear of a number of other "advantages" for staying at a Disney resort. Let's take a look at them:

• **The Disney resort ID card,** allowing you to charge meals and purchases. But surprise—your American Express card works just as well.

• **Use of all Disney recreational facilities** including golf, rental bikes, boat rentals, and water sports. Of course, they all cost extra, even for resort guests, and are often available to non-Disney day guests as well, sometimes for the same price. Disney guests do, however, get preferred tee times.

• **Advance dining reservations,** up to 60 days in advance. Surprise again. Anyone can call 800/WDW–DINE (see Dining) and make their own reservations or secure priority seating arrangements. Besides, do you know anyone who plans meals that far in advance? ("Yes, honey, I think that three months from now, on April 20, I'll be in the mood for sushi.") If your Disney vacation just wouldn't be complete without catching the Hoop-Dee-Doo Revue dinner show, or your pitter-patter heart is absolutely set on dinner at Victoria & Albert's (two of Disney's most popular dinner spots), call ahead. Otherwise, just plan on making reservations at the restaurant of your choice when you get to town; it shouldn't be a problem. With any luck, the starry-eyed couple who made reservations two months ago are now history, and you'll get their corner table at Victoria & Albert's.

• **Early park entrance.** This is a real benefit. Disney's "Surprise Mornings" allow resort guests into a different park each morning at 7:30am, at least a half hour ahead of the maddening crowds. If you're organized about it, this can help you avoid some of the bigger lines. Call Disney (407/824–4321) as soon as you arrive to find out which park has early entry for resort guests the next day. Resort guests can also get E-tickets for after-hours entry into the Magic Kingdom.

• **Guaranteed park entry.** When the parking lots are full, Disney resort guests can still get in using park transportation. Think twice about whether this is a good thing or not—do you really want to enter Magic Kingdom when the sign says "full"? Sounds like a good day to stay at the pool.

• **"Concierge" service.** For about 100 bucks more a night, you (and all the other concierge guests) get a separate concierge entrance with check-in/check-out service, free continental breakfast, and some afternoon cookies and milk. Oh, yeah…you get turndown service, too. For that kind of money, this should be more than a chocolate Mickey Mouse on the pillow. It isn't.

• **"Free" transportation.** Disney resort guests get free transportation via monorail trains, ferryboats, launches, and motorcoach shuttles to all areas in the World. This can be a benefit if you plan to hop from one area to another during the day: Say you want to spend a few hours in the morning at the Magic Kingdom, have lunch at the MGM Grand, and then hop over to Epcot for the afternoon. (Are you nuts?!? This is supposed to be a vacation.) Free transit is also an advantage if you plan to exit and return to the park during the day (a good idea with young ones, since it lets you take a nap, swim in the pool, and return refreshed). There's only one problem: Let's say you're staying at a primo Disney resort but decide to take in another Orlando attraction (as you should)….Just try to get a Disney World bus driver to drop you off at Universal Studios. No way, José. Most non-Disney hotels in the area do offer free shuttle service to the major attractions, including Disney World and Universal Studios, while others charge a nominal fee.

The Lowdown

Only in Orlando… Welcome to total immersion vacationing. Here, you'll not only spend your days in fantasyland, but your nights, too. Take your pick: Are you in the mood for a timber-framed Western lodge, Southwestern haciendas, seaside inns, beach cottages, Caribbean island abodes, a classic Victorian resort, Southern manors on the bayou— or how about a Swiss Family Robinson–style treehouse in the woods? They don't call it the World for nothing. And Disney doesn't have the lock on themed lodging, either; Orlando-area resorts outside Disney World compete with their own faux settings and over-the-top designs. You can't spend the night at Cinderella's Castle in the Magic Kingdom, but if you really want to play in a palace, book a room at **The DoubleTree Castle,** a frivolous, all glitter-and-gold fortress on International Drive. In the spacious rooms here, you'll find upholstered chairs painted purple, with pointy backs, all studded with multicolored stones, plus thrones, headboards, jeweled mirrors, hand-set mosaics of kings, queens, and jesters, and stuffed mystical castle creatures peering around the corners. Even the swimming pool has a fountain and a regal hot tub. Kitschy? Sure; but it is so gloriously over the top, you won't care. Besides, rooms are bright and spacious, the location is great (although the traffic is horrendous), and at $99 to $150, the price is right. You'll pay twice as much at a comparably themed Disney resort. But why settle for a mere room when you can, say, go on an African safari? At the new **Sheraton Safari Resort,** handcrafted wooden animals "graze" in the lobby and leopard-spotted carpeting and sandstone tiles enhance the African safari illusion. The theme is actually tastefully executed—almost elegant. Outside, you'll walk a wooden-planked bridge to the "jungle oasis" and a large pool and water slide, complete with a water-spouting (fake) python. Guests at the **Sheraton Studio del City** even get to time travel, as they are transported to the "homes" of Hollywood stars, complete with 1950s era furnishings, costumed hosts, vintage movies, free popcorn, and more. (The Marilyn Monroe rooms sport zebra-striped shower curtains and oversized, colorful makeup mirrors.)

Tropical delights... It's hot and sultry; so what if there's not a sea in sight? Tropical-themed resorts are big in Orlando. At the **Caribe Royale Resort Suites and Villas,** you'll find a variety of suites and villas, all sitting on a 30-acre parcel of giant palm trees and colorful foliage. Actually, there's not much more to it than the giant pink facade that says "Caribbean," but you could do a lot worse for the money. We also don't find anything particularly tropical (or fun, for that matter) at the **Tropical Palms Fun Resort** in Kissimmee. You do get a lot for your money here, however. The spacious, separate home-style accommodations—which they have dubbed "FunSuites"—include two bedrooms, sleeping loft, a pull-out sofa in the living area, and a full kitchen (enough room for four adults and four children) for about $70 to $100 per night. Perfect for families who like to get away from the mayhem and can live without the whimsy. Disney's **Polynesian Resort** has always been one of their most popular; frankly, we don't see the appeal. The newly renovated lobby hits the mark with trickling waters, South Pacific foliage, island music, and thatched things all about, but the motel-style rooms are only so-so. Plus, you'll drop a load here ($274–530 per night). We like the **Disney's Caribbean Beach Resort** better, for less than half the price ($119–164). This lively and colorful resort sits on a 42-acre lake, surrounded by 200 acres; it also features one of Disney's best pools. You'll find lots of water activities on site, too.

Out of Africa... Here's your chance to stay in a South African game reserve without a passport and hours spent on a plane. All you have to do is book a room at Disney's new **Animal Kingdom Lodge.** Disney has already begun taking room reservations for their newest property, even though it won't open until 2002. The impressive lobby features hand-carved furnishings, a mud fireplace, and stunning views of a 33-acre tropical savannah. You'll find lots of other carvings as well, along with rich jewel-tones, low lighting, and thatched huts, all done very tastefully. (Peter Dominick, of Disney's Wilderness Lodge fame, had his hand in this property, too.) During your stay here, the Disney powers-that-be are hoping you'll catch plenty of sightings of animals and exotic birds from the lodge's large picture windows (some 100 grazers and 130 birds live on the property's private reserve), and forget, for a moment, that you really are in Orlando. Of course, this mind-over-body transportation will cost you; rooms here are at Disney deluxe side of the scale, starting at $179 a night. In the meantime, another option is to follow the leopard carpeting to the front lobby of the **Sheraton Safari Resort.** This out-of-Africa-themed hotel includes fine furnishings, a lush courtyard, and a kid-approval-winning pool. (They'll also like the in-room Sony Playstations.) There are no exotic animals roaming outside, but the prices are tamer ($100–150 per night for rooms and small suites).

La Dolce Vita... The luscious new **Portofino Bay Hotel** at Universal Studios Escape conjures up images of an idyllic Italian fishing village. Never mind that you're mere seconds away from cavorting with Spider-Man and the Incredible Hulk; once here, you'll be enchanted. This Loew's Hotel property—which comes complete with imported Italian cypress and olive trees, elaborate trompe l'oeil paintings created by artists from Portofino, Italy (the real place), a harbor dotted with fishing boats, and an open piazza—is Universal's first on-site hotel, and it's a beauty. Families will like the child-friendly amenities, including special discounts on adjoining rooms and a "kid's kloset" full of games, books, car seats, strollers, potty seats, and more. We like its style and its proximity to Universal parks and CityWalk. There's also a deluxe, full-service European-style spa on the premises. We booked a massage and sent the kids to Universal; life suddenly got better.

Disney's best fantasies... Nestled on the shores of Bay Lake, the **Wilderness Lodge** is a tribute to early 20th-century national park lodges, and is one of Disney's best-executed themes. Okay, maybe its not the sweeping view you'd get if you were looking out the window of the Old Faithful Lodge in Yellowstone, but the hotel lobby elicits more than a few oohs and ahhs: It features a seven-story pine-beamed great hall with an 80-foot quarry-stone fireplace, a giant, carved totem pole, magnificent tepee-like chandeliers, and carved wooden bears, goats, and eagles peering at you from all directions. Bubbling hot springs start in the lobby and cascade outdoors into the pool. In true Disney, let's-take-it-over-the-top fashion, an erupting geyser completes the scene. The rooms are spacious, in Disney terms, done up in Western-style furnishings with plaid bedspreads and buffalo-print sheets, and the surroundings of woods and water give the resort a quiet, secluded feeling. Is that sagebrush we smell? Of course, Mickey sports an Orvis fly-fishing vest here. Then there are the side-by-side **Walt Disney World Dolphin** and **Walt Disney World Swan** hotels—either you hate 'em or you love 'em (we love 'em), but you can't miss them. These striking, postmodern high-rise hotels, their rooftops graced respectively with a giant swan and a whimsical fish (it's definitely *not* a dolphin, as any 10-year-old will be quick to point out), can be seen from miles around. This over-the-top creative extravaganza is obviously what happens when a famous architect is given free rein and a seemingly unlimited budget. **The Swan** boasts a water fantasy theme, all turquoise and coral and oh-so-trendy. Murals line the lobby ceiling, and there are playful touches in all the corners of the lobby and guest rooms—such as parrot lamps, sea horse chandeliers, and swan-shaped benches. **The Dolphin** goes even further: On top of the brightly colored building, you'll see a large fountain cascading into a clamshell. And that's just the beginning. Walk into the lobby and prepare yourself—a giant, striped circus tent drapes the ceiling and walls, and fanciful furnishings are everywhere, including dolphin fountains, fish chairs, tropical headboards, canopy-striped bedspreads. "Unique" is an understatement. The two resorts face Crescent Lake and share a slice of sandy beach—one of the best places in the World to watch Disney World's nightly fireworks. While the decor may sound childishly whimsical, the two resorts are actually quite upscale, and one of the better places to take (or be taken by) your lover.

You won't even know you're in Orlando... Check into the **Hyatt Regency Grand Cypress** in Orlando and you may not even make it to the amusement parks. This 1,500-acre mega-resort is a sports-minded hedonist's wet dream: a grand pool with grottoes and waterfalls, plus a 21-acre lake, 45 holes of championship golf, lush grounds, an equestrian center, tennis courts, racquetball....Need we say more? This place is deluxe, inside and out. Rooms are decorated in soft, tropical hues, and the public areas—the lobby, hallways, restaurants, and outside gardens and walkways—are filled with sunlight and top-notch art and sculpture. The hotel has five restaurants, including Hemingway's, an upscale Key West–style eatery overlooking a free-form swimming pool, waterfalls, and gardens. Also in the get-all-your-needs-met-under-one-roof category is the gigantic **Orlando World Center Marriott**, a 200-acre resortopolis surrounded by tropical foliage, golf fairways, and cascading waterfalls. It boasts one of the largest meeting facilities in the country, so you'll be surrounded by suits and badges. Never mind; they'll all be in meetings while you splash in the gigantic freshwater pool, complete with waterfalls and a water slide (of course), or soak in one of the secluded spas. The building itself—tall, towering cement with a 12-story atrium lobby and glass elevator—is not terribly unique, but the oversized rooms have classy pastel-and-floral-draped furnishings, and the grounds are luscious. Finally, you *definitely* won't feel like you're in Orlando at the **Celebration Hotel** in the Disney-created town of Celebration. In fact, walking the streets in this made-to-be-perfect real town (you can actually buy a house here, if you promise to keep your lawn mowed, the kids' toys inside, and laundry off the line, among other things that we can only imagine) is like being in *The Truman Show Revisited*. Help, I'm stuck in a fantasy and I can't get out....The town, of course, is perfect: perfect little upscale shops, perfect little restaurants, perfect little park on the water, perfect little coffee shop, and so on, and so on. Actually, the Celebration Hotel is quite nice and provides a fabulous escape from theme park frenzy. The place is a flashback to Old Florida, when the pace was slower and the scale much smaller. The four-star boutique hotel borders the lake (what else?) and features an understated clapboard and stucco design, a brick courtyard entrance, and a quiet, elegantly casual atmosphere. (Think Ernest Hemingway, not Jimmy Buffett.) Guest rooms are a palette of brick red and mossy greens, furnished with Old Florida Plantation–style replicas.

Hiding from Mickey... You'll find no cutesy mouse-ear topiaries, gushing geysers, or water-sprouting dragons at the **Star Island Resort and Country Club**. This oasis, located just four miles from the entrance to Disney World off the busy U.S. 192 strip, backs up onto Lake Cecile and is perfect for folks who can't stand another moment of Disneyness. Alas, the resort does succumb to its own kitschy oversell: "Everyone who comes to Star Island is a star." But you'll forgive them once you take a look at what you get for your money. The oversized, one- or three-bedroom/two-bath villas with private patios or porches sleep four to eight people, and run $186 to $255 a night. They also didn't skimp on the furnishings (handpainted mural walls, two-person whirlpool baths) or the amenities. The 65-acre resort includes a spa and fitness center, nine-court tennis complex, a giant pool and spa area, a sand beach on the shores of Lake Cecile, boat rentals, and recreation galore. Book a full-body mud mask and "serenity massage" at the end of your day at Disney—it's the perfect Disney detox, guaranteed to mute that irritating "It's a Small World" tune in your head and ease your frazzled soul. At the **Isle of Bali** resort, you can get a two-bedroom suite (sleeps six), along with fully equipped kitchen and a private patio or balcony, for $131 to $207 a night. (One-bedroom suites sleep four and cost $87 to $153 a night; deluxe two-bedroom and three-bedroom suites are also available.) The resort features spacious one- to three-bedroom villas, spread over private grounds—not unlike an exclusive neighborhood in suburbia—and sits just six minutes from Disney's main gate entrance, also features a massive swimming pool and water park, tennis courts, supervised children's programs—even a pre-arrival shopping service.

Faux pas... Honeymooners and families alike flock to the **Polynesian Resort,** making it one of Disney's most popular places to stay. Can so many people be wrong? Sure. This faux tropical paradise comes about as close to the islands of the South Pacific as Mad Dog 20/20 comes to a fine Cabernet. The lobby, full of lush greenery, misty waters, and island music, is promising, but that's about as far as it goes. The place is always crowded and crawling with overburdened parents herding toddlers and tots. The two-story rows of rooms with outside entrances have the look of a Quality Inn with a thatched roof. The pool is tiny by Florida resort standards, the rooms ordinary at best. Prices range from $269 to $445 a night. Our advice: Save your money for a ticket to Tahiti. **Dixie Landings** also misses the mark. We like the smell of magnolias and the expansive 325-acre grounds at this moderately priced Disney resort (where rooms run from $119 to $164 per night), but the romantic Old South it ain't, no matter how many banjo-toting, blue-jean-clad Mickeys are strolling about. Lodgings are faux-antebellum mansions or Southern-cracker bayou dwellings. While certainly not appalling, we did find the entire resort clichéd and boring, with a capital B.

Overplayed, overpriced... Reeking of class and elegance, the **Grand Floridian Beach Resort and Spa** makes a great first impression: A stately white Victorian-style hotel with a red-shingled roof and a zillion balconies, it sits facing the Seven Seas Lagoon. The lobby is all chandeliers, arched windows, and gold birdcages. High tea is served at 3pm (raise that pinkie, now). But this place tries way too hard. You could forgive its pretentiousness, if not for the $300- to $545-a-night price tag. Disney's **BoardWalk Inn** and **BoardWalk Villas** resort takes the 1930s Atlantic Seaboard scene to the max. The bustling seaside illusion takes place outdoors: Disney's G-rated, golly-gee clubs, street performers, shops, and restaurants are clustered along a lakefront boardwalk. In other words, let the good times roll, and roll, and roll….After a day's worth of fun, fun, fun at the parks, do you really need to come home to more? We don't think so. The smallish, inn-style rooms will set you back a whopping $249 to $490 a night, and the larger Boardwalk villas break the bank—we're talking $249 to $1,300. You're better off renting a room elsewhere and visiting the Boardwalk for an evening.

Where trendoids hang… The Michael Graves–designed **Walt Disney World Dolphin** and **Walt Disney World Swan** hotels are magnets for the oh-so-hip. These outrageously designed hotels have attitudes. Those who really want to impress can book a penthouse suite for a mere $1,500 or so a night, making them some of the most expensive rooms in town. You're likely to see someone you recognize (and who wants to be recognized) lounging in the larger-than-life lobby at the Dolphin, under the striped circus-tent decor, or lying beside the grotto pool. Lots of celebs like to stay at the ultra-private **Villas of del Grand Cypress,** where they can hide from fans and security is tight. You aren't likely to see them lingering around the pool, but you could catch a glimpse of someone famous riding by in a golf cart. The **Grenelefe Golf and Tennis Resort,** located 30 minutes outside of Orlando in Haines City, is a favorite spot with duffers. Often selected as the site of the PGA qualifying finals, Grenelefe features three championship courses, a 6,400-acre lake and marina, tennis courts, a fitness center, and villa-style accommodations. Rooms have been recently updated, but are still fairly basic.

When you want to be seen… For maximum exposure, try the **Cypress Cove Nudist Resort,** about 30 minutes from Disney World. This full-service resort sits on a 50-acre lake and includes a campground, hotel, and lots of recreation, including fishing, boating, tennis, and swimming. Disney's **Grand Floridian Beach Resort and Spa** attracts those who request the best and most expensive place to stay at the World. When money is no object, or, perhaps, more accurately, when money *is* the object, the Floridian is the hotel of choice. It tries to be gracious and elegant—in that Disney faux-style way—with lots of chandeliers, arched windows, and lavish decor. Cutesy shops have been replaced with high-end boutiques, and a Mickey mannequin sports top-of-the-line resort wear in the obligatory Disney store on premises (as opposed to the bandanna and patched overalls he wears at the Dixie Landings resort shop). A more under-stated crowd, sprinkled with Ralph Lauren model wannabes, hangs out at the **Wilderness Lodge.** You'll find celebrities who might otherwise be spending their vacation at, say, Telluride, doing what every parent must do (take the kids to Disney World). Dress like you've just walked off the pages of an Orvis catalog, and you'll fit right in. Look for trendoids to hang instead at Disney's new **Animal Kingdom Lodge** when it opens in 2002. Those who like to be the first on the block and first in line will undoubtedly herd here in hordes, at least for the first few seasons. You may also catch a glimpse of a few hipsters from the entertainment world at Universal Studios Escape resorts, including their upcoming **Hard Rock Hotel.**

When you come to your senses... With so many fam-ilies flocking to Orlando, it makes sense there would be a deal like the **Holiday Inn Sunspree** in Lake Buena Vista. The "kidsuite accommodations" include a playhouse/bed-room for the kids and a mini-kitchenette. The playhouse area sleeps three with a bunk bed and twin, and comes equipped with its own television, VCR, and video-game player. (With all that entertainment, who needs to pay park admissions?) The only thing we don't like about this place is the corporate messages plastered all over the kids' rooms, in the form of giant Coke bottles and Little Caesar decor. If you can look past this (and, of course, the kids couldn't care less), you've got yourself a bargain. (Sunspree room rates start at $100.) Family-friendly perks include free meals (for kids 12 and under), a separate restaurant for kids (what a concept! too bad this hasn't caught on elsewhere), a game room and pool, free nightly entertainment, and planned activities. You can also take advantage of free shut-tle service to the parks, and Camp Holiday, a supervised day camp for children. Europeans and seasoned Disney travelers love the **Summerfield Suites International Drive**—and for good reason: The two-bedroom suites offer lots of space and privacy. Two separate bedrooms, each with private bath and television, a fully equipped, full-size kitchen, and a living room area make these rooms feel like a home away from home. Nothing fancy here, just modest, not unpleasant furnishings, an outdoor pool, hot tub, and on-premises restaurant. It feels like nirvana after a nerve-jangling day at the parks.

Deals at Disney... One of the Epcot resort-area hotels, the lively **Caribbean Beach,** was first to enter Disney's budget category, and it's still a bargain with rooms starting at $119 a night. The price point draws a lot of families, so expect it to be a bit on the noisy and active side. Rent a paddle boat and join the fun. "Colorful" and "energetic" are too-kind words to describe the loud, hurts-your-eyes-just-to-look-at-it decor of the **All-Star Sports, All-Star Music,** and **All-Star Movies** resorts, Disney's entries into the lower-price lodging market. Suffice it to say, the kids will love it here. The Sports resort has giant surfboards, taller-than-the-building football helmets, and stairwells in the shape of soda cans. Things are even wackier at the Music resort: Get ready for three-story cowboy boots, a guitar-shaped pool, and a walk-through, neon-lit jukebox. The newer All-Star Movies resort features a giant-size, 35-foot-tall Buzz Lightyear from *Toy Story,* and the towering bodies of Pongo and Perdita from *101 Dalmations* and Mickey the Sorcerer from *Fantasia.* The icons decorating their facades and the layout of their outdoor areas may differ, but the three resorts are nearly identical in setup: They each have a fast food–style court, in-room refrigerators upon request, and pizza delivery. Rooms are small and sparse, however, and because the resorts are set apart in their own little section of the World, transportation to parks via crowded buses is often time-consuming. But hey, what do you want for $74 to $100 a night? Disney's version of the French Quarter, the **Port Orleans** resort ($119–164 a night) lacks the Big Easy's 24-hour jazz-club hopping, while the legendary New Orleans ladies of the evening have been replaced by squeaky-clean bell captains and the only blues you'll find are the soft pastel colors of the buildings' facades. Still, it has lots of wrought-iron railings, picturesque courtyards, and a marvelous pool—climb up a sea serpent's back and drop out of its mouth into the water. The rooms, unfortunately, are a bit shabby and dark; romance is best found strolling along the cobblestone streets and the meandering river walk. And look, over here....Why, it's a lost Mayan kingdom, complete with a 46-foot pyramid and water rushing down its "ceremonial" stone steps. So goes the fantasy at **Coronado Springs Resort,** Disney's newest themed resort. Of course, Disney's depiction of the Southwest is clichéd and sterile, but we applaud the resort's moderate price tag (rooms start at $119 a night) and obsessive attention to detail. Disney imagineers set out to transport guests to an American Southwest with Mickey Mouse–shaped cactus landscaping, a 15-acre manmade lagoon, and two- and three-story "ranchos" and "cabanas," all draped in desert sand and sunset pink colors, red-tile roofs, and mosaic accents. You can choose between the lively, brightly colored casitas, the quirky beach cabanas, and the earthy, Western-styled ranchos. The lobby and the resort's large food market are built around "La Fuente de las Palomas," a "spring-fed" fountain bubbling up from a Spanish urn. Between the ranchos and cabanas is the towering pyramid, the splashy centerpiece for the pool and water slide. And yes, Mickey wears a sombrero here. Pick up yours in the gift shop. If you picked up arms for Uncle Sam, even Disney will give you a discount, specifically at its **Shades of Green Armed Forces Recreation Center,** a resort reserved for active and retired military personnel and their families. The nondescript, ranch-style accommodations are about as hip and exciting as fatigues. But the place boasts two golf courses, two pools, and the price is right: under $100 a night.

Where to go to get away from other people's kids... The best answer is someplace else, preferably out of state. This is Disney World, folks, where kids rule and parents pool all their resources to (a) pay for the adventure, and (b) keep their cool while doing so. If the tiny bundles of noise and energy really do drive you up the wall, book a room at the quiet and elegant **Peabody Orlando Hotel.** Parents with young ones feel instantly out of place when they walk into what is in fact a very gracious lobby, full of beautiful art, subtle tones, and hushed voices. Spend an afternoon at the Peabody Athletic Club (classes, machines, personal fitness trainers, tennis courts, and a lap pool are all available), and then treat yourself to an intimate dinner at the sophisticated Dux restaurant, on the premises (see Dining). If you must, there's also daily bus transportation to all the theme parks. The **Villas at The Disney Institute** are

excellent adult getaways. They're huge—up to three bedrooms and two baths, with fully equipped kitchens—but
very isolated. The two-story houses on stilts are set in a forest, with a gated entrance. Ask for a tree house overlooking
the waterway. There are pools nearby, a full-service health
spa at the Institute, and the delights of Seasons restaurant
(see Dining). The **Caribbean Beach** resort's budget pric-
ing is popular with families, but if you're craving a sem-
blance of quiet, request a room in Trinidad South, where
guests have their own private beach and pool. At the much
pricier **Walt Disney World Dolphin** and **Walt Disney
World Swan** hotels, you'll find fewer families and over-
the-top decor and architecture. Tip for canoodlers: The
outside bench and pool area can be quite romantic at night.

Tops for toddlers... You'll find tots splish-splashing into
the wee hours at the **Disney Yacht and Beach Club
Resorts.** The two share the coast of Stormalong Bay, a
mini–water park that looks as if it jumped off the pages of
a kid's fantasy tale. Of course, you're likely to go crazy trying to keep your eyes on the little ones as they climb
aboard the pirate ship, zip down the water slide, and cross
the rope bridges of this mega–swimming pool. Forget the
Magic Kingdom; you'll have a tough time coaxing them
out of the water. The offer of an ice cream sundae at the
resorts' Beaches and Cream old-fashioned soda shop
might get them to emerge, though. There is also a reprieve
for parents: Mom and Dad can drop off their progeny at
the supervised SandCastle Club, a child-sitting program
(for ages 4–12) that runs from 4:30pm to midnight.
Families are attracted by the budget prices at the **Port
Orleans** resort, and kids will go for another one of those
themed pools, this one with a giant sea-serpent slide. The
resort's Mardi Gras–style food court is a hit with little
ones, too; it features counter-service restaurants, a Dixieland band, and, if you're lucky, an appearance by a Disney
character or two. Toddlers have their own restaurant, their
own sleeping area in their parents' room, and a separate
adult-supervised activity club at the **Holiday Inn Sun
spree,** which is a whole lot cheaper than any comparable
Disney resort. Kids aged 2 to 12 are welcome at Holiday
Inn's Camp Holiday, open from 8am to midnight. This
hotel is going after young families in a big way: Kids
check in at their own desk and receive a bag of goodies;

outlet covers and shock protectors have been installed in the rooms; cribs, high chairs, and sleeping bags are available; nightly cartoons and movies are shown; and if you really want to traumatize your child, they have a giant racoonlike mascot named Max whose job it is to tuck tykes into bed at night. Even better is the newer **Holiday Inn Family Suites Resort** in Lake Buena Vista, which goes overboard for families. Each suite includes a separate parent's room, a bright-colored kid's room with bunk or twin beds, and a pull-out couch in the sitting area. A small refrigerator and microwave helps families save money on snacks and drinks. There's also a free, all-you-can-eat hot breakfast buffet. Kids have their own check-in, eat free all day, and have a fabulous zero-depth pool to splash around in; there's also a small toddler pool and a separate, more secluded adult pool. The lobby features train station decor, and J.J., a bear dressed as a train engineer, walks around hugging kids and signing autograph books. The resort is located at the doorstep of Disney World and the all-suite rooms are a bargain, starting at $129 a night.

Way cool for teens... If you've got teens, you'll be spending time at the Universal Studios park, where you'll find the fastest, wildest, coolest rides. Look for Universal's newest destination resorts, including the **Portofino Bay Hotel** and the soon-to-be-opened **Hard Rock Hotel** to be the places your brooding brood will most want to be. The resorts offer plenty of atmosphere and amenities, as well as come-and-go, easy access to Universal's Islands of Adventure and Universal Studios. Disney's BoardWalk waterfront resort and entertainment district is also competing to be *the* place for families with teens. Give them a bundle of money and let them go: On the boardwalk, they'll find arcades, carnival-midway games, and assorted shops. When you can't find them, check at ESPN World, where live sports broadcasts are held, and virtual-reality game rooms, TV sporting events, and food keep a young crowd cheering. The resort is within walking distance to Epcot and a boat ride away from MGM Studios, but you can expect to overpay dearly for your room. The **All-Star** resorts **(All-Star Music, All-Star Sports, All-Star Movies)** could also pass muster, with their arcade-game rooms, and End Zone food courts serving pizza, pasta, sandwiches, hamburgers, ribs—all the staples of the basic teen diet. But there are lots of toddlers here, too, and teens may have a tougher time getting away on their own—transportation to the theme parks is via a motor coach. Definitely not cool. Access to the parks is better at the **Contemporary Resort,** where older kids can hop on the monorail and come and go as they please. The Contemporary manages to avoid being too corny, and its Food 'n' Fun Center features all-day counter-style eating and video games. International Drive hotel locations are also popular choices for parents with teens. Try **The DoubleTree Castle,** where the decor of jewels, jesters, and jugglers is quite a trip. Buy them an I Drive bus pass and they'll be happily busy for hours. They can hit just about any diversion they want on this strip—mini-golf, go-carts, shops, restaurants, the Wet 'n' Wild water park. Give them lunch money and send them over to the Race Rock restaurant or Friday's Front Row. They'll love it.

For honeymooners and romantics... First, don't even think about Disney's **Polynesian Resort.** This is the top choice for honeymooners visiting Disney World, for no apparent reason. Only thing we can figure is that this is what Disney pushes, and folks just don't know any better. It sounds so romantic—a touch of the French Polynesian islands, warm breezes, thatched roofs. What you'll actually get is a mediocre room and a resort packed with diaper-clad crawlers and hot, harried parents. Watch out for the stroller traffic jams at the door.

Then there's the **Walt Disney World Dolphin** and the **Walt Disney World Swan** resorts—quaint and cozy they're not, but romantic they can be. Sure, they're a bit much. But if you have a bit of the flamboyant in you, you'll fit right into this whimsical, outrageous environment. The large pool, full of waterfalls and spas, is a perfect place to linger an afternoon away. Later, take a stroll on the beach, a sandy sliver shared by the two resorts, and grab a swing under a palm tree to watch the nightly fireworks. The romance and lure of the Wild, Wild West lives on at Disney's **Wilderness Lodge.** So it's full of pretend hot springs and manufactured geysers—it's still one of Disney's best. The surrounding woods and somewhat secluded setting on Bay Lake Beach give a sense of privacy. Rent a bike and take a ride in the pines, or paddle a boat at twilight around Discovery Island, where giant turtles, tropical birds, and florid flamingoes thrive. The Wilderness is a great place to come home to—the towering wood-and-stone lobby is stunning. Wait until the sun starts to head for the other side of the world, then find a table for two at the small, upscale Hemingway's restaurant in the **Hyatt Regency Grand Cypress** resort. After a fine dinner, stroll the lush grounds and then pick a private spot at the giant grotto pool. Listen to the waterfalls, and sneak into one of the tucked-away spas.

Aquatic wonderlands... The Orlando area has to have the largest concentration of swimming pools per square mile in the world. Every hotel, motel, campground, and resort has at least one, and oftentimes five or six. Lots of these may be your basic, dip-your-feet-in models, but there are also plenty of the spare-no-expense, over-the-top examples sure to fulfill your wettest and wildest dreams....Kids take one look at the gigantic, free-flowing fantasy pool shared by the **Disney Yacht and Beach Club Resorts,** and they forget all about Mickey Mouse. In the middle of the 3-acre pool is a giant pirate ship; kids climb in and zip down the water slide. Meanwhile, parents can relax in the spas tucked away in rockscapes. The Doubloon Lagoon theme pool at Disney's **Port Orleans** resort is a hoot, with its alligator fountains and a colorful dragon slide that looks like a Mardi Gras float. (The slide, which takes up most of the room in the pool, is a bit slow, according to our experienced sources, but that may suit you just fine if your children are younger.) If you prefer languorous soaks in the sun and sensuous cool floats on the sparkling water, check out **Orlando World Center Marriott,** where guests have a choice of four pools—indoor, children's, sport, and the sprawling freshwater pool with its rock-framed waterfalls, four secluded spas, and fast-moving water slide. At the **Hyatt Regency Grand Cypress,** there's a stunning free-form pool with grottoes, cascading waterfalls, and a water slide, all surrounded by a maze of tropical foliage and meandering walkways. You'll find spas tucked away in corners and hidden under waterfalls. If you like the feel of sand between your toes, stroll over to the beach, where you can build your own castle, go sailing, or take a dip in the lake. Parents with young children will love the zero-depth entry pool at the **Holiday Inn Family Suites Resort.** The pool is quite large and features a bunch of fun stuff, like spouting animals, gushing waterfalls, and squirting holes. There's also a smaller toddlers' pool and a separate lap pool, with steaming spas for the adults.

More wet dreams... The **Isle of Bali** resort went to a top aquatic recreational architect to design its Liki Tiki Lagoon and Water Park. While others are forking over big bucks, waiting in line, and fighting the soggy crowds at Disney's Blizzard Beach (their "melting snow" water park), Isle of Bali guests have their own private little water paradise. In fact, the company that built Liki Tiki also designed and built Water Country USA in Williamsburg, Virginia, and served as a consultant for Blizzard Beach. The one-and-a-half-acre park is surrounded by tropical plants and stocked with animated birds and fish that spit water and make noises. The main pool features five water slides, an erupting volcano that shoots water and smoke five stories in the air, a wave pool, waterfalls, and an in-water sports area. Or walk the plank to **Sheraton Safari Resorts'** Olympic-size pool, where you'll find a massive 79-foot serpent water slide rising 13 feet from the water. The watering hole is surrounded by tropical plants and lush greenery. They're trying to emulate an African jungle, and while it's not an over-the-top water wonderland— there are better pools in Orlando—it's one of the best to be found at a moderately priced resort.

Pamper palaces... Another day of jostling among the sweating masses, waiting in line for Dumbo rides and Goofy roller coasters?!! Fuhgeddaboudit....Instead, sign up the kids for one of the dozens of children's camps or programs and book a few hours at the spa. At the **Portofino Bay Hotel,** you'll find a very deluxe, full-service European-style spa that offers feel-good treatments like the flower acid peel, moor mud balneotherapy, body polishes, wraps, and more. Stay at Disney's **Grand Floridian Beach Resort and Spa** or the **Villas at The Disney Institute** and you'll have the luxury of a full-service spa on site. Both have relaxing settings and all the standard treatments. The services and amenities at the **Wyndham Palace Resort & Spa** are top-notch. Of course, you don't have to be a guest here to partake of the spa—but oh, how much easier it is to pop in for a wonderful massage and foot rub when it's only two floors away.

Simple and cheap... Grottoes, waterfalls, fake environments, doting bellcaps? Hell, you just want a regular room with two beds, a pool, and an ice machine nearby. And you want to pay a reasonable price (reasonable by tourist-town standards, anyway). No problem. For starters, you can't beat the **Wynfield Inn Westwood,** a pleasant motel-style accommodation that always gets top marks with returning travelers on a budget. Who can argue with clean, bright rooms, a heated pool, snack bar, free continental breakfast, and free shuttles to Disney World and Sea World—all for around $50 to $90 a night? Its convenient location, just off I Drive, is another plus. For a little more expense and a lot more charm, consider the **Country Hearth Inn,** located on International Drive. Despite its high-powered address, this homey inn-style hotel is surprisingly tranquil. Rocking chairs line the veranda, and the lobby is all Laura Ashley–style flowers and prints. The rooms are a bit dark, though, and as atmospheric as its ceiling fans may look, they're a poor substitute for air-conditioning. It can get hot here in the summer, but there's always a pool in the back. **Larson's Inn Family Suites,** near Disney World on U.S. 192, always books up fast. Newly renovated rooms feature a mini-fridge and microwave in the room. Kids stay free in the same room as their parents, or you can opt for the larger suites. Ignore the din of traffic and the music blaring from the water park next door, and count the ways you're saving money. The rooms at the **Radisson Barcelo Hotel** on International Drive won't charm your pants off, but they're okay, if a little musty. Management has tried to spruce up the outdoor pool area with some trees and flowers, and you do get a refrigerator in the room and a restaurant on the premises (not that you'll need it—you're within walking distance of at least 50 other eating establishments). One great perk at the Radisson is that guests get free passes to the YMCA Aquatic Center, located right behind the hotel. The center has an excellent fitness area, two Olympic-size pools, a lap pool, and more. Just up the street, the family-friendly **La Quinta Inn at International Drive** has some extra niceties. Standard rooms feature a small cooktop and

ACCOMMODATIONS | THE LOWDOWN

refrigerator, and outside there's a good-size pool, a spa, and a small putting green that will keep the kids amused while you sip a strawberry daiquiri at the poolside lounge. The **Golden Link** motel is a U.S. 192 favorite. There's a heated pool facing the busy road, but most guests hang out behind the motel at the small beach on Lake Cecile. Skip going to the parks one day and take waterskiing lessons instead, or rent a jet boat for zipping around the lake. The rooms are nothing to write home about, but the price is—$29 to $79 a night. Also on Lake Cecile is the nothing-fancy **Park Inn International**, offering fishing, waterskiing, beach barbecues, and a pool. It's a real noise-fest—U.S. 192 traffic competing with the outboards on the lake—but cheap and only minutes from Disney World. Bargaining for the best rate when choosing between these two will probably make your decision for you; otherwise, there's not much difference. Another nondescript but okay lodging on U.S. 192 in the watching-your-wallet category is the **Orlando/Kissimmee Maingate Knights Inn,** a pleasant one-story motel so bare-bones that it boasts about marginal amenities like free coffee, free ice, free local calls, and free in-room movies. There's a **Hampton Inn** on U.S. 192, but we prefer the ones in the I Drive area, near Universal Studios, because the location is more convenient. Other I Drive budget-watchers include the **Gateway Inn,** which offers unlimited buffet dining (good for families with big eaters), and **Quality Inn Plaza,** which offers free breakfasts and shuttles to the amusement parks.

And cheaper still... If you're really looking to spend micro-bucks, your best bets are the small, locally owned U.S. 192/Kissimmee motels; all of the following establishments charge less than $50 a night. The modest and not-so-tiny **Econolodge** features recently refurbished rooms, a pool, a laundry, a game room, and a free shuttle to Disney parks. **Record Motel** has the all-important basics: clean rooms, a pool, and friendly service. As one guest explained, "We get up early; we're gone all day. When we return, we take a dip in the pool and fall asleep. Why pay for a fancy place to stay?" The **Sun Motel** is another three-C property (as in clean, comfortable, and convenient), cut from the same tourist-town mold. Its short list of amenities boasts free HBO and ice, which gives you an idea of what to expect. The downtrodden **Hosteling International Orlando Downtown** has seen better days. This Spanish-style home, with private family rooms available in addition to the standard dormlike accommodations of a hostel, sits across from Lake Eola in downtown Orlando. Check it out first. They keep promising a refurbishing, but who knows when that will be? You can stroll the walkways around the lake, take a swan-boat ride, and walk to restaurants and bars favored by the locals. The **Hosteling International Orlando Resort** in Kissimmee features a lakefront, a beach, a pool, paddle boats, and private family rooms, as well as dorm rooms. Be aware that at both of these hostels you'll be mingling plenty with your fellow vacationers.

I want to be alone... If privacy is what you seek in Orlando, you'll have to stay in your room and lock the door. Otherwise, no matter when or where, you'll be in a crowd. That said, there are a few spots that are more secluded than others. **Westgate Lakes** suites and villas, though popular with families, are spread out enough to provide a sense of seclusion. Each cluster of townhouses on the wooded 97 acres has its own spa, and a walk along the edge of the lake at night should give you a bracing shot of peace and quiet. **The Villas at The Disney Institute** range over a large chunk of property and are thankfully devoid of Disney clutter and clatter. Unfortunately, they're also devoid of much personality and charm. But quiet they are, and the tree houses, nestled in the woods, are especially private. The **Hyatt Regency Grand Cypress** is big enough to let you remain incognito—it's quite possible to check in next to people you'll never see again until checkout time. While you're golfing, they're horseback riding. While you're playing tennis, they're at the driving range. While you're in one restaurant, they're in another. Hell, you could both be at the pool at the same time and not bump into one another— the resort is that big.

Suite deals... Suite accommodations are a big deal in the Orlando area. No wonder; after battling the masses all day, the idea of waiting in line for dinner and then bunking down with the kids in a tiny hotel room may not sound like your idea of a vacation. You want a place to sprawl out and relax, with a separate room for the kids and a cold beer in the fridge. Even if you pay a little more for the room itself, just think of what you could save by purchasing snacks and meals from the grocery store instead of some overpriced restaurant. At **Summerfield Suites International Drive,** you get a spacious living area, full kitchen, two bedrooms, and two baths for less than you'd pay for a tiny room at the deluxe Disney properties and plush Orlando resorts. There's also a small pool and an on-premises restaurant and lounge, and you're within walking distance to about a hundred restaurants and shops. One- and two-bedroom suites, a free continental breakfast, and free shuttles to Disney World and Orlando International Airport make this a great deal for families. You'll pay more at the **Buena Vista Suites** on International Drive, just a mile or so from Disney World, where rooms are smaller, the suites have only one bathroom, and there's a mini-kitchen setup (small fridge, microwave oven, and coffeemaker). On the other hand, the public areas are more deluxe; they include a large swimming pool, exercise room, and tennis courts. **The Blue Tree Resort at Lake Buena Vista** features generously sized one- and two-bedroom suites with a country club atmosphere. You'll feel pampered here with the well-equipped sparkling new rooms, four pools (one heated), luxurious grounds, and a welcome sense of privacy considering the proximity to Walt Disney World. For a more tropical-flavored escape, try the **Caribe Royale Resort Suites and Villas.** It's all pink and green with lots of foliage, giant palm trees, and pretty flowers spread out on a 30-acre parcel just outside Disney World. Unfortunately, the high-rise buildings give it away—no, Dorothy, you're not in the Caribbean, either. Still, the suites offer a bit more space than a standard hotel room, plus kitchen facilities. They come in lots of variations; the standard package is living room plus bedroom, while the deluxe suite gives you a pull-out couch in the living area. What the designers saved on the suites (they kept them pretty basic, with just enough room), they put into the public areas. The free-form swimming pool has a 75-foot water slide, whirlpools, and a poolside bar and grill, and there is a separate children's pool (with built-in squirt guns), plus adults' and children's sundecks.

Home away from home... What? No cartoon characters, no overdone themes, no giant water slides? It doesn't even feel like Disney at **The Villas at The Disney**

Institute. In fact, these quiet town houses look more like a bland condo subdivision than a resort. There are five major types of accommodations: bungalows, one- and two-bedroom town houses, tree-house villas, fairway villas, and grand vista homes, ranging from about $200 to $1,150 a night and sleeping from four to eight people. The tree houses are the only ones with any real personality: They're little houses on stilts tucked in the woods that sleep up to six and cost $365 to $399 a night. There's an 18-hole golf course on site, six swimming pools, and lots of walking and biking trails. If you're traveling with kids, though, they'll give it a big B for boring. The **Old Key West Vacation Club** resort is Disney's answer to time-sharing. They've taken the already tricky concept and complicated it even further, so the ownership system is about as easy to understand as a computer manual. Forget trying to get a place here during peak season; they're booked up for years to come. But if you go off-season you might get lucky, so ask about it when you call Disney reservations. The resort offers the best of two worlds: a Disney theme property with a giant pool and lots of activities and amenities, and home-style accommodations. The suites are roomy, bright, and airy, with a choice of studios, one-bedrooms, two-bedrooms, and grand villas. For a real oasis in the middle of madness, check into **Westgate Lakes,** a surprisingly serene 97-acre lakefront property that attracts a loyal following of returnees. Don't be fooled by the understated decor of its one- and two-bedroom villas—they have lots more comforts than you're likely to have at home, including swimming pools, spas, tennis courts, a fitness center, a beach with water sports, plus a restaurant, lounge, and maid service—all within a few minutes' drive of major attractions.

Fairways in the foreground... If your idea of the perfect vacation spot includes an 18-hole golf course outside your door and a pro on staff, start packing your clubs. The Orlando area has a number of top-ranked golf resorts. Only minutes from Disney is **Arnold Palmer's Bay Hill Club and Lodge,** consistently ranked one of the top courses in the country. If you have that obsessive, gotta-golf-every-day passion, you'll fit right in at Bay Hill. The lodge-style rooms at the resort are modest, but nobody notices. They come for Palmer's renowned golf academy, in hopes of shaving off a few strokes from their score, and for the demanding play on 27 championship holes. At the very swanky **Grenelefe Golf and Tennis Resort,** a half hour away from Orlando, you have a choice of three championship courses. One- and two-bedroom fairway villas are set alongside the rolling fairways. Slicing, hooking, just can't get it right? Take time off for a game of tennis (Grenelefe has 20 courts), try some bass fishing, take a lake cruise, or go for a walk on one of the many nature trails. If you can pull yourself away from the sporting life, Disney and Orlando attractions are only about a half hour's drive away. The Spanish-style **Mission Inn Golf and Tennis Resort** offers challenging golf in a serene setting. Traditionalists will appreciate the El Campeon course, designed in 1926 by C. E. Clarke of Troon, Scotland, which features rolling hills, peninsula greens, and tee boxes up to 85 feet in elevation—when did we leave the flats of central Florida? When you tire of El Campeon (you won't), try the resort's links-style Las Colinas course, which follows the more natural lay of the landscape. The Mission Inn offers lots of lodging/golfing packages, and attracts a number of businesspeople with its conference center. It's clear from the plain-jane, no-frills room decor that most folks come here for the golf, but Sea World, Universal Studios, and I-Drive restaurants and shops are close by as well. The **Poinciana Golf and Racquet Resort** is a semiprivate resort (open to guests and day visitors for golf) featuring large two- and three-bedroom villas. You'll have room to practice your swing in these spacious digs, then you can take it outdoors to the 18-hole, par-72 course. Golfers like the look of the course, a beautiful layout sculpted from an old cypress forest; lots of day guests come to play, too, so consider this an option even if you're staying somewhere else. Poinciana also has an on-premises restaurant, lounge, and pool, and a very friendly staff. Nongolfing partners will not have to pray for rain when they decide to stay at the **Hyatt Regency Grand Cypress**—there's plenty to keep everyone busy at this opulent, anything-your-little-heart-desires resort. First, the golf course: a Nicklaus-designed championship layout, inspired by Scotland's classic St. Andrews links, with lots of vistas and heathered fairways. Second, the golf school: one of the best, with state-of-the-art teaching techniques. Finally, the resort: one of the finest around, with sprawling grounds, a giant pool, fine restaurants, tasteful accommodations, and more activities than you'll be able to handle in one vacation. In the same class is **Orlando World Center Marriott,** a spectacular high-rise hotel with six restaurants, eight tennis courts, and expansive, free-flowing pools with slides and spas. Did we mention golf? Marriott's Golf Club is situated on 130 acres, with lots of water. Improve your game at John Jacob's School of Golf, which boasts once having been named the "Golf School of Choice" by *Golf Magazine.* The course also offers practice and driving ranges, private or group clinics, and one of the best pro shops in the country. The resort sits at the door of Disney, if you can tear yourself away. There are five championship courses at Disney World itself: Eagle Pines, Palm, Magnolia, Osprey Ridge, and Lake Buena Vista, offering a total of 99 holes, as well as 3 pro shops and 15 pros on hand. (See Getting Outside for details.) Stay at any Disney resort, and you'll receive preferred tee times. Hint: If you plan to go golfing more than amusement park–hopping, look into one of Disney's Golf Getaway packages. These start at $269 per person and include choice of Disney accommodations, unlimited golf, and transportation to courses.

Quaint and cozy... In Orlando? Even in this mega-land of chain hotels and fantasy resorts, there's a handful of small B&Bs and inns for travelers who seek down-home, sweeter-than-molasses hospitality. The **Perrihouse Bed & Breakfast** sits on a 4-acre oasis just outside of Disney World. Rooms are pleasant, and there's a pool and spa and lots of peace and tranquility. The **Country Hearth Inn** on busy I Drive is a breath of fresh air. Flowered wing chairs, chintz coverings, hardwood floors, and ceiling fans create a cozy atmosphere. It's a low-key kind of place, for adults seeking a blend of quaint and quiet.

Condo-mania... Condos and rental homes are often the cheapest way to go for families and groups. It's possible to rent a two- or three-bedroom condo or house with a community pool for less than $100 a night, though you can certainly spend more if you want even more space and amenities (even within a given property, there's usually a wide range of price options). The word about these bargains has been slow to get out, but this type of lodging is definitely catching on. The disadvantage is that it feels like, well, a home, instead of a resort—the maid service is usually minimal—and if you have teenagers, they'll hate it; there's not enough action on the premises. Spending all your waking hours at the attractions (that's why you came here, isn't it?) might help. **All Florida Vacations** (407/852–6117) offers a large selection of villas, town houses, and elegant single-family homes in Kissimmee, all within a few minutes of Disney World. Spacious living quarters, fully equipped kitchens, washers and dryers, air-conditioning, a community pool, a clubhouse, and rec areas are often part of the package. At **Orlando Sun Village,** you'll find snowbirds hunkering down for the long winter months as well as short-term vacationers. This lakefront property, encompassing three freshwater lakes, has 376 two- and three-bedroom town houses clustered in small villages. Some are for sale, others for rent. Everything you need is here (probably a lot more than you have at home), including seven pools, a spa, tennis courts, and a lakefront clubhouse. It's quite an elegant neighborhood, especially for the U.S. 192 side of town, but it feels more like a slow-moving retirement center than a vacation resort. For more condominium info, ask for the Orlando/Orange County Convention and Visitors Bureau's free accommodations guide. It lists several other condo and vacation-home rental agencies in the area.

Taking care of business... The **Hyatt Regency Grand Cypress** is a favorite among the working crowd—well, among those who are supposed to be working, anyway. It's tough to put the nose to the grindstone when you're surrounded by 1,500 acres of lush grounds, waterfalls, a massive swimming pool, world-class golf, an equestrian center, and more. But, hey, if the company's paying, why not? Meeting planners have 65,000 square feet of space to play with, including a 25,000-square-foot ballroom, an exhibit hall, and 18 meeting rooms. Within walking distance of the golf club and villas, the executive meeting center offers an additional 7,000 square feet, with seven meeting and banquet rooms. If your VIPs need to helicopter in, you can arrange landing clearance at the resort's helipad. Only a bit less sybaritic, with more than 200,000 square feet of meeting space, **Orlando World Center Marriott** ranks as one of the largest meeting resorts in Florida; it's a magnet for really big groups. The individual business traveler is provided for, too, with a complete business center—equipped with fax, copy machine, and

IBM and Macintosh computers—and a full-service audio/visual production unit. Off hours, the resort offers more recreational opportunities than you'll have time for: swimming, golf, a driving range, tennis courts, a health club, and, of course, all those Orlando/Disney attractions nearby. Bet you end up playing hooky. Not quite in the same class is the **Wyndham Palace Resort & Spa,** a 27-acre property near Disney Village, which features translation and secretarial services, fax, computers, and photocopying at its business center. The resort has 44 meeting rooms, a ballroom, and a conference/exhibit hall. This place looks all business—low ceilings, dark halls—until you get to the spa. Be sure to schedule a visit to this full-service pamperatorium for a massage, body wrap, facial, or a hydrotherapy treatment—way more fun than catching the bus to Disney World on your afternoon off. The prices are kinda high for the ho-hum rooms, but the outside swimming area and walkways are pleasant, and you'll get a good view of sunsets against the skyline (and, later, the nightly fireworks) from the lounge on the 27th floor. High-powered executives favor the posh, subdued **Peabody Orlando Hotel,** right across from the Convention Center. Its pale and plush surroundings are very soothing to come home to after a day on the convention floor, and buttoned-down types may well prefer such traditional decor to the tropical riot of most other Orlando lodgings. The high-rise **Renaissance Orlando Resort** is a major convention facility, catering more to business than pleasure, but it's near Sea World, and they make it easy to take the kids along on a business trip (would you even think of going to Orlando without them?) by offering a full-day kids' program of supervised activities. The Renaissance also features the world's largest atrium lobby, with a $600,000 tropical aviary and a pool of more than 200 rare Japanese koi. Lots of business travelers who are tired of the same-old same-old opt for the **Country Hearth Inn,** right across from the Convention Center on I Drive. With rocking chairs on the front porch and wingback chairs around the lobby fireplace, it's a refreshing alternative to sterile high-rises and plush theme resorts. The low prices are refreshing, too, if you're not on an expense account.

Up and coming... 99,000 rooms and counting....Look around Orlando and you'll see new construction going on everywhere, as "Opening Soon" signs announcing new hotels dot the already crowded landscape. In addition to the recently opened **Portofino Bay Hotel** and soon-to-be-opening **Hard Rock Hotel,** Universal plans to open the **Royal Pacific Resort** in 2001. Look for **Opryland Hotel Florida** to follow suit in early 2002. In addition, Disney will be expanding its **Wilderness Lodge** property, offering larger villa accommodations in 2001.

Happy campers... Let's suppose your blood is already thin and you can handle the sweatbox conditions of central Florida (and let's suppose the bugs don't bother you)—well, then, camping just may be the way to go. Or perhaps you have one of those traveling homes on wheels, and just need a place to plug in. If so, you're in luck. Disney's **Fort Wilderness Campground** is downright plush by camping standards. More than 700 acres of woods surround the campground, where you'll find sites for tents, homes, and cabins. There are still a number of Wilderness Homes for rent—trailer-type homes that accommodate up to six people, with separate living space, fully equipped kitchens, telephone, and daily housekeeping—but they're disappearing fast. It turns out that trailer-style vacationing is not cool enough for Disney. (Where's the theme, here?) So they've begun to remake the park, turning the trailers into log cabins. It's actually a major improvement. Of course, prices have gone up, but the cabins are still a deal in Disney dollars. Call way ahead, because these spots fill up months in advance; campsites and hookups run about $35 to $58 a night, while homes rent for $185 to $215. At this huge campground, you'll find snack bars, restaurants, bike and boat rentals, game rooms, horseback riding, nightly campfires, movies and entertainment, tennis, two swimming pools, and a small beach. Not exactly roughing it! You'll also have access to theme parks by boat or bus. Don't expect much in the way of nature and greenery at the **Orlando-Kissimmee KOA Kampground,** but you can't beat the close-to-Disney location. There are lots of paved pull-throughs for those big RVs, as well as tent sites and air-conditioned cabins for rent. There's a pool and playground, too, but you'll likely do what most folks do—head for the theme parks with the money you saved on lodging. (A shuttle runs to Disney World, Universal Studios, and Sea World.) There's nothing rustic at all about **Yogi Bear's Jellystone Park,** just off I Drive.

Campers (we use the term lightly) can enjoy a pool, shuttle to attractions, a restaurant, mini-golf, and cable TV, as well as full RV hookups. On the U.S. 192 strip, the **Tropical Palms Fun Resort** borders Disney World. While the term "resort" is really stretching it, this property has campsites for motor homes, trailers, and pop-ups. You'll be close to loads of shops, restaurants, and entertainment. Both Jellystone and Tropical Palms are pretty densely populated, with bumper-to-bumper hook-up sites. If you're looking for more of a back-to-nature thing, the closest you'll get is the much-smaller **Katie's Wekiva River Landing,** out in Sanford, 45 minutes away. It ain't hiking the backwoods, but you can camp on the banks of a real river. Modern, full-hookup RV sites are available at dirt-cheap rates: $18 to $20 a night.

Doggie digs... This is Orlando, folks, where kids and dogs reign supreme. If you can't bear to leave Fido at home, you'll find lots of places where he's welcome here. Traveling pets finally get the respect they deserve at the **Holiday Inn Hotel & Suites** on U.S. 192 in Kissimmee. Pets receive a welcome snack, in-room dog and cat beds, and a special bag of treats and toys—all at no extra charge. It's part of the PAW program: "Pets Always Welcome." What else would you expect in a town that worships a giant mouse? Other hotels that allow pets include **Caribe Royale Resort Suites and Villas, Days Inn Airport, Days Inn International Drive, Days Inn Kissimmee East, Days Inn Lake Buena Vista, Days Inn Lodge Maingate, Embassy Suites Orlando North, Holiday Inn Express at Universal Studios, Holiday Inn Hotel & Suites Maingate East, Holiday Inn International Drive Resort, Holiday Inn Kissimmee Downtown, Holiday Inn Maingate West, Holiday Inn Orlando North, Holiday Inn Sunspree, La Quinta Inn at International Drive, La Quinta Inn & Suites Orlando, Larson's Inn Family Suites, Red Roof Inn, Residence Inn Marriott Convention Center, Residence Inn Marriott Lake Buena Vista, Residence Inn Marriott International Drive.** Disney resorts, except for the **Fort Wilderness Campground,** do not allow pets. However, on-site kennels are available at Epcot, Magic Kingdom, and MGM Studios. None are available at the three Disney water parks or Discovery Island; and no overnight accommodations are offered. Kennels for day use are also available at Sea

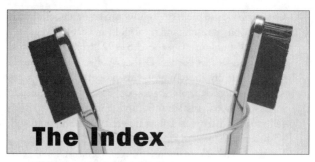

The Index

World and Universal Studios.

$$$$$	over $200
$$$$	$150–$200
$$$	$90–$149
$$	$50–$89
$	under $50

All-Star Movies Resort. Giant-size characters from Disney movies adorn this hotel, Disney's latest budget-priced All-Star property. Loud, busy, and bright.... *Tel 407/934–7639. www.disneyworld.com. 1991 W. Buena Vista Dr., Lake Buena Vista 32830–1000. 1,920 rms. $$–$$$* **(see pp. 32, 35)**

All-Star Music Resort. Kitschy, but a real kid pleaser, and a wallet-pleaser, too, at least for a Disney property.... *Tel 407/ 939–6000; fax 407/939–7222. www.disneyworld.com. 1801 W. Buena Vista Dr., Lake Buena Vista 32830–1000. 1,920 rms. $$–$$$* **(see pp. 32, 35)**

All-Star Sports Resort. Disney's salute to big-league sports is one of the World's cheaper digs.... *Tel 407/939–5000; fax 407/939–7333. www.disneyworld.com. 1701 W. Buena Vista Dr., Lake Buena Vista 32830–1000. 1,920 rms. $$* **(see pp. 32, 35)**

Animal Kingdom Lodge. Disney's latest deluxe resort takes on an African theme, offering panoramic views of its 33-acre tropical savannah brimming with birds and animals.... *Opening in 2002. www.disneyworld.com. Disney World Resort, Lake Buena Vista 32830. 1,300 rms. $$$–$$$$* **(see pp. 25, 31)**

Arnold Palmer's Bay Hill Club and Lodge. This mini-resort is a favorite among golfers, who come to test their skill on the top-rated golf courses and to attend Palmer's Academy.

Lots of packages available.... *Tel 407/876–2429, 888/ 422–9445; fax 407/876–1035. www.bayhill.com. 9000 Bay Hill Blvd., Orlando 32819. 59 rms. $$$–$$$$*
(see p. 43)

Best Western in WDW Resort. Located at Downtown Disney, this 18-story high-rise hotel is best for travelers willing to pay a little more for convenience. The hotel sits on a pretty lake, and many rooms offer great views of water and the World.... *Tel 407/828–2424, 800/348–3765; fax 407/828–8933. www.orlandoresorthotel.com. 2000 Hotel Plaza Blvd., Lake Buena Vista 32830. 325 rms. $$$–$$$$* **(see p. 19)**

Blue Tree Resort at Lake Buena Vista. A resort that offers all-suite accommodations with a five-star rating from an industry trade group, Intervals International. *Tel 407/238– 6000, 800/688–8733; fax 407/238–6014. www.blue treere sort.com. 12007 Cypress Run Rd., Orlando 32836. xxxrms. $$$–$$$$$* **(see p. 42)**

BoardWalk Inn. Disney's entertainment center/resort area try- ing to re-create the Atlantic Seaboard in the 1930s. Inn rooms are smack-dab in the middle of all the action.... *Tel 407/939–5100. 2101 N. Epcot Resorts Blvd., Lake Buena Vista 32830–1000. 378 rms. $$$$$* **(see pp. 29, 35)**

BoardWalk Villas. These pricey Disney rooms range from small studios to three-bedroom villas. Tucked around a faux 1930s Atlantic Seaboard scene, they're best for those who like to be around a lot of action and aren't in the habit of looking at the price tag.... *Tel 407/934–7639. N. Epcot Resorts Blvd., Lake Buena Vista 32830–1000. 532 villas. $$$$$* **(see pp. 29, 35)**

Buena Vista Suites. This somewhat boring all-suites property has nothing distinct going for or against it. AAA gives it three diamonds; free breakfast and free shuttle to Disney parks make it a bit more attractive.... *Tel 407/239–8588, 800/537–7737; fax 407/239–1401. www.buenasuites.com. 8203 World Center Dr., Lake Buena Vista 32830. 280 2- room suites. $$$$* **(see p. 42)**

Disney's Caribbean Beach Resort. In the Epcot resort area, this island-themed property is family-friendly. Activity and noise levels are high; there are six pools, a small beach,

boat rentals, and a food court, on more than 200 acres.... *Tel 407/934–7639; fax 407/934–3288. 900 Cayman Way, Lake Buena Vista 32830–1000. 2,112 rms. $$$*
(see pp. 25, 32, 34)

Caribe Royale Resort Suites and Villas. Lushly planted grounds surround this high-rise suite property. Large swimming pool, water slide, kids' pool, and sun decks.... *Tel 407/238–8000, 800/823–8300. www.caribe-royale.com. 8101 World Center Dr., International Dr., Orlando 32821. 1,218 suites and 120 2-bedroom villas. $$$–$$$$*
(see pp. 24, 42, 49)

Celebration Hotel. Elegant and lovely old-Florida-style hotel, perfect for adults who want to get away from tack and madness. Too bad it's in Disney's manufactured, too-perfect town of Celebration.... *Tel 407/566–6000; fax 407/566–1844. www.celebrationhotel.com. 770 Bloom St., Celebration 34747. 115 rms. $$$$$* **(see p. 27)**

Comfort Inn. If you're looking for a nondescript room, a pool, and an on-site restaurant close to Disney World, you'll find it here at a bargain price. Comfort Inn also has six other properties in the area, including three all-suite accommodations. All are about the same.... *Tel 800/223–1628; fax 407/396–7497. 757 West Irlo Bronson Hwy., Kissimmee 34747. 640 rms. $–$$* **(see p. 16)**

Contemporary Resort. Once futuristic, now it just looks bland, but this towering A-frame with wings remains popular. Some rooms have views of the Magic Kingdom, Bay Lake, and Seven Seas Lagoon, but those will cost you even more.... *Tel 407/824–1000; fax 407/824–3539. 4600 N. World Dr., Lake Buena Vista 32830–1000. 1,053 rms. $$$$$* **(see p. 36)**

Coronado Springs Resort. This latest entry into the moderately priced lodging category is also one of Disney's best values. It's bright, colorful, and lively—the surrounding grounds include waterfalls, a swimming pool with giant pyramid and water slide, and a 15-acre lagoon.... *Tel 407/828–1818; fax 407/828–2184. www.disney world.com. 1000 W. Buena Vista Dr., Lake Buena Vista 32830. 1,967 rms. $$$–$$$$* **(see p. 33)**

Country Hearth Inn. Down-home, country-style hotel on I-Drive, right across from the Convention Center.... *Tel 407/447–1890, 800/848–5767; fax 407/352–5449. www.countryhearth.com. 9861 International Dr., Orlando 32819. 150 rms. $$$* **(see pp. 39, 45, 47)**

Courtyard by Marriott. You've seen them before; they're all the same. This one is an "Official Hotel of Walt Disney World," located adjacent to the Downtown Disney resort area, so you'll pay more for less. Marriott has six additional properties in the area, including its fabulous Orlando World Center Marriott....*Tel 407/239–6900, 800/787–3636. 8501 Palm Parkway, Orlando 32836. 323 rms. $$$–$$$$* **(see p. 19)**

Cypress Cove Nudist Resort. For those who like to be seen. The resort includes a hotel and campground and is 30 minutes from Disney World.... *Tel 407/933–5870, 888/683–3150. www.suncove.com. 4425 Pleasant Hill Rd., Kissimmee 34746. 90 rms, 100 campsites. $$$* **(see p. 30)**

Days Inn Lake Buena Vista. Days Inn goes deluxe at this 8-acre resort with pools. Close to Sea World and I Drive. Days Inn has 14—and counting—hotels in the area. All have pools; most have free shuttles and discounted tickets to attractions.... *Tel 407/239–0444, 800/645–7666; fax 407/239–1778. www.daysinnorlando.com. 12490 Apopka Vineland Rd., Orlando 32836. 496 rms. $$$* **(see p. 49)**

Days Inn Lakeside. Families flock to this hotel on the lake—don't even consider it unless you love other people's kids. Three pools, playgrounds, lake recreation, kids eat free at the cafeteria. Efficiencies and suites are available; reserve them now.... *Tel 407/351–1900, 800/777–3297; fax 407/352–2690. www.thhotels.com. 7335 Sand Lake Rd., Orlando 32819. 695 rms. $–$$* **(see p. 16)**

Days Suites East Maingate. Days Inn's budget answer to home away from home—pull out all the couches, cots, and beds and you can sleep a scout troop here. Ask about free attraction tickets when you book.... *Tel 407/396–7900, 800/327–9126; fax 407/396–1789. www.thhotels.com. 5820 W. Irlo Bronson Hwy. (U.S. 192), Kissimmee 34746. 603 suites. $$–$$$$* **(see p. 16)**

Disney Yacht and Beach Club Resorts. These are Disney's attempt to mimic the New England seacoast cottages and grand summer hotels of the 1870s. They do a decent job with the theme, but it'll cost you. Rooms go for $260–455. The best thing about these places is the mini–water park/pool they share. This is the place your kids would select in a heartbeat.... *Tel 407/934–7000. Disney Yacht Club, 1700 Epcot Resorts Blvd., Lake Buena Vista 32830–1000. 630 rms. Tel 407/934–8000. Disney Beach Club, 1800 Epcot Resorts Blvd., Lake Buena Vista 32830–1000. 589 rms. www.disneyworld.com. for both.* $$$$$ **(see pp. 34, 37)**

Dixie Landings. One of Disney's better values, this Southern-style resort offers lovely grounds, airy rooms with simple but tasteful decor, six swimming pools, boat and bike rentals, and restaurants.... *Tel 407/934–6000; fax 407/934–5777. www.disneyworld.com. 1251 Dixie Dr., Lake Buena Vista 32830–1000. 2,048 rms.* $$$ **(see p. 29)**

The DoubleTree Castle. This towering purple and pink hotel makes for a fun place to stay, if you like this sort of thing. Inside, you'll find a whimsical decor (think jester colors and jewel-bedecked headboards), a backdrop of Renaissance music, and the chirping of crickets and birds. International Drive location, and a bargain in the theme category.... *Tel 407/345–1511, 800/952–2785; fax 407/248–8181. 8629 International Dr., Orlando 32819. 216 rms.* $$–$$$ **(see pp. 23, 36)**

DoubleTree Guest Suites Resort. Bilevel suites with kitchen, living area, and patios sleep two to eight guests.... *Tel 407/ 934–1000, 800/222–8733; fax 407/934–1015. www.do bletreehotels.com. Downtown Disney Resort, Lake Buena Vista 32830. 229 suites.* $$$$–$$$$$ **(see p. 16)**

Econolodge. When all you really want is a room and a pool, close to Disney. Free breakfast and bus shuttles.... *Tel 407/ 396–1890, 800/523–8729; fax 407/396–8336. www.enjoyfloridahotels.com. 4669 W. Irlo Bronson Hwy. (U.S. 192), Kissimmee 34746. 99 rms.* $ **(see p. 40)**

Embassy Suites International Drive. The basic suite design features a private bedroom and a separate living space with pull-out couch. Complimentary breakfast, afternoon beverages, free parking.... *Tel 407/345–8250, 800/327–9797; fax 407/352–1463. www.embassy-suites.com/orlando-jamaican. 8250 Jamaican Court, Orlando 32819. 246 suites. Embassy Suites Orlando Convention Center. 244 suites, tel 407/352–1400, 800/433–7275; fax 407/363–1120; 8978 International Dr., Orlando 32819. Embassy Suites Resort Lake Buena Vista. 280 suites, tel 407/239–1144, 800/257–8483; fax 407/239–1718; 8100 Lake Ave., Lake Buena Vista 32836. $$$–$$$$* **(see p. 16)**

Fort Wilderness Campground. Disney does it right for campers at this 700-plus-acre campground. Lots of campsites, RV hookups, and homes available to rent; walking and biking trails, boating, fishing, horseback riding, swimming, restaurants, snack bars, pools, campfires, dinner shows, and more.... *Tel 407/824–2900; fax 407/824–3508. www.disneyworld.com. 4510 N. Fort Wilderness Trail, Lake Buena Vista 32830–1000. 784 campsites. $–$$$$$* **(see pp. 48, 49)**

Gateway Inn. This family-friendly I-Drive budget hotel has a pool, lounge, restaurant, shuttle, and convenience store on premises.... *Tel 407/351–2000, 800/327–3808. www.all-floridaresorts.com. 7050 Kirkman Rd., Orlando 32819. 354 rms. $$–$$$* **(see p. 40)**

Golden Link. A real deal in the budget category, this motel on the U.S. 192 strip backs up onto pretty Lake Cecile.... *Tel 407/396–0555, 800/654–3957. 4914 W. Irlo Bronson Hwy. (U.S. 192), Kissimmee 34746. 84 rms. $–$$* **(see p. 40)**

Grand Floridian Beach Resort and Spa. Oh-so-elegant Disney resort with lavish Victorian design.... *Tel 407/824–3000; fax 407/824–3186. 4401 Grand Floridian Way, Lake Buena Vista 32830–1000. 900 rms. $$$$$* **(see pp. 29, 30, 38)**

Grenelefe Golf and Tennis Resort. Fancy villa-style digs on the fairway, with three championship courses plus swimming, nature trails, tennis, boating, and fishing, just a half hour's drive from Orlando.... *Tel 941/422–7511, 800/237–9549; fax 941/421–1694. www.grenelefe.com. 3200 State Rd. 546, Haines City 33844–9732. 950 units. $$$–$$$$* **(see pp. 30, 44)**

Grosvenor Resort. Pricey Downtown Disney resort. Surroundings are bit more hushed and elegant than at other high-rise lodgings in the area, but the rooms are standard fare. It's conveniently located next to the Downtown Disney entertainment complex.... *Tel 407/828–4444, 800/624–4109; fax 407/828–8192. www.ten-io.com/disneyvha/gros. 1850 Hotel Plaza Blvd., Lake Buena Vista 32830. 626 rms. $$$$–$$$$$* **(see p. 21)**

Hampton Inn. Looks like about a zillion other hotels nearby. The chain has eight properties in the area. All have pools and offer free breakfast and shuttles to main attractions.... *Tel 800/763–1100. www.hampton-inn.com. 7110 Kirkman Rd., Orlando 32819. 170 rms. $$* **(see p. 40)**

Hilton in the Walt Disney World Resort. One of Disney's "official" Village Resort Hotels. It's a Hilton; what more can we say? Expect to pay more for its affiliation and location near the Downtown Disney entertainment area.... *Tel 407/827–4000, 800/782–4414; fax 407/827–3805; www.hilton.com. 1751 Hotel Plaza Blvd., Lake Buena Vista 32830. 814 rms. $$$$* **(see p. 16)**

Holiday Inn Family Suites Resort. A top-notch place for families, conveniently located on the doorstep to Disney World, with plenty of kid- and parent-friendly amenities. A real bargain.... *Tel 407/387–KIDS, 800/HOLIDAY. www.hifamilysuites.com. 14500 Continental Gateway, Lake Buena Vista 32821. 800 rms. $$$$* **(see pp. 35, 38)**

Holiday Inn Hotel & Suites. If you have a picky pet in your entourage, this is the place to stay. There are a few things for two-legged guests, too, like a comfortable room, kitchenettes, a kids' program, a pool, and a shuttle to Disney. Holiday Inn has 16 properties in the Orlando area. Most offer a kids-eat-free program, pools, and shuttles to attractions.... *Tel 407/396–4488, 800/306–5437; fax 407/396–8195. www.familyfunhotel.com. 5678 W. Irlo Bronson Hwy. (U.S. 192), Kissimmee 34746. 200 rms. $$–$$$* **(see p. 49)**

Holiday Inn Nikki Bird Resort. Kids love this hotel's cast of too-cute-for-words characters, like Zucchini the Clown and Nikki the Bird. Pools, playgrounds, arcade, Nikki's gift shop.... *Tel 407/396–7300, 800/206–2747; fax 407/396–7555. www.hionline.com 7300 W. Irlo Bronson Hwy. (U.S. 192), Kissimmee 34747. 529 rms. $$–$$$* **(see p. 16)**

Holiday Inn Sunspree. Can't beat this close-to-Disney hotel for vacationing families. Book a Kidsuite—separate rooms for parents and kids, and a mini-kitchen—for optimum value. Free shuttle service, large pool, and kids' day camp.... *Tel 407/239–4500, 800/366–6299; fax 407/239–7713. www.kidsuites.com. 13351 State Rd. 535, Orlando 32821. 507 rms. $$–$$$* **(see pp. 31, 34, 49)**

Hosteling International Orlando Downtown. Drab accommodations in a dreary Spanish-style home in downtown Orlando. Transportation to most attractions is available.... *Tel 407/843–8888; fax 407/841–8867. 227 N. Eola Dr., Orlando 32801. 90 beds. $* **(see p. 41)**

Hosteling International Orlando Resort. This lakefront property offers dorm-style rooms (separate women's and men's quarters), six to a room; private family rooms are also available. Minutes from Disney World.... *Tel 407/396–8282, fax 407/396–9311. 4840 W. Irlo Bronson Hwy. (U.S. 192), Kissimmee 34746. 41 rms. $* **(see p. 41)**

Hotel Royal Plaza. Not a bad deal for a Disney-affiliated hotel. Rooms are basic, but the location in the Downtown Disney area and the pool, tennis courts, and five championship golf courses nearby make it a better deal than others. The prices are a bit lower, too.... *Tel 407/828–2828, 800/248–7890; fax 407/827–3977. www.royalplaza.com. 1905 Hotel Plaza Blvd., Lake Buena Vista 32830. 394 rms. $$$–$$$$* **(see p. 19)**

Hyatt Regency Grand Cypress. This mega-resort is in its own not-so-little world. A half-acre swimming pool, an equestrian center, 45 holes of Jack Nicklaus–designed golf, a 21-acre lake, and a kids' program.... *Tel 407/239–1234, 800/233–1234. www.hyatt.com. 1 Grand Cypress Blvd., Orlando 32836. 750 rms. $$$–$$$$* **(see pp. 27, 37, 41, 44, 46)**

Isle of Bali. This value-packed resort property features one-, two-, and three-bedroom villas, sleeping four to ten people. Fully equipped kitchens, lots of room, and minutes from Disney World. A giant swimming pool and private, for-guests-only waterpark on the premises are tops with kids. You get lots for your money here.... *Tel 407/239–5000, 800/634–3119. 17777 Bali Blvd., Kissimmee 32741. 250 villas. $$–$$$$$* **(see pp. 28, 38)**

ACCOMMODATIONS | THE INDEX

Katie's Wekiva River Landing. This no-frills camping site may appeal to budget-minded, back-to-nature types who don't mind driving 45 minutes to attractions.... *Tel 407/628–1482; fax 407/322–6766. 190 Katie's Cove, Sanford 32771. 55 sites. $* **(see p. 49)**

Orlando/Kissimmee Maingate Knights Inn. A budget-priced motel on U.S. 192 with park-at-the-door units and a small pool. Free shuttles to attractions and breakfast. Two other fewer-frills Knights Inns are also located in Kissimmee.... *Tel 407/396–4200; fax 407/396–8838, 888/511–7082. 7475 W. Irlo Bronson Hwy. (U.S. 192), Kissimmee 34746. 120 rms. $* **(see p. 40)**

Orlando-Kissimmee KOA Kampground. A close-to-Disney campground with recreation, shuttle service, pool, cabins, and store on premises.... *Tel 407/396–2400, 800/562–7791; fax 407/396–7577.www.koakampgrounds.com. 4771 W. Irlo Bronson Hwy. (U.S. 192), Kissimmee 34746. 300 sites. $* **(see p. 48)**

La Quinta Inn at International Drive. This hotel is affiliated with Universal Studios and Sea World (check package deals). Not a bad place for the money. Bright rooms, pool, spa, in-room refrigerators, on-site restaurant.... *Tel 407/351–1660, 800/332–1660; fax 407/351–9264. www.laquinta.com. 8300 Jamaican Court, Orlando 32819. 200 rms. $$* **(see pp. 39, 49)**

Larson's Inn Family Suites. Traveling families will find in-room refrigerators and microwaves, small suites, a guest laundry, restaurant, and pool here on busy U.S. 192.... *Tel 407/396–6100, 800/327–9074; fax 407/396–6965. www.larsoninnfamilysuites.com. 6075 W. Irlo Bronson Hwy. (U.S. 192), Kissimmee 34746. 128 rms. $–$$* **(see pp. 39, 49)**

Mission Inn Golf and Tennis Resort. This first-class Spanish-style resort offers two outstanding championship golf courses set on 625 acres.... *Tel 352/324–3101, 800/874–9053; fax 352/324–2636. www.missioninnresort.com. 10400 County Rd. 48, Howey-in-the-Hills 34737. 187 rms. $$$$–$$$$$* **(see p. 44)**

Old Key West Vacation Club. Sunny, large rooms, furnished in light woods and subtle island prints; fully equipped kitchens and deluxe bathrooms. Lots of Disney activities include kids' programs, character meals, boating, beaching, and more. Villas accommodate four to 12 people.... *Tel 407/827–7700; fax 407/827–7710. www.disneyworld.com. 1510 N. Cove Rd., Lake Buena Vista 32830–1000. 497 rms. $$$$$*   **(see p. 43)**

Orlando Sun Village. Long-term renters and short-term vacationers share the streets of this faintly geriatric lakefront townhouse property. Tennis, three freshwater lakes, boating, pools, spas, clubhouse.... *Tel 407/396–4000, 800/642–8918; fax 407/390–9335. 4403 Sun Village Blvd., Kissimmee 34746. 72 units. $$$$–$$$$$*   **(see p. 46)**

Orlando World Center Marriott. One of the top places to stay in Orlando. You'll love the grotto swimming pool with waterfalls and hidden spas. All the amenities—and perfect for those seeking refuge from the Disney theme thing. Rates range from $125 to $230.... *Tel 407/239–4200, 800/333–3333; fax 407/238–8777. www.orlando. com/owcm. 8701 World Center Dr., Orlando 32821. 1,503 rms. $$$$–$$$$$*   **(see pp. 27, 37, 45, 46)**

Park Inn International. Bargain-priced motel on Lake Cecile, where you'll find a tiny beach, waterskiing, jet-boat rentals, and barbecue pits. There's also a pool, free breakfast, and a shuttle to attractions.... *Tel 407/396–1376, 800/432–0276; fax 407/396–0716. 4960 W. Irlo Bronson Hwy. (U.S. 192), Kissimmee 34746. 197 rms. $–$$*   **(see p. 40)**

The Peabody Orlando Hotel. This gracious and elegant hotel across from the Convention Center is made for those wanting to get away from Disney madness and other people's kids. Its I-Drive location is close to the action without being smothered by it. Rates range from $190 to $240.... *Tel 407/352–4000, 800/732–2639; fax 407/351–9177. www.peabodyorlando.com. 9801 International Dr., Orlando 32819. 891 rms. $$$$–$$$$$*   **(see pp. 33, 47)**

Perrihouse Bed & Breakfast. If you're the B&B kind of traveler, consider this homey, simple inn just outside of Disney World. There's a pool, spa, 4 acres of quiet—about as far to the other end of the spectrum from Orlando's themed resorts.... *Tel 407/876–4830, 800/780–4830; fax*

407/876–0241. www.perrihouse.com. 10417 Centurion Ct., Lake Buena Vista 32830. 8 rms. $–$$ **(see p. 45)**

Poinciana Golf and Racquet Resort. This friendly semi-private resort offers an 18-hole, par-72 course, popular with golfers of all abilities. Full-service restaurant, lounge, pool.... *Tel 407/933–0700, 800/331–7743. www.poin cianaresort.com. 500 E. Cypress Pkwy., Kissimmee 34759. 56 villas. $$$–$$$$* **(see p. 44)**

Polynesian Resort. One of Disney's favorite resorts, full of tots and honeymooners. Go figure.... *Tel 407/824–2000; fax 407/824–3174. 1600 Seven Seas Dr., Lake Buena Vista 32820–1000. 853 rms. $$$$$* **(see pp. 24, 29, 36)**

Portofino Bay Hotel. Universal Studios' first on-site resort hotel. This lush and lovely Italian-themed hotel features imported paintings and plantings, butlers, water taxis, and a full-service spa.... *Tel 407/224–7117; 888/837–2273. www.loewshotels.com. 5601 Universal Blvd., Orlando 32819. 750 rms. $$$$$* **(see pp. 25, 35, 38, 48)**

Port Orleans. This Disney-themed riverside resort offers poolside gaiety at a good address in Disney World. Wrought-iron railings, courtyards, and old-fashioned street lamps help make up for small, modest rooms.... *Tel 407/934–5000; fax 407/934–5024. 2201 Orleans Dr., Lake Buena Vista 32830–1000. 1,008 rms. $$$* **(see pp. 32, 34, 37)**

Quality Inn Plaza. Simple rooms, pool, restaurant, and lounge on premises, shuttle service to attractions. There are four other properties in the area, including three all-suite accommodations.... *Tel 407/345–8585, 800/999–8585; fax 407/352–6839. www.tamainns.com. 9000 International Dr., Orlando 32819. 1,020 rms. $–$$* **(see p. 40)**

Radisson Barcelo Hotel. This budget-priced chain hotel on International Drive has a good location and free membership to the YMCA Aquatic Center next door.... *Tel 407/ 345–0505, 800/333–3333; fax 407/352–5894. www.radisson.com. 8444 International Dr., Orlando 32819. 300 rms. $$–$$$* **(see p. 39)**

Record Motel. A bargain property on U.S. 192, with a friendly staff, clean rooms, and a modest pool.... *Tel 407/396–*

8400, 800/874–4555; fax 407/396–8415, 800/843–7663. www.orlando.com/record. 4651 W. Irlo Bronson Hwy. (U.S. 192), Kissimmee 34746. 57 rms. $–$$ **(see p. 40)**

Red Roof Inn. No frills, just a clean room and a pool out back, plus it's near the Convention Center.... *Tel 407/352–1507; fax 407/352–5550, 800/843–7663. www.redroof.com. 9922 Hawaiian Court, Orlando 32819. 134 rms. $–$$*
(see p. 49)

Renaissance Orlando Resort. This high-rise hotel, located directly across from Sea World, has large rooms, four on-site restaurants, an adjacent golf course, swimming pool, and fitness center.... *Tel 407/351–5555, 800/327–6677; fax 407/351–4618. 6677 Sea Harbor Dr., Orlando 32821–8092. 780 rms. $$$$–$$$$$* **(see p. 47)**

Shades of Green Armed Forces Recreation Center. This out-of-the-way, no-frills Disney resort is reserved for active and retired military personnel and their families. The hotel has about as much style as a private's uniform, but there are two golf courses and it's a bargain.... *Tel 407/824–3600; fax 407/824–3665. www.disneyworld.com. 1950 W. Magnolia Palm Dr., Lake Buena Vista 32830. 288 rms. $$* **(see p. 33)**

Sheraton Safari Resort. Why should Disney have the lock on themed housing? This fanciful hotel gives the African Safari motif full play, with leopard-spotted carpeting, wood carvings, African prints, a python water slide, and Olympic-size pool. All tastefully done. You can't beat the location (there are lots of restaurants and shops nearby), and the price is right.... *Tel 407/239–0444, 800-423–3297; fax 407/239–1778. 12205 Apopka-Vineland Rd., Orlando 32836. 394 rms. $–$$*
(see pp. 24, 25, 38)

Sheraton Studio City. Can't miss this 21-story towering tower of steel. The property was recently renovated into Art Deco decor and a 1940s movie star theme. Good location if you're doing the Universal parks.... *Tel 407/351–2100, 800/327–1366; fax 407/352–8028. www.grandthemehotels.com. 5905 International Dr., Orlando 32819. 302 rms. $$$* **(see p. 24)**

Star Island Resort and Country Club. Away from the commotion....One hundred spacious, nicely appointed villas, Celebrity Spa and Fitness Center, tennis complex, swimming pool, a sand beach on Lake Cecile with marina, boat rentals, and activities. All in all, a private retreat, just 4 miles from Disney World.... *Tel 407/396–8300, 800/ 423–8604. 5000 Ave. of the Stars, Kissimmee 34746. 100 villas. $$$$–$$$$$* **(see p. 28)**

Summerfield Suites International Drive. This I-Drive all-suite hotel hosts lots of value-minded vacationers. Modest furnishings, full-size kitchens, and more-than-adequate facilities make it a bargain. We like their newest property in Lake Buena Vista, too.... *Tel 407/352–2400, 800/ 830–4964; fax 407/352–4631. www.summerfieldorlan do.com. 8480 International Dr., Orlando 32819. 150 suites. $$$$–$$$$$* **(see pp. 31, 42)**

Sun Motel. A clean, basic U.S. 192 budget property.... *Tel 407/396–2673, 800/541–2674; fax 407/396–0878. www.usvacationguide.com. 5020 W. Irlo Bronson Hwy. (U.S. 192), Kissimmee 34746. 106 rms. $* **(see p. 40)**

Tropical Palms Fun Resort. If you're traveling in a motor home, trailer, or pop-up, you'll find lots of inexpensive hookups here. Or, if the camping life isn't your thing, stay in one of their spacious funsuites. It's in the middle of the U.S. 192 strip.... *Tel 407/396–4595, 800/647–2567; fax 407/396–8938. www.superpark.com. 2650 Holiday Trail, Kissimmee 34746. 500 sites. $* **(see pp. 24, 49)**

Villas of Grand Cypress. This top-notch, world-class resort caters to the rich and famous, offering luxury, privacy, and championship golf. Mediterranean-style suites and one-, two-, three-, and four-bedroom villas are tucked away on 1,500 acres. A Mobil four-star property.... *Tel 407/ 239–4700, 800/835–7377; fax 407/239–7219. www. grandcypress.com. One N. Jacaranda Ave., Orlando 32836. 146 villas. $$$$$* **(see p. 30)**

Villas at The Disney Institute. Quiet, out-of-the-way, and a little dull. Features all-suite accommodations, including studios, one- and two-bedroom town houses, tree houses and fairway villas, and homes.... *Tel 407/827–1100; fax 407/934–2741. www.disneyworld.com. 1901 Buena Vista*

Dr., Lake Buena Vista 32830–1000. 585 units. $$$$$
(see pp. 33, 38, 41, 43)

Walt Disney World Dolphin. One of the most unique properties in the area. If you don't want to put up the bucks to stay here, at least come by for a peek at the Michael Graves design. Spacious rooms sport whimsical touches, and the outdoor pool area is great.... *Tel 800/227–1500. www. swandolphin.com. Epcot Resorts Blvd., PO Box 22653, Lake Buena Vista 32830. 1,510 rms. $$$$$*
(see pp. 26, 30, 34, 36)

Walt Disney World Swan. This high-priced Disney property, also designed by architect Michael Graves, screams to be noticed. The Swan shares the sandy beachfront plaza with the Dolphin (see above).... *Tel 800/248–SWAN, 800/ 228–3000. www.swandolphin.com. 1200 Epcot Resorts Blvd., PO Box 22786, Lake Buena Vista 32830–2786. 758 rms. $$$$$* **(see pp. 26, 30, 34, 36)**

Westgate Lakes. Woodsy town houses (a welcome relief from the nearby I-Drive surroundings) are popular with families. Full kitchens, spacious living areas, and lots of room to roam outside, plus a beach, lake activities, swimming pool, restaurant, kids' program, and a number of tucked-away spas.... *Tel 407/345–0000, 800/424–0708; fax 407/ 345–5384. 10000 Turkey Lake Rd., Orlando 32819. 340 suites. $$$–$$$$$* **(see pp. 41, 43)**

Wilderness Lodge. The romance of the West is alive and well at this spectacular Disney theme resort on Bay Lake.... *Tel 407/824–3200; fax 407/824–3232. www.disneyworld.com. 901 Timberline Dr., Lake Buena Vista 32830–1000. 728 rms. $$$$–$$$$$*
(see pp. 26, 31, 36, 48)

Wyndham Palace Resort & Spa. Formerly the Buena Vista Resort & Spa, this 27-acre resort is a Disney affiliate. Pleasant and nice service, but average rooms; you'll pay more because it sits on Disney property. Nice on-site spa, though.... *Tel 407/827–2727; fax 407/827–6034. www. wyndham.com. 1900 Buena Vista Dr., Lake Buena Vista 32830. 1,014 rms. $$$$* **(see pp. 38, 47)**

Wynfield Inn Westwood. A bargain favorite, this agreeable little spot just off I Drive has all you really need: clean rooms, a swimming pool, a good location, free continental breakfast, and shuttles to attractions.... *Tel 407/345–8000, 800/346–1551; fax 407/345–1508. www.orlando.com/wynfield. 6263 Westwood Blvd., Orlando 32821. 299 rms. $$–$$$*

(see p. 39)

Yogi Bear's Jellystone Park. Lots of big motor homes pull into this place, which also has furnished cabins. Don't have your own home on wheels? You can rent one, too. Free cable TV, swimming pool.... *Tel 407/351–4394, 800/776–9644; fax 407/351–9221. 9200 Turkey Lake Rd., Orlando 32819. 500 sites. $* **(see p. 48)**

Orlando/Walt Disney World Area Accommodations

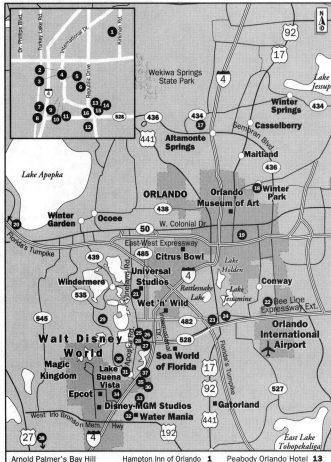

Arnold Palmer's Bay Hill
  Club and Lodge **24**
Buena Vista Suites **37**
Caribe Royale Resort
  Suites and Villas **36**
Comfort Inn **31**
Country Hearth Inn **15**
Courtyard by Marriott **4**
Days Inn Lake
  Buena Vista Village **28**
Days Inn Lakeside **23**
DoubleTree Castle **6**
DoubleTree Guest Suites **34**
Embassy Suites **2, 10, 26**
Gateway Inn **27**
Grenelefe Golf and
  Tennis Resort **40**

Hampton Inn of Orlando **1**
Holiday Inn Family Suites **32**
Holiday Inn Sunspree **35**
Hosteling International
  Orlando Downtown **19**
Hyatt Regency
  Grand Cypress **30**
Katie's Wekiva
  River Landing **17**
La Quinta Inn at I Drive **3**
Mission Inn Golf and
  Tennis Resort **20**
Omni Rosen Hotel **14**
Orlando Sun Village **18**
Orlando World Center
  Marriott **33**

Peabody Orlando Hotel **13**
Perrihouse Bed and
  Breakfast **29**
Portofino Bay Hotel **21**
Quality Inn Plaza **11**
Radisson Barcelo Hotel **9**
Red Roof Inn **16**
Renaissance Orlando Resort **22**
Sheraton Safari Resort **25**
Summerfield Suites
  I Drive **5**
Westgate Lakes **8**
Wynfield Inn Westfield **12**
Yogi Bear's Jellystone Park **7**

Walt Disney World Accommodations

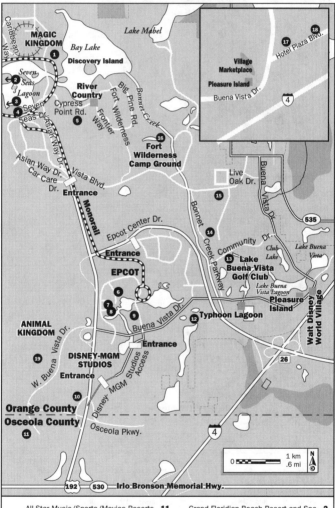

All-Star Music/Sports/Movies Resorts **11**
Animal Kingdom Lodge **19**
Best Western Lake Buena Vista Hotel **18**
BoardWalk Villas **9**
Contemporary Resort **1**
Coronado Springs Resort **10**
Disney's Caribbean Beach Resort **12**
Disney Yacht and Beach Club Resorts **6**
Dixie Landings **15**
Fort Wilderness Campground **16**

Grand Floridian Beach Resort and Spa **2**
Old Key West Vacation Club **13**
Polynesian Resort **4**
Port Orleans **14**
Shades of Green **3**
Walt Disney World Dolphin **7**
Walt Disney World Swan **8**
Wilderness Lodge **5**
Wyndham Palace Resort & Spa **1**

Kissimmee Area Accommodations

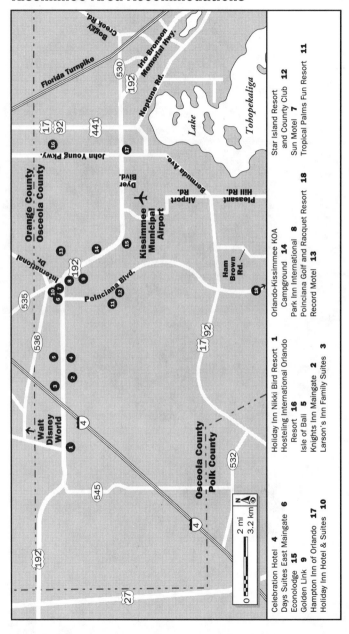

Celebration Hotel **4**
Days Suites East Maingate **6**
Econolodge **15**
Golden Link **9**
Hampton Inn of Orlando **17**
Holiday Inn Hotel & Suites **10**

Holiday Inn Nikki Bird Resort **1**
Hosteling International Orlando
Resort **16**
Isle of Bali **5**
Knights Inn Maingate **2**
Larson's Inn Family Suites **3**

Orlando-Kissimmee KOA
Campground **14**
Park Inn International **8**
Poinciana Golf and Racquet Resort **18**
Record Motel **13**

Star Island Resort
and Country Club **12**
Sun Motel **7**
Tropical Palms Fun Resort **11**

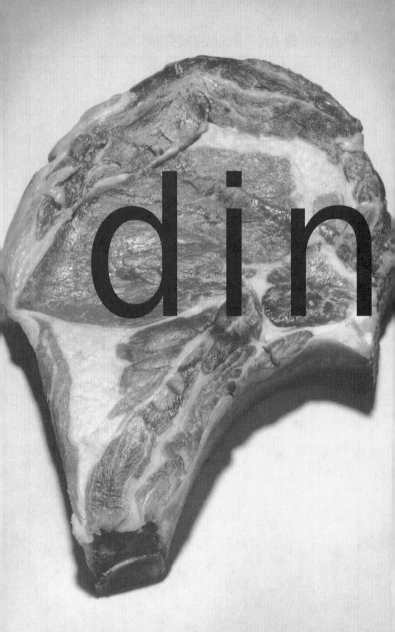

ing2

Wanna ditch that
too-friendly
couple you met in
line at Pirates of
the Caribbean?
Just say, "Meet us
at Taco Bell."

Wink-wink. You'll have 'em driving around in circles, trying to figure out which of the five dozen or so Taco Bells you meant. Would that we were exaggerating. Orlando's tourist strips boast more fast-food outlets than you could shake a deep-fried jalapeño-burrito-on-a-stick at. Given that Orlando is America's top tourist destination, it's only natural that the city is a proving ground for the fast-food giants. Dying to test the latest culinary inspiration from America's major Mcfood chains? Pull into any drive-thru. And where but Orlando would you expect to find the World's Largest McDonald's?

Suffice it to say that homey little one-of-a-kind eateries are as endangered as alligators here. Still, for those diners who bother to sleuth 'em out, the local haunts that have survived the fast-food onslaught are gems indeed. Example: the arroz con pollo at downtown Orlando's Numero Uno rivals Downtown Disney's Bongos Cuban Cafe, quality-wise; plus, with the cash you've saved, you can top off dinner with an aperitif at the cigar-and-martini bar.

If you're itching to ditch the tourist scene and dine where the locals do, hit Orange Avenue and environs, also home to the club scene for Orlando's twentysomething set (see Nightlife and Entertainment). Plus, good eats crop up in places where you'd least expect them; who'da thunk upscale mall Pointe*Orlando would house three better-than-average options (Dan Marino's Town Tavern, Lulu's Bait Shack, and Monty's Conch Harbor)? Then again, it also has a Hooter's.

Within the parks, the real excitement is happening at the "dining and entertainment zones," Downtown Disney's new West Side and standby Pleasure Island, and Universal's new CityWalk. Yes, they're themed to the max, yes, they're full of polyester-wearing yokels from Dubuque, and yes, they're cheek-by-jowl with way too many Hard Rock Cafes (is there anybody out there who doesn't think Hard Rock is, like, *so* over?), but where else can you sample Emeril Lagasse one night, Wolfgang Puck the next?

You'll also find credible eats at Disney's BoardWalk (Spoodles, Flying Fish Cafe) and, of all places, Disney's eerily perfect Town of Celebration (Front Street Grill and Columbia Restaurant).

It's a good bet that you'll also, out of sheer weariness or curiosity, grab a meal or two in your hotel, should you be staying in a full-service place. Lucky you if you're ensconced in the

Peabody Orlando (home of top-rated **Dux**) or Universal's Portofino Bay Hotel, which offers two highly regarded Italian eateries.

Out of consideration for the honeymoon crowd, or those who have no trouble paying upward of $80 for dinner (that's *per person,* darlings) without breaking into a cold sweat, we'll say a word about Disney's gushingly romantic, ultra-gourmet Victoria & Albert's: Ugh. Sorry, it's not that we have anything against elegance—you can indeed dress us up and take us out—but all the wretched excess is a trifle too much. The personalized menus, thespian servers (all of whom are named Victoria or Albert, natch), and over-the-top Victorian frippery make us want to take off our Manolo Blahniks and run, not walk, to the nearest Shoney's.

Dining Disney

Good-bye, Mickeyburger. Hello, potato-wrapped bass with leek fondue and Cabernet sauce. Disney dining ain't what it used to be. Thanks to an ambitious plan to upgrade their food, Disney restaurants now offer creative, tasty repasts to rival anything you'll find in your favorite hometown restaurant. That's the good news. The bad news is, you'll pay handsomely for it. If home is Manhattan or Marin County, you might not experience sticker shock when you open your menu; otherwise, ouch! Dinner for two at Disney restaurants will typically set you back $50 to $75; kids' menu prices, for the 11-and-under set, hover around $15 for two. Lunch prices are 20 to 30 percent lower for adults; kids' menus are generally the same at lunch and dinner. Nearly everywhere, though, you can get a basic burger for ten bucks. You, and about 6,999,999 others—Walt Disney World sells about 9 million burgers and 7 million hot dogs each year, proof that not everyone is ready, or willing, to pay for pecan-crusted salmon and goat cheese. Consider, though, that you get more for your money here than mere Food. You get Fun: Chefs who whip up your dinner with great fanfare while you watch. Waiters who dance the Hokey-Pokey. Tables shaped like mouse ears. A dining room designed like a drive-in movie. You want basic, go to Taco Bell.

On the whole, Disney hotel resort dining is better than its theme-park dining. The one exception is Epcot, where, for the price of admission (around $40) you get the privilege of dropping still more cash at the restaurants in World Showcase, a round-the-world pastiche of pavilions representing France, Germany, Mexico, China, Norway, Canada, the United Kingdom, Italy, Japan, Morocco, and the good ol' U.S. of A. (No poor or war-torn nations need apply.) Sure, Epcot has rides and exhibits and such, but most people come for the food and the Disneyesque appeal of visiting scads of foreign countries without so much as a tetanus shot. (They even give you little passports that they'll stamp at each "country.") Take your time strolling around Epcot's re-created villages to fantasize where you'll eat next. You'll notice that the architecture is painstakingly authentic, and the young servers are actually from the countries they represent. A tip for moms and dads: Most of Epcot's sit-down restaurants offer Mickey's Child Deals for kids 9 and under, with a choice of three kid-friendly entrées, soft drink, and ice cream for under five bucks.

Regarding Reservations

If you're the plan-every-last-detail, anal type, you'll love Disney's take on this. They'll tell you to make your dining plans when you book your visit, even if that means deciding if you'll be in the mood for surf or turf six months from now. During high season (see "When is the best time to visit Disney World?," p. 7), you absolutely have to call ahead. Ditto if you have your little hearts set on a certain restaurant, or if your party numbers six or more. If you covet seats at the Chef's Table (warning: they're $160 a pop) in the kitchen at Victoria & Albert's, or want to whoop it up at the **Hoop-Dee-Doo Revue,** reserve six months in advance (call 407/WDW–DINE.) Be aware, though, that not all Disney restaurants accept reservations. Some, like Bongos Cuban Cafe, are walk-in only. Others offer priority seating. This is a sort-of reservation that you make up to 60 days in advance (or a day or two in advance, if you feel lucky); it entitles you to the next available table if you show up at a given time. Confused yet? The folks on the other end of the WDW–DINE number handle all of this, and can fill you in on the drill at restaurants in all the various Disney theme parks, resorts, and Downtown Disney and environs. Best bet for spontaneous types: Downtown Disney (great eats, lighter traffic than the theme parks, geared toward walk-ins, but expect a wait) and Epcot, which has so many restaurants you can often march right up and be seated (sooner or later) when hunger pangs strike—if you're not too picky. This is especially true of stunning, value-priced Restaurant

Marrakesh at Morocco Showcase, which is a tad too exotic for many Disney guests. Here they practically have to drag unsuspecting diners in from the plaza and adjacent souk (shades of *Casablanca*). Don't resist; it's a good spot, and the jingle-belled belly dancers are a nice touch.

How to Dress

What's to say? The most obvious thing about the dress code at Orlando eateries is the lack of one. At the majority of eating spots, when they say "casual," they mean cover up that beer belly with a T-shirt and put on some flip-flops. Lighten up and have fun with Orlando's loosey-goosey, laid-back style—this is the time to throw on that eye-popping Hawaiian shirt or the Day-Glo flowered number you bought on your honeymoon, and hey, why not order a tropical drink to match your ensemble? Even in Orlando, though, it's considered tacky to show up in beach wear at any of the upscale restaurants. Also keep in mind that Orlandoans (and all Floridians, for that matter) dress seasonally just like folks from colder climes, so if you wear a tank top in February, you'll look just plain goofy. And don't let the heat fool you; even when it's 90 degrees and sweltering outdoors, it's sweater weather inside Orlando restaurants, thanks to overzealous air-conditioning.

When to Eat

Need you ask? This is Florida, where the state bird is the Early Bird Special. Since so many visitors dine *en famille*, earlyish eating—say, from 4 to 6pm—is the norm. Even those folks who are anxious to make the scene at Disney's Pleasure Island nightclub complex and downtown Orlando's Church Street Station tend to eat before they go, the better to squeeze in lots of shows between 8pm and midnight. Looking for a late-night bite? Disney restaurants within the theme parks close when the parks close. Eateries at Disney resort hotels generally close around 10 or 11pm, pretty standard for Orlando. After that, you must venture into the Denny's zone.

The Lowdown

Cheap eats... After a day or two of sticker shock at Disney, **Denny's** and **Shoney's** will start to look damn good. If you'd like something a tad less "All-American" than the Grand Slam breakfast, consider one of these wallet-friendly spots. The classic American "cheap eats" is the diner, and while the theme parks are loaded with diner knockoffs, Orlando's Orange Avenue boasts the real thing: a greasy spoon called **Brian's.** Decorated in early Garage Sale, Brian's is a local fave, where you can get breakfast anytime (especially desirable after a night of club-hopping). The city's hole-in-the-wall ethnic places are also good for a cheap bite; downtown-way, **Numero Uno** makes a great Cuban sandwich, while **Olympia** offers all the Greek classics—stuffed grape leaves, moussaka—plus belly dancers on weekends. On the tourist track, **Café Tu Tu Tango,** a funky little artists' loft on I Drive, serves a sampling of tasty tapas; cheap, unless you're ravenous. Best deal at Disney? The smoked turkey legs sold from little stands around the Magic Kingdom. Approximately the size of your head (how they grow these giant mutant turkeys, we don't wanna know), these succulent drumsticks make a great meal on the run for less than five bucks. Surprise! You'll also find same at Universal Islands of Adventure. Bonus: at the **Enchanted Oak Tavern and Alchemy Bar,** you get some atmosphere along with your turkey leg; it's all very Sherwood Forest. But the ultimate cheap eats honors go to **Giraffe Tavern** at the Hotel Royal Plaza. The Giraffe offers a free buffet Monday through Friday during Happy Hour (4–7pm). This is no secret among Orlandoans, so you're bound to meet a (penny-pinching) local or two.

When you'd rather not slip 'em a Mickey... If your kids are too old to be enthralled by a mute grown-up in a mouse suit, show your groovessence by taking 'em to one of O-Town's sports- or music-themed eateries. **The Player's Grill,** at Pointe*Orlando, is jam-packed with memorabilia from NFL greats. Testosterone-drenched as the atmosphere is, you can't go wrong with the food, created by famed Nawlins restaurateur Ralph Brennan. If Josh and Jessica are more into roundball than pigskin, try **NBA City,** at Universal Studios CityWalk. Here, homage is paid to hoopsters, plus, you can play interactive, sports-themed games. And lest you think Disney hasn't got game, there's **All-Star Cafe Orlando** at Disney's Wide World of Sports complex. Here, you'll sit in baseball mitt–shaped booths surrounded by enough memorabilia to fill Yankee Stadium. At all of the above, count on huge video screens blaring live-action games and Memorable Moments in sport, along with the glorified pub grub. If music is more your kids' scene, head to **Hard Rock Cafe** at Universal Studios CityWalk. We know; you've been there, done that, but this *is* the world's largest Hard Rock, dontcha know, and where else can you see makeup-smudged costumes worn by the members of KISS? Elvis, they say, has left the building, but his pink Caddy perches precariously over the bar. Other options at CityWalk: **Bob Marley—A Tribute to Freedom,** sort of a restaurant-cum-museum-cum-reggae jam; or, for junior Parrotheads, **Jimmy Buffett's Margaritaville.** For a post-IMAX-movie bite at Pointe*Orlando, there's always **Johnny Rockets,** which offers kid-friendly grub like chili-cheese fries, good 'n' greasy hamburgers, and malted milkshakes. (Next stop: the antacid aisle at Walgreen's.)

Where to go if someone else is paying... You've really arrived when an Orlandoan invites you to **Manuel's on the 28th,** boasting the loftiest views in the city, from the 28th floor of the Bank of America Building, downtown. Owner Manuel Garcia trumped Arthur's 27 restaurant (in the Wyndham Palace Resort) by setting *his* place one floor higher. Here, altitude is everything, although the food often rises to tantalizing heights, offering the likes of seared lamb loin in cayenne and Scotch-whiskey sauce, or pecan-cilantro-crusted rack of lamb, with a cabernet-tinged chocolate torte for dessert. The tab can easily run to $120 for two. If you're paying, suggest **Pebbles,** also operated by Manuel Garcia. Less flash, to be sure, but reliably good food and decidedly down-to-earth prices.

Best place to take your lover... Planning to pop the question? Hedge your bets at **Victoria & Albert's** at Disney's Grand Floridian Resort, where every conceivable romantic cliché is trotted out—all *you* have to do is show up with a glittery bauble (and an American Express card with a high limit). A harpist or violinist will set the proper mood, as will fresh flowers, Royal Doulton china, personalized menus, and a seven-course feast featuring luxe 'n' lusty choices like veal sweetbreads and roast duckling. This is considered the most romantic, intimate venue at Disney, so the servers are well versed in the art of hide-the-ring-in-the-Grand Marnier soufflé, or whichever ploy you choose. Looking to be a little more, shall we say, discreet? The best place for a romantic lunchtime tête-a-tête may well be **White Wolf Cafe,** downtown. Our sources tell us you can be hidden in plain sight here, behind the potted plants at a sidewalk table or indoors, among the antiques in the cafe's numerous nooks and crannies. The food is good, should you notice. Other spots that rank high on the Love-o-meter are the **Wolfgang Puck Café** at Downtown Disney West Side and the **Sci-Fi Dine-In Theater Restaurant** at Disney-MGM. At Puck's, skip the elegant upstairs and head downstairs, where you get cool Art Deco digs and lakefront views. If you don't get lucky, at least you've had a good meal. And we mention the Sci-Fi simply because it's set up like a '50s-era drive-in—your "table" is a cherry-red convertible (and, yes, those scratchy metal speaker-boxes are hung on the doors). There's something deliciously naughty about "making out" at the drive-in, under the glow of hundreds of twinkling fiber-optic stars....

Best place to take your mother... After all the years she cooked for you, let her watch someone else do the dirty work. At the award-winning **California Grill,** at Disney's Contemporary Resort, the onstage kitchen is the centerpiece. Watch the chefs roll sushi, toss pizza, pipe pastry, and stuff Sonoma goat cheese into ravioli. Another good bet is to treat Mum to teatime at a grand hotel. High tea at the **Garden View Lounge** at Disney's Grand Floridian Resort and Spa is extremely mom-worthy; fill a plate with fresh-baked scones and Devonshire cream, top it off with a little dollop of English trifle, pour yourselves a spot of lemon verbena tea, and settle in for a chat. Teatime treats are offered daily from 3 to 6pm. If you and Mom have been doing some museum-hopping in Winter Park, treat her to a meal at the pretty **Park Plaza Gardens,** where the chief draw is a lush New Orleans courtyard-style setting; the menu features both Florida and continental dishes, of above-average quality.

Feed your foodie fantasies... Who knew that Orlando would end up a not-bad place to eat? Then again, with 3,800 restaurants, there are bound to be some stand-outs. New-toque-in-town Emeril Lagasse, of New Orleans and Food Network fame, is giving Wolfie Puck some competition in the Superstar Chef category with **Emeril's Restaurant Orlando** at Universal Studios

CityWalk. Lagasse, named one of *Food & Wine* magazine's Top 25 chefs, has created a restaurant with an open kitchen, where chefs whip up Creole-based dishes like Louisiana oyster stew in full view of the patrons. Puck, meanwhile, has lent his cachet to a sprawling complex called **Wolfgang Puck Café** at Downtown Disney, where you can get anything from Puck's signature pizzas to sushi to pasta to a fluffernutter. Locals rave about **Le Coq au Vin** in south Orlando; it's French with a Cajun kick, minus the attitude. This is where the chefs go on their nights off, we're told. If it were located on Disney property, they'd charge twice as much. Speaking of which, if you want to sample the ultimate in Disney dining, try the **California Grill** at the Contemporary Resort, considered by WDW brass to be the best eats at Disney. Chef Clifford Pleau has won beaucoup awards—among them, "Top Meal in America" by *USA Today*. Try the lemongrass risotto with grilled shrimp; skip the pizza topped with chicken caesar salad (creativity run amok).

Theme me, feed me, touch me... Is there some sort of local statute that requires every restaurant to have a gimmick? Orlando now boasts not one, but two, racecar eateries: **Race Rock Supercharged Restaurant,** on I Drive, owned by 13 celebrity racing legends (who knew Mario Andretti could heat up the kitchen as well as the track?) and **NASCAR Cafe Orlando** at Universal Studios CityWalk, featuring NASCAR Winston Cup cars. If this kind of thing revs your engine, you auto love it. Want tunes with your tuna? The number of music-themed restaurants in O-Town is off the charts. Universal's CityWalk is home to several of these, including **Motown Cafe Orlando, Jimmy Buffett's Margaritaville, Hard Rock Cafe,** and more; Disney weighs in with **Bongos Cuban Cafe, Wildhorse Saloon** (country-western), and **House of Blues,** still a standout in this crowded category. Its famous gospel brunch is offered daily, while the bluesmen hit the mike around elevenish at night. We've never been able to sustain a good case of the blues after a dose of HOB's jambalaya, with a bread-pudding-in-whiskey-sauce chaser. Since nothing aids the digestion like the sight of hairy, sweaty armpits on a wall-size TV screen, you can bet your jockstrap that there's a sports-themed restaurant, or 10, in the hood. Currently on the field are the official eateries of the NFL, the NBA, and ESPN (see "When you'd rather

DINING | THE LOWDOWN

not slip 'em a Mickey," p. 74); our fondest hope is that the WWF stays out of the restaurant biz while we're still covering the beat. If you've come for the food, not the frat-party atmosphere, try **Dan Marino's Town Tavern** at Pointe*Orlando, where, in addition to macho-man-size hunks of meat, you'll find delicate sesame tuna and wood-roasted, barbecue-rubbed salmon.

It's a zoo in there... Kids feeling a little, shall we say, spirited? Take 'em someplace where their animal antics only add to the ambience. At **Rainforest Cafe,** part of a national chain, the small fry may be too distracted by the gigantic flapping butterflies, chest-thumping gorillas (automated), and intermittent thunderstorms to remember what they were fighting about. They can be as rowdy as they please: No one will hear 'em over the shrieking parents—oops, parrots—that are part of the din. (Warning: This wild scene may be a bit too much for babies and toddlers.) Don't expect the food to be as exotic as the decor, though—it's a kid-pleasing lineup along the lines of pizzas, pasta, and other casual fare. Look for outposts at Disney's Animal Kingdom, natch, and Downtown Disney. Lotsa cute (stuffed) animals and fewer scary special effects await at **Jungle Jim's,** a low-tech version of Rainforest Cafe, with lower prices to match. The menu teems with so-so burgers, chicken sandwiches, and fruity drinks.

Honey, I ditched the kids... You're probably paying dearly for a rent-a-sitter (or you'll owe Grandma and Grandpa big time), so make the most of that evening sans offspring. You'll probably want to choose a place where you won't be surrounded by other people's children, who are undoubtedly even more poorly behaved than your own. While we can't promise that *nobody* will brazenly smuggle a colicky tot into one of these restaurants, your odds of avoiding kids are better than average at **Fulton's Crab House,** on the lagoon at Disney's Pleasure Island, and at **Pebbles,** a local favorite that's as un-themey as you'll get in these parts. Like its namesake, San Francisco's Fulton Street Fish Market, Fulton's offers fresh fish, flown in from all over the world, and house specialties like mustard-crusted trout. You'll never go wrong with Fulton's "crab experience," a crab combo platter with Alaskan king, Dungeness, and snow crab (even tastier when there are no kids around to go, "Ewww…yuck!"). Pebbles, owned by the same guy who owns pricey, gushed-over Manuel's on the 28th, offers a toned-down atmosphere (blond wood, plants) where the food takes center stage. Pebbles is a decent choice if you're in the mood for something inventive—say, smoked duck and scallops with hot Asian spices—at prices that won't break the bank. Another place where the kids are few and far between is Disney's Celebration. If you can get past the eerie perfection of this Disney-created "small town," you'll find a couple of good restaurants. Even Orlandoans grudgingly admit that **Front Street Grill** is an acceptable choice for creative/casual cuisine. **Columbia Restaurant** is an outpost of the famous Cuban place in Tampa's Ybor City that claims to be Florida's oldest restaurant. Afterward, you can take a horse-and-carriage ride, or stroll around the lake.

Conched out… If you, like most sophisticated travelers, like to sample the local specialties while on vacation, we're here to tell you…fuhgeddaboudit. The closest thing you'll find to regional cuisine here is grouper, a mild, white fish (that, when blackened, has no discernible flavor whatsoever), and some savory treats that have migrated north from the Keys: hearts of palm, conch, stone crabs, and Key lime pie. Fresh hearts of palm, from the tree, are a staple at most upscale restaurants; even casual **Pebbles** offers a house salad that includes hearts of palm and artichokes, tomatoes, and sesame sticks. Conch, a bivalve that has the consistency of a teething ring when not prepared correctly, appears in a multitude of guises: in seviche-like salads, breaded and fried like calamari rings, and tucked into chowder. A logical place to sample this South Florida delicacy: **Monty's Conch Harbor** at Pointe*Orlando, also a good bet for stone crabs, when in season (October to March). And if the "Floribbean" cuisine at **Jimmy Buffett's Margaritaville** doesn't quite live up to the raucous gaiety of the scene, so what? Knock back a couple of neon-hued 'ritas, and you won't give a jolly goddamn.

Vegging out… Even Disney World has gotten the message that not everyone devours animal flesh. At the **Crystal Palace,** in the Magic Kingdom, the dreary cafeteria service has been replaced by a buffet, with make-your-own salad among the options. Meanwhile, at **Cosmic Ray's Starlight**

Cafe (Tomorrowland), guests can order a variety of freshly tossed salads and veggie burgers, along with the typical burgers and fries. **Sleepy Hollow,** in Adventureland, serves veggie chili in a bread bowl, while the **Commissary** at Disney-MGM offers healthy, meatless selections like vegetarian chili pie and citrusy salads. **Electric Umbrella,** near Epcot's Innoventions, offers a veggie wrap with tabouleh and hummus, plus a good-size, fresh-tasting caesar salad

World Showcase winners... Where else but Disney could you walk a mere mile and sample the cuisine of 11 nations? In theory, anyway. Most of the food at World Showcase aims for authenticity—and is pretty good, if not exactly cutting-edge. (With one exception; read on.) Forgot to make a reservation with WDW–DINE (shame on you for being spontaneous!) and feeling hunger pangs? Try the underrated **Restaurant Marrakesh** at Morocco Showcase. Since the average American isn't familiar with Moroccan cuisine, people stay away in droves. Their loss; the dishes are mildly spiced, quite tasty, and inexpensive (for Epcot) to boot. Plus, the chef was personally recommended by King Hassan II. Try the *berber* (feast) for two, the tasty platter of veggie couscous, and a Florida-meets-Morocco dish, tagine of grouper, where the fish is poached in a flavorful mix of lemon and vegetables. Kids can order safe-looking shish kebabs. The Moroccan palace setting is a stunner, and Moroccan musicians and bejeweled belly dancers add an exotic element. Most foodies take direct aim at Epcot France, where three famous owner-chefs lend their gastronomic éclat to Disney dining. Culinary artistes Paul Bocuse, Roger Vergé, and Gaston Lenotre developed the menu, trained the chefs, and drop in on a regular basis to supervise the kitchen at **Les Chefs de France.** The place has an authentic brasserie feel, and you won't be disappointed with the classic coq au vin or pot-au-feu. And ooh-la-la! That pastry cart! Nice as this is, skip it, and go where the real action is, upstairs to **Bistro de Paris.** Surprise: The Three Chefs have lent their magic touch to this less-expensive eatery as well, and seemed to have had a bit more fun with the menu. Call it Country French with an edge. All this, and no snotty waiters like you'd get in the *real* France. *Do* drink the water—or better yet, the Dos Equis—and treat yourself to a meal at Epcot's Mexico Showcase. It's twilight time again (and again and again) at the **San Angel Inn Restaurant,** set along the boat-ride route of El Rio de Tiempo (The River of Time), a man-made indoor river. Even at high noon it's deliciously cool here. Some quibbles: The tables are too close together and the service can be annoyingly slow, but mostly this one rates high on our list. The chicken with spicy mole (chocolate-infused) sauce is soul-satisfying, especially when paired with an ice-cold *cerveza.* Across the "street," the **Cantina de San Angel,** an outdoor cafe overlooking the World Showcase Lagoon, serves the best cheap eats at Epcot—burritos, tostadas, tacos, and the like. A decent place to escape the heat and hoist a pint is the **Rose & Crown Pub and Dining Room** at Epcot's United Kingdom Showcase. Let's not kid ourselves; the Brits aren't known for dazzling cuisine. This clubby spot, though, is positively brill ("brilliant," in Brit-speak) by Epcot standards. It has cunning waterfront tables outdoors, and a menu that relies on pub grub standards like cottage pie and beef with Yorkshire pudding. (We don't believe anyone actually orders the latter; it must be on the menu strictly for effect.) The runaway best-seller is fish and chips. And, by the looks of things at the elbow-to-elbow bar, the ales, lagers, and stouts are a big draw—you can even ask to have them served authentically, at room temperature. This lagoon-front pub always hops (sorry), especially at night when Epcot's IllumiNations laser show is happening, since this is the only full-service restaurant on Epcot's World Showcase Lagoon. (Tip for singles looking for a perky companion: Some WDW cast members hang out here after work.)

World Showcase losers... When in Rome, do as the Romans do—sashay right by **L'Originale Alfredo Di Roma Ristorante** (Italy World Showcase). Yeah, we know, it's based on the original Roma ristorante where fettuccine Alfredo originated. But all that heavy cream is a bit passé, and you can find homemade pasta almost anywhere for half the price you'll pay here. (Gotta have a pasta fix? Try **Pasta Piazza Ristorante,** at Epcot's Innoventions Plaza in Future World—it's cheerful, unpretentious, and cheap, and the pasta is fresh. If the "American Adventure" show has whipped you into such a patriotic frenzy you're thinking of dining at the white-pillared **Liberty Inn,** don't say we didn't warn you. Let's not encourage Disney to dole out burgers and fries and call it "American cuisine." Puh-leeze! Would it be too much to ask for a clambake, or a stainless-steel dining car with Mom's meat loaf and real mashed potatoes? Or at least a Philly cheese-steak? If you feel it's your duty to "buy American," head to the funnel-cake stand.

Best place to escape at Epcot... It's 90 degrees in the shade (or it would be, if there *were* any shade), you've stood on the pavement with approximately 20,000 other sweaty souls to hear the Pipes of Nova Scotia and the Drums of Congo (still ringing in your ears)....Where to make it all go away? Sneak away to the **Matsunoma Lounge,** on the second floor of the Mitsukoshi Department Store in Epcot Japan, where they've got a sake martini (vodka or gin) with your name on it. Passable sushi, too. You can also get away from it all in the deliciously dungeonlike bar at **Le Cellier Steakhouse** in Epcot Canada, where an ice-cold Labatt's never tasted so good. We can't vouch for the eats, though.

Quick bites at Islands of Adventure... So busy will you be at Universal's Islands of Adventure, what with waiting in line for Spider-Man and the Hulk coaster, that you won't want to waste precious minutes eating. Just as well. While the restaurants fit in perfectly with the themed Islands—could there be a place cuter than **Green Eggs & Ham Cafe** at Seuss Landing?—the cuisine is Basic Chicken Fingers and BBQ ribs. Universal probably figures its CityWalk restaurants will look real good to you after a day on the fast-food track. The secret to survival here: the fruit cup. At around $3.50 a pop, it's not bad, and a far more heart-healthy alternative than **Wimpy's** burger baskets, bologna-laden Dagwood sandwiches at **Blondie's,** and, yes, Green Eggs & Ham. We confess we didn't try Islands' high-end eatery, **Mythos,** but it looked empty every time we poked our heads in. Completely irresistible, though, is the **Enchanted Oak Tavern and Alchemy Bar,** located in the Lost Continent. This one is hard to miss: It's shaped like an enormous, gnarly oak tree. Feel like a Viking as you gnaw a giant turkey drumstick (wonder where they got that idea?) and hoist a pint. Tip: This is a great place to duck inside while the kids are in line for the Dueling Dragons coaster across the way. You'll have an hour to yourself, one of the few times you'll be grateful for long lines at the attractions. Another place to grab something that actually resembles real food: **Croissant Moon Bakery,** near the park entrance, where you can get a specialty sandwich on fresh bread. The pastry is better than the surly service.

Dining with character at Universal... If the kids are clamoring to dine on roast beast with the Grinch, Universal makes it easy. Everyone from Rocket J. Squirrel to Olive Oyl eats at the same place: **Confisco Café,** at Islands of Adventure. Daily, from noon to 2pm, characters meet, greet, and pretend to eat as your enthralled kids look on. Don't think this is your only chance to see the Universal characters, however—at Islands of Adventure, you'll practically trip over them. They're everywhere. We saw Spider-Man hold his famous squat pose for an hour, till the last snapshot was snapped. And everywhere we went, we saw that fun couple, Popeye and Olive Oyl, strolling hand in hand. Look for the Grinch—appropriately cranky—and the rest of the Seuss gang in front of the bookstore in Seuss Landing.

Table-hopping at CityWalk... Where to go to forget you're in theme park land? **Emeril's Restaurant Orlando.** The room is delightfully airy and subtly done, so that chef Emeril Lagasse's Creole cuisine takes center stage. The "Bam!" guy from *Emeril Live* shows he's no flash in the pan—his signature Louisiana oyster stew and succulent "mudbug" (crayfish) creations are soul-satisfying eats. Book your table a month in advance. If you can't get into Emeril's, the next best thing is **Pat O'Brien's Orlando,** a replica of the legendary New Orleans bar, where they don't stint on the firepower. Everybody orders a big ol' Hurricane to wash down the spicy Cajun catfish fillets. An older crowd grooves to the dueling boogie-woogie pianists. We're waiting till they jazz up the menu at the **Latin Quarter** before giving it a thumbs-up; with 21 Latin countries to choose from, you'd think they could've come up with a more scintillating bill of fare than flan and rib-eye steaks. And what's with the crowds at **Jimmy Buffett's Margaritaville**? Maybe it's the Florida heat, and the rel-

DINING | THE LOWDOWN

ative proximity to Key West, that makes this one so alluring. The menu offers nothing outrageous—fresh fish, conch fritters, Key lime pie—but it's a lively scene, with chairs fashioned from surfboards, an erupting volcano, and everybody's favorite billionaire pirate, appearing larger-than-life via video (projected onto a sail, not a screen). Pure fun, and *the* place to dine if you're traveling *en famille.* We had a better-than-expected meal at **NBA City,** where diners sit in a semi-circle around a megasize video screen showing—surprise!—great moments in basketball. This is the first NBA City restaurant, with more to follow, created by the National Basketball Association and the Hard Rock Cafe. The menu features pasta, chicken, salads, and sandwiches; skip dessert and order a milkshake with your meal. Our only beef: In the waiting area, you have to pay to play the b-ball skill games. (What else are you gonna do while you wait for a table? Go into the gift shop and buy a jersey with your name on the back for fifty bucks? On second thought, that $5 game ticket doesn't seem so pricey.) Considering that they've already got you for dinner, this policy seems nickel-and-dimey to us.

Dining with character, Disney-style... If you have small fry in tow, you'll be Mom and Dad of the Year if you treat 'em to a Disney Character Dining Experience (Disney's caps, not ours). Meals are generally buffet-style, and every character, it is promised, stops at each table. (Imagine the psychic damage of being ignored by Eeyore! Yikes!) Character meals are held at the theme parks and at WDW hotel restaurants. Note: You'll be required to pay park admission, in addition to your meal tab, at theme park restaurants. You don't have to be a Disney resort guest to partake in a character meal at a resort. The lineup of who's where may change, so be sure to reconfirm when you call to make your rez with 407/WDW–DINE. Here's a quick rundown of who's currently appearing on the Disney celebrity dining circuit. In the Magic Kingdom: Cinderella and friends at **Cinderella's Royal Table** in Cinderella Castle ("Once Upon a Time" breakfast, daily 8–10am, $14.95, $7.95 ages 3–11, plus park admission). Winnie the Pooh, Eeyore, Piglet, and Tigger join you for breakfast ($14.95/$7.95); lunch ($15.50/$7.95); and dinner ($19.95/$9.95) at **Crystal Palace** (no wonder he's a "tubby little cubby"). Minnie, Pluto, and Goofy dine nightly (does Mickey know?) at **Liberty Tree Tavern** in Liberty Square from 4pm; cost is $19.95/$9.95 plus park admission. At Epcot: Join Mickey and friends at the **Garden Grill Restaurant** in The Land. Breakfast ($14.95/$8.25); lunch ($16.95/$9.95); and dinner ($18.95/$9.95) plus park admission. At Disney-MGM Studios: Minnie, Goofy, Pluto, and Chip 'n' Dale make the scene at **Hollywood & Vine** for breakfast ($14.95/$7.95) and lunch ($15.95/$8.95) plus park admission. At Disney's Animal Kingdom: The "A" List (Mickey, Goofy, Donald, Pluto) turns up at Donald's Breakfastosaurus buffet at **Restaurantosaurus** in Dinoland U.S.A. Cost is $14.95/$8.95 plus theme park admission.

In the resorts: Beach Club Goofy and friends table-hop at **Disney's Beach Club Resort,** Cape May Cafe. Breakfast, $14.95/$8.50. Mickey, Minnie, Chip 'n' Dale, and Pluto turn on the charm at **Chef Mickey's Buffet,** Disney's **Contemporary Resort,** at breakfast ($14.95/$7.95) and dinner ($19.95/$8.95). Who knew Mary Poppins and Alice in Wonderland were tight? Join the homegirls, plus the Mad Hatter and friends, at **1900 Park Fare,** Disney's **Grand Floridian Resort & Spa,** for breakfast ($15.95/$9.95). At dinnertime, Belle, the Beast, and friends show up there; cost is $21.95/$12.95. Join Minnie and friends at Minnie's Menehune Character Breakfast at 'Ohana, Disney's **Polynesian Resort.** Cost is $14.95/$8.95. Dine with Tigger and Pooh at Disney's **Old Key West Vacation Club,** Sunday, Monday, and Wednesday only. Cost is $13.95/$8.50. Breakfast with Winnie the Pooh, Tigger, and Eeyore at Artist Point, Disney's **Wilderness Lodge Resort** (you've gotta see this place anyway; it's gorgeous). Cost is $14.50/$8.75 (see Accomodations for all resorts).

Under the boardwalk, they were having grub...

Can there be a place more Disney than **Flying Fish Cafe?** It's worth a trip to Disney's BoardWalk (Atlantic City minus the sin) to check out this lively spot with a Ferris wheel motif and bustling show kitchen (open for dinner only). Chefs ham it up while slinging grits alongside grilled quail; all this and a dessert called lava cake, complete with erupting white chocolate. It's a carnival ride, all right, and some diners will need an Alka Seltzer chaser at the end of the evening. The menu lives up to the atmosphere here, relying mostly on seafood and seasonal fruits

DINING | THE LOWDOWN

and vegetables. Try the signature dish, potato-wrapped striped bass with leek fondue and Cabernet Sauvignon sauce, and just try to get away without at least sampling that lava cake. What do tapas have to do with Atlantic City? We give up. But that didn't stop Disney from plunking down a Mediterranean restaurant, called **Spoodles,** in the middle of their so-called Jersey coast. Tapas, as everybody must know by now, are small nibbles ordered for sharing or sampling. With combinations like tomatoes and Spanish chorizo sausage, and Spanish lamb pinchos (skewers) with grilled veggies and sumac, this concept won't be a hit with the kids in your party, but Disney's thought of that: They offer "you make it, we bake it" personal pizzas for small fry. Here, too, there's an open kitchen. And then there's Wilderness Lodge—Disney's version of a turn-of-the-century national park lodge is so dazzling to look at, we had high hopes for **Artist Point,** its high-end restaurant. But the huge, high-ceilinged dining room lacks character (except when Pocahontas and friends show up for breakfast) and the Pacific Northwest–inspired cuisine doesn't strike us as particularly Pacific Northwest or inspired. Better to camp out at the family-friendly **Whispering Canyon Cafe,** where you can gaze at the slash pines outside and enjoy the woodsy aroma of meats roasting inside. Or skip dinner altogether and slurp up a thick malted milkshake from the **Beaches and Cream Soda Shop,** alongside Disney's Yacht and Beach Club resorts. Do these stir up memories of your own youth, or Archie and Veronica's? Either way, this is what vacation is all about.

Chowing down at Downtown Disney... Lest anyone dare sneak off the Disney property to spend money at a non-Disney nightclub or eatery, WDW created **Downtown Disney,** an entertainment zone encompassing the old Pleasure Island. Since "hip Disney" is an oxymoron, they've enlisted some star power, from the likes of Gloria Estefan, Dan Aykroyd, Aerosmith, and Wolfgang Puck. Estefan and husband Emilio created **Bongos Cuban Cafe,** a Latin-themed restaurant/nightclub at Downtown Disney West Side. Granted, the food is no better than what you'd get at other Cuban restaurants in town, but the room is lively (dig the bongo seats at the bar), the salsa rocks, and the patio tables (overlooking Seven Seas

Lagoon) are the place to be on a sultry night. Also, the presence of Bongos gives at least a passing nod to Florida's cultural melting pot, something all too rare at the World. **Wolfgang Puck Café** is Florida's first restaurant by the big-name West Coast chef. Skip the upstairs, formalish dining room (Wiener schnitzel is not what California cuisine is all about); instead, opt for an interesting pasta concoction or one of Puck's famous pizzas, far better than the California-style pies concocted at California Grill, at Disney's Contemporary Resort. Praise the Lord and pass the pork chops. At **House of Blues,** created by Dan Aykroyd, Jim Belushi, and Aerosmith, grub and gospel are an inspired pairing. This restaurant/concert hall boasts a menu indebted to the Mississippi Delta, and cooked with more spice and gumption than you'd expect. Think jambalaya with dirty rice, étoufée, and—a must—bread pudding with whiskey sauce. The musical acts—all top-flight—run the gamut from blues to jazz, R&B to fusion, Sammy Hagar to Fiona Apple. The House of Blues gospel brunch, with all-you-can-eat vittles, proved so popular it's now offered daily. Reservations aren't accepted for the dining room, but are recommended for the gospel brunch. Meanwhile, at Pleasure Island, Nashville comes to town in all its big-haired, spangle-shirted glory at **Wildhorse Saloon,** a two-level country music, dance, and entertainment venue. The mix includes a barbecue joint, filling the boots of the defunct Fireworks Factory. This is the place to hear the next Shania Twain or Alan Jackson (you sure won't hear your dining companion amid the din) while barbecue sauce dribbles down your chin.

Meat me in Orlando... Central Florida in the 1800s was cowboy country, and those wild-assed Florida cowboys carried braided buckskin whips that made a loud crack when snapped—ergo, the "cracker cowboy." (That's why Florida natives are called "crackers.") You can still find their modern-day, Stetsoned counterparts, minus the whips, line dancing in country-western clubs around town. And, generally speaking, where there are cowboys, there are steak houses. (Never mind if the beef actually comes from Colorado or Nebraska.) The Orlando area has several choices for committed carnivores. The poshest choice (and the most manly-man steak house in town) is **Morton's of Chicago,** boasting generous, expensive cuts of meat and smoke in the air so thick you could cut it. Dark wood, soft lighting, and white tablecloths make this an appropriate atmosphere for power dining. But hey, this is Orlando, and unless you're deal-making with Disney bigwigs, why not be a bubba? **Wild Jack's** is a hoot, with cowhide seats, horseshoe bar, and frothy brew, served in a glass cowboy boot. So what if they sell T-shirts, hats, and BBQ sauce? You'll forgive 'em when you dig into their melt-in-your-mouth, dictionary-thick filet mignon. Arrive hungry; what with sides, salad, and an irresistible loaf of warm bread, you'll finish the evening as stuffed as the steer that adorns the bar. Purists will appreciate **Charley's Steak House,** named one of America's top 10 steak houses, where the steaks are aged 4 to 6 weeks, then cooked in a wood-fired pit over 1,100-degree heat. Perhaps all you need with that is a good scotch and a cigar, but, for the record, Charley's also has an outstanding wine list. We'd sail right on past **Yachtsman's Steakhouse** at Disney's Yacht Club Resort, with its glassed-in butcher shop (haven't they carried that "behind the scenes" stuff a little too far?).

Fishing for compliments... Never mind that the Atlantic Ocean is nowhere in sight. You come to Florida, you gotta have grouper, or mahi-mahi, or red snapper. Down Disney way, the fish fly out of the open kitchen at **Flying Fish Cafe** at BoardWalk. Maybe our appetites were whetted by the aroma of saltwater taffy in the air (this is the Disneyized version of Atlantic City), but damn, did that fritto misto taste good. The **California Grill** at Disney's Contemporary Resort also displays some skill with the gilled. Grilled tuna is the top-selling item on the menu. You think *you* brought a lot of luggage to Orlando? **Fulton's Crab House** flies in tons of fish daily to Orlando International Airport, from all over the world. Like its namesake, San Francisco's Fulton Street Fish Market, this restaurant has a waterfront location, on the lagoon at Disney's Pleasure Island. House specialties include charcoal-grilled gulf shrimp, calamari steak, and mustard-crusted trout, but you'll never go wrong with Fulton's "crab experience," a crab combination platter with Alaskan king, Dungeness, and snow crab. Another place to spend your hard-earned clams: the **Coral Reef Restaurant,** at Epcot, which features a huge floor-to-ceiling saltwater aquarium—you can go eye-to-eye with a 500-pound grouper while eating a less-lucky member of the same species. Subdued lighting adds to the intriguing undersea feel. Pricey, but worth it.

Viva Italia... The Loews hotel group has gone to great lengths to replicate their namesake Italian port city with the Portofino Bay Hotel at Universal. Makes sense that they'd aim for the same authenticity in the kitchen. And, mama mia! (Or should we say, Mama Della!) do they ever. **Mama Della** herself presides over the restaurant of the same name, decorated in homey style with mismatched chairs and china. Get your family-style cannoli and cacciatore here, served in big bowls. A local newspaper recently named this one "Best Italian" in Orlando. Perhaps that's why Mama is occasionally prone to burst into song. Portofino Bay Hotel's splurgey option, **Delfino Riviera,** features Ligurian specialties like pesto-stuffed ravioli, roasted veal with porcini mushrooms, and other decidedly non-red-sauce options. Ask for a table on the outdoor terrace, listen to the piped-in Andrea Bocelli music, and you'll be transported to the Italian Riviera. **Bergamo's** has an authentic southern Italian menu and a wait staff inclined to hop up to the piano and belt out show tunes, Italian love songs, and operatic arias—it seems totally appropriate that Bergamo's offers a dish called pasta alla Norma (named for Verdi's opera). Don't miss the white bean, fennel, and radicchio salad, a tangy blend of assertive flavors. For an entirely different feel—one more New England than Naples—there's the **Portobello Yacht Club** at Disney's Pleasure Island. Photos of classic sailing yachts and yacht-club burgees adorn the walls of this expansive lagoonside restaurant, where a long mahogany bar is the centerpiece. Brick-oven pizzas are a light choice here, but they're nothing special; Portobello does a lot better with northern Italian–influenced pasta dishes like farfalle primavera (butterfly pasta tossed with vegetables) and *bucatini all' Amatriciana* (tube pasta with plum tomatoes, pancetta, garlic, and fresh basil). Portobello leans toward the creative side of Italian, and offers several low-fat choices, which sets it apart from much of the competition. And once you've had a virtuous low-fat meal, you can blow it away with the signature dessert: cioccolato paridiso—a rich layer cake with chocolate ganache, toffee pieces, and caramel sauce. This place can be noisy and crowded, so show up late (it stays open till 1:30 most nights) or come for lunch, when prices are lower and crowds are sparser.

Feeding time at Future World... If you agree with Sebastian the Crab that "life is much bettah, down where it's wettah," crab-walk your way to the **Coral Reef Restaurant** at Epcot's Living Seas pavilion. The dining room is bathed in dreamlike blue light, with the left side flanked by a creature-filled saltwater tank. And the food is up to the setting—simply but wonderfully prepared fresh and "jet fresh" (i.e., flown in) seafood. A mixed shellfish grill, pan-smoked grouper, and Maine lobster pie are menu perennials. So what's the catch? The prices, alas— you'll be fishing deep in your pocketbook to pay that $100-for-four luncheon tab. Opportunities to see Disney characters are virtually nil at Epcot, except at the revolving **Garden Grill Restaurant** at The Land pavilion. Here, Mickey and friends mingle over family-style American breakfasts and lunch and dinner platters of garden-variety chicken, steak, and fish. If you do a big breakfast here (they even serve grits and biscuits), you can get some new signatures in your autograph books, then hit Epcot's most popular attractions—e.g., Test Track (see Diversions)— when everyone else is eating lunch. Whatever you do, steer clear of Future World's **Pure & Simple,** Epcot's nod to healthful dining. Wholesome it may be, but who sticks around long enough to find out? It sorta defeats the purpose when the display case offers up brown-edged lettuce and dried-out chicken salad (as it did the day we visited). One look at this will make you queasier than a ride on the Tower of Terror.

Magic Kingdom grub... Disney is upgrading its food service offerings, but you'd never know it at the Magic Kingdom. Until Tinkerbell sprinkles a little fairy dust (or a handful of fresh cilantro) on 'em, you'll do best to steer clear of the sit-down restaurants here. While they're not horrible, they're just average and expensive. The least offensive of the lot these days is **Crystal Palace,** off Main Street, U.S.A., but only if you stick to simple fare like the make-your-own salad fixings or fajitas. Otherwise, you might want to just snack your way around the Magic Kingdom. Adopt the strategy developed by Magic Kingdom veterans: Eat a big breakfast, then hit the push-carts as necessary. The street vendors even sell fresh fruit these days, not to mention awesome popcorn. That said, we know you'll still be seduced by the idea of eating a big, sit-down meal at **Cinderella's Royal Table,** since it's the only way to actually get inside Cinderella's Castle. Resist! So what if a caesar salad has been added to the menu at this royal rip-off—you'll still pay a princely sum for eats that are bibbidy-bobbidy bad. You'll get a way-better deal at the **Turkey Leg Wagon** at Frontierland, where five bucks buys you a tasty smoked drumstick approximately the size of your head. (You can get the same drumsticks at the Lunching Pad Cafe in Tomorrowland.) Top it off with a chocolate-chip cookie from **Main Street Bakery,** hosted by Nestlé (if they can't make Toll House cookies, who can?), or an ice-cream sandwich made with vanilla ice cream and two big cookies, and you've bought yourself the best meal to be had at the Magic Kingdom.

TV dinners at Disney-MGM... Dining at this park is like traveling through a time-warp to the '50s. It's all Mom, meat loaf, and drive-in movies. You'll feel as if you've landed in a vintage TV sitcom at **50's Prime-Time Cafe/Tune In Lounge,** where the decor runs to Formica and knickknacks, and Beaver Cleaver is forever ageless on the black-and-white Philco. This concept seemed a little fresher a few years ago, before Nick at Nite introduced a new generation to Rob and Laura Petrie, but it's kinda cute. The food is just what you'd expect: pot roast, meat loaf with gravy (the mega-seller here), and chicken pot pie, and it's not bad. Either that, or we've just forgotten what this stuff is supposed to taste like. Way cooler, and more appropriate to the movie-mad theme of Disney-MGM, is the **Sci-Fi Dine-In Theater Restaurant,** a tribute to the glory days of the drive-in movie. You'll sit in a faux '55 convertible and watch sci-fi movie trailers on a giant screen, under fiber-optic twinkling stars. Kind of puts one in the mood to cop a...meal. Alas, the food is barely a step up from concession stand fare, and you can be sure they charge more than five bucks a carload. Yes, here's another chance to order that basic $10 burger. At least it's big. The Oriental salad with grilled chicken is a good option. Kids' choices are lame—for $7.50, couldn't they at least garnish the watery spaghetti with a slice of watermelon?—but the kids will forgive 'em when dessert arrives, a cupcake served on a glow-in-the-dark Frisbee (it's a keeper). Get your name on the list early for these two eateries because, with good reason (that being, the competition stinks), they fill up fast. Another diner with great nostalgia appeal is **Mel's Drive-In** at Universal Studios Florida. A replica of the hangout in *American Graffiti,* complete with red Naugahyde stools at the counter and a vintage car parked out front, Mel's features burger baskets and wonderful, frosty shakes. The **Hollywood Brown Derby** can be enjoyable—it's all very Old Hollywood in feel, and kinda classy, right down to the white-jacketed waiters and potted palms— but if you're *en famille,* the kids won't sit still for Cobb salads and movie-star caricatures (bor-ring!) and the slow-paced service. That leaves **Mama Melrose's Ristorante Italiano,** where the brick-oven pizza is always a good, and filling, choice: We vote for the 4-Star Pizza, topped with Brie, Romano, mozzarella, and Gorgonzola. With hardwood floors, red-and-white-checked tablecloths, and hanging Chianti bottles, it's your classic trattoria movie set, and the smell of the hickory wood–burning oven will drive you crazy if you're really hungry. We'd give a pass to Disney-MGM's cafeteria-style restaurants; what fun is a commissary if no movie stars show up? The stars do make guest appearances at **Soundstage Restaurant,** a quick-service restaurant that offers safe choices like deep-dish pizza and deli turkey sandwiches. Disney characters greet guests at breakfast (reservations only) officially, but they've also been known to drop by during lunchtime and dinner. If it's strictly sustenance you're after, head to **Sunset Ranch Market,** where you can find six kinds of hot dogs. Choose a Rosie's Red Dog (or a turkey dog, if you actually believe there's such a thing as a healthful wiener), pile it high with sauerkraut, chili, and chopped onions, and we'll bet you get as much personal space as you desire in the Tower of Terror elevator.

Epcot for hearty eaters... If the gang is hot, tired, and famished, consider one of Epcot's all-you-can-eat buffets. **Restaurant Akershus,** at the Norway pavilion, probably scares people off, thanks to Norway's reputation for creamed-herring cuisine. To counter this, Epcot has installed smiling Norsk gals with peaches-and-cream complexions to beckon you inside this medieval fortress–style dining room. The food isn't so bad if you like hearty fare: lots of salads and deli, plenty of fresh fish, macaroni and cheese with ham, meatballs in gravy. And, yes, herring. Every day is Oktoberfest at Germany's **Biergarten,** with all that implies: polka dancing, accordions, and lederhosen. If that sounds enticing, get in line for the all-you-can-eat buffet. It's not all sausage, spaetzle, and sauerkraut; the groaning buffet table also has roasted chicken and lots of salads, all uncomplicated and pretty uncontroversial grub. We suspect many guests are drawn by the 33-ounce steins of bier. Not the wurst place to spend an hour or two.

For do-it-yourselfers... Here's an insider's tip: Do as the locals do, and haunt the local supermarkets. **Publix** doesn't stay open till 11 every night for nothing. Both Publix and **Winn-Dixie** offer an astonishing array of prepared foods—from lemon-poppyseed muffins to antipasti to whole roasted chickens. Pick up a pack of plastic cutlery and you're on your way. Cheap (compared with restaurant fare, anyway), filling, and available anytime hunger strikes. A couple of close-to-Disney options: **Goodings Supermarket,** in Crossroads Shopping Center (also open 24 hours), and, in a pinch, **Gourmet Pantry,** at Downtown Disney, for the makings of a quick feed or picnic-to-go.

The Index

$$$$	over $25
$$$	$15–$25
$$	$7–$14
$	under $7

Per person for dinner entrées plus drink, not including tax or tip.

All-Star Cafe Orlando. They shoot, they slide, they slam-dunk, and they sink their millions into theme restaurants. This "ultimate sports cafe" (their words), complete with baseball mitt–shaped booths, is the "brainchild" of Tiger Woods, Shaq, Joe Montana, Wayne Gretzky, Monica Seles, and Andre Agassi. It joins the roster of All-Star Cafes in Las Vegas, Myrtle Beach, Melbourne, Australia, and elsewhere. Worth a visit if you're a fan.... *Tel 407/827–8326. Disney's Wide World of Sports complex, Walt Disney World.* $$
(see p. 74)

Artist Point. This Pacific Northwest–themed restaurant doesn't live up to the rest of the wonderful Wilderness Lodge.... *Tel 407/WDW–DINE. Wilderness Lodge, Walt Disney World.* $$$ **(see pp. 85, 86)**

Beaches and Cream Soda Shop. Slip into this cool, old-fashioned soda shop for a Milky Way sundae, a fudge "mud-slide," or a thick malted.... *Tel 407/WDW–DINE. Yacht and Beach Club Resorts, Walt Disney World.* $ **(see p. 86)**

Bergamo's. The menu and wine list span several regions of Italy; the singing servers throw in Italian ballads, show tunes, and opera. Dinner served after 5pm nightly; music starts at 7.... *Tel 407/352–3805. The Mercado, 8445 International Dr., Orlando. Reservations recommended.* $$$ **(see p. 89)**

Biergarten. Accordion playing, lederhosen, hearty fare—and, of course, *bier*—reign supreme at this German banquet hall.... *Tel 407/WDW–DINE. Germany Showcase, Epcot. Reservations recommended. $$$* **(see p. 93)**

Bistro de Paris. Despite its name, le Bistro is a bit more upscale than its downstairs Epcot neighbor, Chefs de France, which also draws on the creations of top French chefs Paul Bocuse, Roger Vergé, and Gaston Lenotre.... *Tel 407/WDW–DINE. France Showcase, Epcot. Reservations recommended. $$$* **(see p. 80)**

Blondie's. Home of the Dagwood, named in honor of comic-strip protagonist Dagwood Bumstead (remember his towering sandwiches?). Buy a stacked sandwich, by the inch.... *Tel 407/363–8000. Toon Lagoon, Universal Studios Islands of Adventure. $* **(se p. 82)**

Bob Marley—A Tribute to Freedom. A re-creation of the King of Reggae's home in Kingston, Jamaica, with lush greenery and authentic eats/drinks like roasted plantains, Jamaican beef patties, and Red Stripe Beer.... *Tel 407/363–8000. Universal Studios CityWalk. $$* **(see p. 75)**

Bongos Cuban Cafe. Disney goes Cuban, enhanced by the star-power of celeb-owner Gloria Estefan and hubby Emilio. The food's fine, but the setting's better, especially if you sit on the patio.... *Tel 407/828–0999. www.bongoscubancafe.com. Downtown Disney West Side. $$–$$$* **(see pp. 77, 86)**

Brian's. Cheap eats, cheesy decor; just what you want in an All-American diner.... *Tel 407/896–9912. 1409 N. Orange Ave., Orlando. $* **(see p. 74)**

Café Tu Tu Tango. This funky little artists' loft serves a super tapas menu; everything costs $3.25 to $7.95.... *Tel 407/248–2222. 8625 International Dr., Orlando. $–$$* **(see p. 74)**

California Grill. Disney goes hip with this stylish restaurant atop the Contemporary Resort.... *Tel 407/WDW–DINE. The Contemporary Resort, Walt Disney World. Reservations recommended. $$$* **(see pp. 76, 77, 88)**

DINING | THE INDEX

Cantina de San Angel. Quick, grab one of the umbrellaed tables and a Mexican fast-food lunch. Or come for dinner and a margarita and watch the nightly IllumiNations laser show. Arrive early; other people have caught on to this strategy.... *Tel 407/WDW–DINE. Mexico Showcase, Epcot. $* **(see p. 81)**

Charley's Steak House. A bastion of big beef, award-winning Charley's serves flavorful, well-aged Western steaks and has an outstanding wine list.... *Tel 407/855–7130. 6107 S. Orange Blossom Trail, Orlando. Reservations recommended. $$$* **(see p. 88)**

Chef Mickey's Buffet. Join the world's favorite rodent as he whips up breakfast and dinner at Disney's Contemporary Resort. Breakfast served 7:30 to 11:30am; dinner from 5 to 9:30pm.... *Tel 407/WDW–DINE. The Contemporary Resort, Walt Disney World. $$* **(see p. 85)**

Cinderella's Royal Table. Dining here is the only way to get inside Cinderella's Castle at the Magic Kingdom, but you'll pay a princely sum for food not even fit for commoners.... *Tel 407/WDW–DINE. Cinderella's Castle, Magic Kingdom. $$$* **(see pp. 84, 91)**

Columbia Restaurant. Direct from Tampa's Ybor City (Cuban district) comes a spin-off of Florida's oldest restaurant, to, of all places, Disney's Town of Celebration. Try the paella and the irresistible Cuban bread.... *Tel 407/566–1505. www.columbiarestaurant.com. 649 Front St., Celebration. $–$$* **(see p. 79)**

Commissary. How does Snow White keep her girlish figure? She noshes on the salads here. The healthier-than-average fare makes up for the lack of ambience.... *Tel 407/WDW–DINE. Disney-MGM Studios, Walt Disney World. $$–$$* **(see p. 80)**

Confisco Café. Where else can you dine with such fun couples as Rocky and Bullwinkle and Popeye and Olive Oyl? The one and only place to dine with the stars at Universal's Islands of Adventure, daily from 12 to 2. Pasta, steak, burgers, salads.... *Tel 407/363–8000. At park entrance, Universal Studios Islands of Adventure. $–$$* **(see p. 83)**

Coral Reef Restaurant. The pan-seared swordfish with Thai curry lobster sauce here may well be the best meal you'll eat at Epcot.... *Tel 407/WDW–DINE. The Living Seas, Epcot. Reservations recommended. $$$–$$$$*

(see pp. 88, 90)

Cosmic Ray's Starlight Cafe. Beat the fast-food blues with a fresh tossed salad—in the Magic Kingdom, no less. Reward yourself with one of those giant chocolate-chip cookies.... *Tel 407/WDW–DINE. Tomorrowland, the Magic Kingdom. $–$$*

(see p. 79)

Croissant Moon Bakery. Fresh-baked pastries, cappuccino, gourmet sandwiches.... *Tel 407/363–8000. At park entrance, Universal Studios Islands of Adventure.*

(see p. 83)

Crystal Palace. One of the least offensive dining options at the Magic Kingdom; just to play it safe, stick with the do-it-yourself salad or the fajitas.... *Tel 407/WDW–DINE. Main Street U.S.A., Magic Kingdom, Walt Disney World. $$*

(see pp. 79, 84, 90)

Dan Marino's Town Tavern. Don't count on seeing owner Marino (although they say he does pop in on occasion). The big draw is steaks and ribs, oak-grilled in the open kitchen, and—we suspect—the big TVs behind the football-shaped bar.... *Tel 407/363–1013. Pointe*Orlando, International Dr., Orlando. $$–$$$* **(see p. 78)**

Delfino Riviera. Named "most romantic" by a local newspaper, this high-end restaurant at Universal's Portofino Bay Hotel boasts views of the harbor and Ligurian specialties like minestrone à la Genovese.... *Tel 407/224–9255. Universal Studios Plaza. $$$–$$$$* **(see p. 89)**

Denny's. No one actually admits they eat at this fast-food diner chain, but get a load of the long lines at the I-Drive outpost on a Sunday morning.... *Tel 407/352–9335. 7960 International Dr., Orlando. $* **(see p. 73)**

Dux. A seasonally changing menu offers a creative international mix of ingredients.... *Tel 407/352–4000. 9801 International Dr., Orlando. Reservations recommended. $$$*

(see p. 71)

Electric Umbrella. Surprisingly good, cheap eats at Epcot, with little waiting (everybody else is at the World Showcase). Head toward the giant silver Spaceship Earth globe and you'll find it.... *Tel 407/WDW–DINE. Innoventions, Epcot. $* **(see p. 80)**

Emeril's Restaurant Orlando. Hotshot chef Emeril Lagasse created this culinary cousin of his New Orleans restaurant. They say he's around; we didn't see him bustling around the open kitchen. But once the food came, we were happily distracted.... *Tel 407/224-2424. www.emerils.com At Universal Studios CityWalk. $$$–$$$$* **(see pp. 76, 83)**

Enchanted Oak Tavern and Alchemy Bar. A cool example of Universal's playful approach to theme-park dining. Sit inside a giant faux oak tree, dig into some hickory-smoked chicken and a Dragon Scale Ale, and wait for Merlin to appear.... *Tel 407/363–8000. The Lost Continent, Universal Studios Islands of Adventure. $–$$* **(see pp. 74, 82)**

50's Prime-Time Cafe/Tune In Lounge. All pastel formica and chrome, in tune with the black-and-white sitcoms on the TVs—but as for the diner-type food, if Father knew best, he'd never show.... *Tel 407/WDW–DINE. Disney-MGM Studios. $$* **(see p. 91)**

Flying Fish Cafe. Lively, carnival-like setting and creative cuisine (try the oak-grilled scallops with lobster risotto) make this one worth a visit. Disney resort dining at its best.... *Tel 407/939–2359. Disney's Boardwalk, Walt Disney World. $$$* **(see pp. 85, 88)**

Front Street Grill. Disney's small-townish Celebration is the setting for this pleasant little place. Simple grilled chicken and fish preparations are the bill of fare.... *Tel 407/566–3448. Front St., Disney's Town of Celebration. $$–$$$* **(see p. 79)**

Fulton's Crab House. This West Coast transplant is right at home here on the Buena Vista Lagoon. Navigate the lengthy menu till you find your favorite shellfish.... *Tel 407/934-2628. www.fultonscrabhouse.com. Pleasure Island, Walt Disney World. $$$–$$$$* **(see pp. 78, 88)**

Garden Grill Restaurant. The fare runs to family-style American breakfasts and big platters of chicken, ribs, and fish.... *Tel 407/WDW–DINE. The Land pavilion, Future World, Epcot.* $$
(see pp. 85, 90)

Garden View Lounge. This sunlit spot overlooking formal gardens offers daily high tea—scones, jam tarts, those cunning little sandwiches, even strawberries and champagne.... *Tel 407/WDW–DINE. Grand Floridian Beach Resort, Walt Disney World.* $$–$$$
(see p. 76)

Giraffe Tavern. The ultimate cheap-eats venue in O-Town, where you'll find local folk and tourist types scarfing down free nachos, tacos, and burgers at the Happy Hour buffet, Mon–Fri from 4 to 7.... *Tel 407/828–2828; 800/248–7890. www.royalplaza.com. Hotel Royal Plaza, 1905 Hotel Plaza Blvd., Lake Buena Vista.*
(see p. 74)

Goodings Supermarket. 24-hour supermarket directly across the highway from the entrance to Disney Village Marketplace.... *Tel 407/827–1200. Crossroads Shopping Center, State Rd. 535, Lake Buena Vista.*
(see p. 93)

Gourmet Pantry. Besides gourmet goodies like garlic-infused olive oil and Mickey-shaped pasta, this shop also has a few necessity items, like snack packs of cereal, milk, cheese, even baby food.... *Tel 407/828–3486. Downtown Disney Marketplace, Walt Disney World.*
(see p. 93)

Green Eggs & Ham Cafe. At this green ham–shaped cafe, you can get real green eggs and ham, or a normal-hued breakfast. Cute as can be.... *Tel 407/363–8000. Seuss Landing, Universal Studios Islands of Adventure.* $
(see p. 82)

Hard Rock Cafe. The world's largest Hard Rock seats 2,000 for concerts, serves burgers 'n fries, pie a la mode.... *Tel 407/351–7625. Universal Studios CityWalk* $$ (see pp. 75, 77)

Hollywood Brown Derby. A replica of the original Brown Derby in California (same menu, too), with irritatingly slow service.... *Tel 407/WDW–DINE. Hollywood Blvd., Disney-MGM Studios.* $$$
(see p. 92)

DINING | THE INDEX

Hollywood & Vine. Minnie goes glam, Chip 'n' Dale don bow ties at character breakfasts here, daily. Buffet-style eats.... *Tel 407/WDW–DINE. Disney-MGM Studios, Walt Disney World. $$* **(see p. 85)**

Hoop-Dee-Doo Revue. *The* most popular dinner show at Walt Disney World. It's corny, it's country; it's so cute it'll make your teeth hurt....Family-style vittles include ribs, fried chicken, and corn on the cob.... *Tel 407/WDW–DINE. Three shows nightly at Pioneer Hall, Fort Wilderness Campground, Walt Disney World. Reservations required. $$$$*
(see p. 72)

House of Blues. Terrific musical acts and delicious Southern comfort food (with a contemporary slant) make this house one you'll want to hang out in. The Sunday Gospel Brunch is not to be missed.... *Tel 407/934–2583. www.hob.com. Downtown Disney West Side, Walt Disney World. Must be over 21 for evening performances. Ticket prices and meal prices are separate. $$ (performances), $$ (meals), $$$ (gospel brunch)* **(see pp. 77, 87)**

Jimmy Buffett's Margaritaville. Wasting away again is right. You could wait forever for a cheeseburger in paradise here; it's that busy. Count on lotsa families with preteens, an erupting volcano (of Margarita mix) when the blender needs refilling, and "Floribbean" cuisine.... *Tel 407/363–8000. Universal Studios CityWalk. $$–$$$ (plus $10 cover charge nightly after 10pm)* **(see pp. 75, 77, 79, 83)**

Johnny Rockets. Yes, it's part of a national chain, but you'll relish the idea of spending chump change on a chili dog if you've just blown a wad at FAO Schwarz or the Disney Store.... *Tel 407/903–0762. Pointe*Orlando, 9101 International Dr. $* **(see p. 75)**

Jungle Jim's. The jungle theme is fun and the menu is absolutely foolproof if you've got persnickety kids in tow: burgers and chicken sandwiches in a zillion variations.... *Tel 407/827–1257. Crossroads Shopping Plaza, State Rd. 535, Lake Buena Vista. Tel 407/872–3111. 55 W. Church St., near Church Street Station, Orlando. $$*
(see p. 78)

Latin Quarter. Somehow, the shortish menu claims to repre-
sent 21 Latin nations. Look for snapper Veracruz, black
beans and rice, and plaintains and flan, all spiced up with
live music and impromptu merengue lessons.... *Tel 407/
363–5922; 888/745–2846. www.thelatinquarter.com.
Universal Studios CityWalk. $$–$$$ (plus cover charge of
$4 Sun–Thur; $10 Fri.–Sat.)* **(see p. 83)**

Le Cellier Steakhouse. Cool, dark, and the food has
improved.... *Tel 407/WDW–DINE. Canada Showcase, Epcot.*
$$$ **(see p. 82)**

Le Coq au Vin. Rustic French food and not a smidgen of snob-
bery. No wonder in-the-know locals have made this their
favorite haunt.... *Tel 407/851–6980. 4800 S. Orange Ave.,
Orlando. $$$* **(see p. 77)**

Les Chefs de France. Foodies make this restaurant their first
priority at Epcot. The bill of fare features dishes created by
three top French chefs—Paul Bocuse, Roger Vergé, and
Gaston Lenotre—at their own restaurants in Paris and
Lyons.... *Tel 407/WDW–DINE. France Showcase, Epcot.
Priority seating recommended. $$$* **(see p. 80)**

Liberty Inn. Epcot's casual American restaurant serves sorry
old hamburgers and hot dogs. Give it a miss.... *Tel 407/
WDW–DINE. American Adventure pavilion, Epcot. $*
(see p. 82)

Liberty Tree Tavern. Goofy goes Patriotic at this faux Colonial
cafe. Character dinners nightly from 4 pm.... *Tel 407/WDW–
DINE. Magic Kingdom, Walt Disney World. $$* **(see p. 85)**

L'Originale Alfredo di Roma Ristorante. Heavy food, overly
fussy decor, and strolling opera singers.... *Tel 407/WDW–DINE.
Italy Showcase, Epcot. Reservations recommended. $$$*
(see p. 81)

Main Street Bakery. We dare you to pass by on your way into
the Magic Kingdom—the aroma of freshly baked chocolate-
chip cookies and pastries and fresh-brewed coffee is irre-
sistible.... *Tel 407/WDW–DINE. Main Street U.S.A., Magic
Kingdom. $* **(see p. 91)**

DINING | THE INDEX

Mama Della's Ristorante. Mama Della welcomes you to her "home" at the Portofino Bay Hotel, pushing pasta on you with a "Mangia! Mangia!" Sounds hokey, but who care's when the food's so good?.... *Tel 407/224–9255. Portofino Bay Hotel, Universal Blvd. $$–$$$* **(see p. 89)**

Mama Melrose's Ristorante Italiano. A casual trattoria with great pizza—and shorter lines than at other Disney-MGM Studios eateries.... *Tel 407/WDW–DINE. New York Street back lot, Disney-MGM Studios. $$–$$$* **(see p. 92)**

Manuel's on the 28th. Splurge-worthy dining atop the Barnett Bank Building in downtown Orlando. The city lights sparkle, the Asian-spiced rack of lamb sizzles.... *Tel 407/246–6580. www.culinaryconceptsinc.com. Suite 2800, 390 N. Orange Ave., Orlando. Jackets preferred. $$$$* **(see p. 75)**

Matsunoma Lounge. One of Epcot's best-kept secrets (till now); sneak away to the second floor of the Mitsukoshi Department Store at World Showcase Japan, nibble sushi, and sample a sake martini.... *Tel 407/WDW–DINE. World Showcase Japan, Epcot. $* **(see p. 82)**

Mel's Drive-In. Da Fonz would approve of this cool classic diner at Universal Studios.... *Tel 407/363–8000. Hollywood Blvd., Universal Studios Florida. $* **(see p. 92)**

Monty's Conch Harbor. With its giant-shark motif, this wouldn't be out of place at the theme parks. Part of a South Florida chain, Monty's does a good grouper sandwich and stone crab claws (in season).... *Tel 407/354–1122, 888/584–3555. www.montysstonecrab.com. Pointe*Orlando, 9101 International Dr. $$* **(see p. 79)**

Morton's of Chicago. The thick, expensive steaks and testosterone—er, smoke-filled air make this a real manly-man dining spot.... *Tel 407/248–3485. The Marketplace at Dr. Phillips, 7600 Dr. Phillips Blvd., Orlando. $$$$* **(see p. 87)**

Motown Cafe Orlando. Don't expect soul food—the closest you'll get is sweet potato fritters (on the appetizer menu)—but, if you're a fan, you'll get a kick out of the Motown cover bands and '60s memorabilia. Entrees include grilled chicken fettucine, steak, and prime rib....

Tel 407/224–2500. Universal Studios CityWalk, Universal Escape. $$–$$$ **(see p. 77)**

Mythos. The Mediterranean-influenced menu looks dandy, but who has time for a fancy sitdown meal when the line at Doctor Doom's Fearfall is growing longer by the minute?.... *Tel 407/363–8000. The Lost Continent, Universal Studios Islands of Adventure. $$* **(see p. 82)**

NASCAR Cafe Orlando. Raise the checkered flag—uh, table-cloth—and dig into "down-home American" cuisine amid grease-monkey decor. If the thought of this makes your heart race, have at it.... *Tel 407/224–7223. www.nascar cafe.com. Universal Studios CityWalk. $$* **(see p. 77)**

NBA City. Even if you think "music" when you hear the word "Celtic," you won't mind the food at this shrine to round-ball. Thankfully, it's more restaurant than sports bar, with some tasty pasta dishes, good sandwiches, and killer milkshakes.... *Tel 407/363–5919. www.NBACity.com. Universal Studios CityWalk. $$* **(see pp. 74, 84)**

1900 Park Fare. This buffet-style restaurant, dominated by Big Bertha, a century-old band organ built in Paris, offers breakfast with Mary Poppins and dinner with Mickey and Minnie.... *Tel 407/WDW–DINE. Grand Floridian Beach Resort, Walt Disney World. $$* **(see p. 85)**

Numero Uno. Succumb to the urge for a Cuban sandwich, yellow rice and chicken, or black beans and rice, made right, at this friendly hole-in-the-wall.... *Tel 407/841–3840. 2499 S. Orange Ave., Orlando. $* **(see p. 74)**

Olympia. You'll experience everything Athens except the pollution at this friendly Greek restaurant.... *Tel 407/273–7836. 8505 E. Colonial Dr., Orlando. $$* **(see p. 74)**

Park Plaza Gardens. Eat al fresco, in a New Orleans-style courtyard setting.... *Tel 407/645–2475. 319 Park Ave. South, Winter Park. $$$* **(see p. 87)**

Pasta Piazza Ristorante. A nice, cheap spaghetti-and-lasagna place at Epcot.... *Tel 407/WDW–DINE. Innovations West, Future World, Epcot. $* **(see p. 81)**

Pat O'Brien's Orlando. An authentic reproduction of the original in New Orleans. On offer are the usual Creole faves (catfish, jambalaya), plus the famous Hurricane drink concoction and dueling pianos (a concept dreamed up by Pat O'Brien's, they say).... *Tel 407/224–2690. Universal Studios CityWalk. $$–$$$* **(see p. 83)**

Pebbles. Our antidote to theme-park/theme-restaurant over-load—not a kooky costume or wild animal to be found, just pale wood and plants and really tasty food.... *Tel 407/827–1111. www.pebblesrestaurant.com. Crossroads Shopping Plaza, State Rd. 535, Lake Buena Vista. Tel 407/839–0892. 17 W. Church St., Orlando. Tel 407/839–0892. At junction of I-4 (exit 49) and State Rd. 434, Orlando. $$–$$$* **(see pp. 75, 78, 79)**

The Player's Grill. Home of the NFL Players, with a menu created by New Orleans restauranteur Ralph Brennan. More than 300 NFL players visited in the last couple of years, they say, so you know the portions must be gigantic, and lean toward manly-man choices like steaks, ribs, and surf-and-turf. Some Nawlins faves, too.... *Tel 407/903–1974. Pointe*Orlando, 9101 International Dr. $$–$$$* **(see p. 74)**

Portobello Yacht Club. Styled in New England nautical, this Pleasure Island restaurant can be bustling and noisy, but the northern Italian cuisine compensates.... *Tel 407/934–8888. www.portobellorestaurant.com. 1650 Buena Vista Dr., Pleasure Island, Walt Disney World. $$$* **(see p. 89)**

Publix Supermarkets. Go ahead, sneak one of their rotisserie chickens into your hotel room. Known for great bakery goods, too. Open late.... *Tel 407/351–6745. 7733 Turkey Lake Rd.; Tel 407/397–1171. Xcentury City Center, 2925 International Dr., Kissimmee; plus other locations* **(see p. 93)**

Pure & Simple. Epcot's nod to healthful dining features tuna and chicken salads, turkey sandwiches, and fruit smoothies.... *Tel 407/WDW–DINE. Future World, Epcot. $* **(see p. 90)**

Race Rock Supercharged Restaurant. A shrine to motor sports, decked out with race cars, race boats, and *Bigfoot,*

the world's largest monster truck. Fare runs to sandwiches, salads, pasta, pizza, and prime rib.... *Tel 407/248–9876. www.racerock.com. 8986 International Dr., Orlando.* $$
(see p. 77)

Rainforest Cafe. P.C. to the max, this eatery at Downtown Disney Marketplace is a simulated tropical rainforest environment.... *Tel 407/827–8500. www.rainforestcafe.com. Disney Downtown Marketplace, Walt Disney World. Tel 407/938–9100. Disney's Animal Kingdom, Walt Disney World.* $$
(see p. 78)

Restaurantasaurus. The Big Cheese, Goofy, Donald, and Pluto entertain the young'uns at this bountiful breakfast buffet.... *Tel 407/WDW–DINE. Disney's Animal Kingdom, Walt Disney World.* $$
(see p. 85)

Restaurant Akershus. An all-you-can-eat Norwegian buffet, called a *koldtbord*, in a large, medieval fortress–style dining room.... *Tel 407/WDW–DINE. Norway World Showcase, Epcot.* $$–$$$
(see p. 92)

Restaurant Marrakesh. Some Epcot guests may need a little nudge to try this adventurous cuisine, but it's a gem—a palatial dining room serving distinctive food.... *Tel 407/WDW–DINE. Morocco Showcase, Epcot.* $$
(see p. 80)

Rose & Crown Pub and Dining Room. Cottage pie, fish and chips, and other British pub standards are served here. The pub, in the front part of the restaurant, pours ales, stouts, and lagers; high tea, served daily at 3:30pm, is very popular.... *Tel 407/WDW–DINE. United Kingdom Showcase, Epcot.* $$–$$$
(see p. 81)

San Angel Inn Restaurant. This enchanting Mexican restaurant serves up specialties like *huachinango a la Veracruzana* (red snapper poached in wine with onions, tomatoes, and chilies) and *mole poblano* (chicken with mole sauce).... *Tel 407/WDW–DINE. Mexico Showcase, Epcot.* $$–$$$
(see p. 81)

Sci-Fi Dine-In Theater Restaurant. Cool—this place really does feel like a drive-in, as you slip into a convertible and watch sci-fi movies playing on the giant screen. Alas, no magic happens in the kitchen.... *Tel 407/WDW–DINE. Disney-MGM Studios. $$* **(see pp. 76, 91)**

Shoney's. This casual Southern family restaurant chain offers low prices and diner-type food—get your patty melt here. There are at least 10 of 'em in the Orlando area (we stopped counting).... *Tel 407/248–9050. 7437 International Dr., Orlando, and other locations. $–$$* **(see p. 73)**

Sleepy Hollow. Skip the Mickey-on-a-stick ice cream and have a real (quick) lunch, here, say a veggie chili and an iced capuccino.... *Tel 407/WDW–DINE. Disney-MGM Studios, Walt Disney World. $* **(see p. 80)**

Soundstage Restaurant. If you're doing the Disney-MGM Studios thang and dying to see the Disney gang, this one's a sure bet. Characters show up to meet and greet at the breakfast buffet.... *Tel 407/WDW–DINE. Disney-MGM Studios, Walt Disney World. Reservations only. $$*
(see p. 92)

Spoodles. Dig into a platter of tapas grandes and some sweet sangria, and you'll swear you're in Costa del Sol, not Costa del Disney.... *Tel 407/939–3463. Disney's BoardWalk, Walt Disney World. $$–$$$* **(see p. 86)**

Sunset Ranch Market. Hot diggity dogs. Six kinds of hot dogs here, with all the necessary add-ons like chili and sauerkraut. Cheap eats (but you'll pay for it later).... *Disney-MGM Studios, Walt Disney World. $* **(see p. 92)**

Turkey Leg Wagon. Forget the Magic Kingdom's mediocre sit-down restaurants—nosh here on a hefty, meal-size smoked turkey leg.... *Tel 407/WDW–DINE. Frontierland, The Magic Kingdom. $* **(see pp. 74, 91)**

Victoria & Albert's. Overstuffed Victorian restaurant featuring luxury dishes like sweetbreads and roast duckling. Romantic elegance is laid on with a trowel by way of floating violinists, fresh flowers, gleaming china, and low lighting.... *Tel 407/WDW–DINE. Grand Floridian Beach Resort, Walt Disney World. Reserve as far in advance as possible. $$$$* **(see p. 75)**

Whispering Canyon Cafe. A rustic setting (complete with views of slash pines) and wood-smoked meats and chicken make this family-friendly restaurant the best bet at the Wilderness Lodge. Food is all-you-can-eat, served family-style on big platters.... *Tel 407/WDW–DINE. Wilderness Lodge, Walt Disney World. $$–$$$* **(see p. 86)**

White Wolf Cafe. A real gem on N. Orange Ave., with inspired choices for vegetarians and meat-eaters alike. Open for lunch and dinner. Try the Moroccan chicken salad with honey-curry dressing or the veggie black bean soup. Soon to come at White Wolf: a wood-burning pizza oven.... *Tel 407/895–5590. 1829 N. Orange Ave. (downtown Orlando.) $–$$* **(see p. 76)**

Wildhorse Saloon. Dig into some all-American BBQ while watching the next country music superstar strut his/her stuff.... *Tel 407/824–4321. Downtown Disney Pleasure Island, Walt Disney World. $$* **(see pp. 77, 87)**

Wild Jack's. Where to go for great steaks and too much food; make sure to try the Tex-Mex treats.... *Tel 407/352–4407. 7364 International Dr., Orlando. $$–$$$* **(see p. 88)**

Winn-Dixie Supermarkets. Suffering from restaurant burn-out? Get dinner-to-go here, where the goods include lots of prepared deli items, salads, and a fresh fruit bar. Pharmacy and one-hour photo, too.... *Tel 407/859–4013. 2103 Americana Blvd. (off I-Drive), and several other area locations. $* **(see p. 93)**

Wimpy's. Listen to the squeals of the river-rafters braving Popeye and Bluto's rapids as you dig into your burger basket, chicken fingers, or (amen) fruit cup. Haute cuisine, no, but not bad for theme-park fast-food fare.... *Tel 407/363–8000. Toon Lagoon, Universal's Islands of Adventure. $–$$* **(see p. 82)**

Wolfgang Puck Café. Sample signature dishes created by superchef Puck, including wood-fired pizzas and pastas. Head downstairs for elegant Art Deco digs and a little peace and quiet.... *Tel 407/938–9653. Downtown Disney, Walt Disney World. $$–$$$* **(see pp. 76, 77, 87)**

DINING | THE INDEX

Yachtsman's Steakhouse. Yacht club burgees (flags) and a glassed-in butcher shop alone can't make this into a tempting option. For hard-core preppies only.... *Tel 407/WDW–DINE. Disney's Yacht Club Resort, Walt Disney World. $$$* **(see p. 88)**

Orlando/Walt Disney World Area Dining

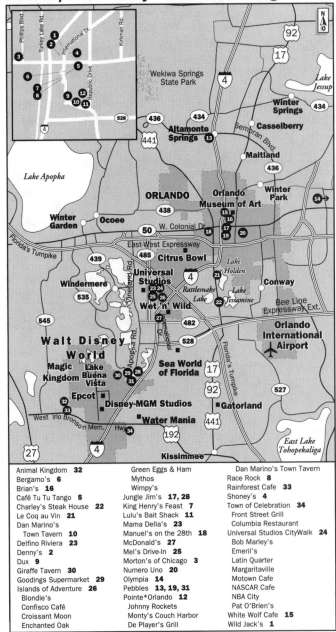

Animal Kingdom **32**	Green Eggs & Ham	Dan Marino's Town Tavern
Bergamo's **6**	Mythos	Race Rock **8**
Brian's **16**	Wimpy's	Rainforest Cafe **33**
Café Tu Tu Tango **5**	Jungle Jim's **17, 28**	Shoney's **4**
Charley's Steak House **22**	King Henry's Feast **7**	Town of Celebration **34**
Le Coq au Vin **21**	Lulu's Bait Shack **11**	Front Street Grill
Dan Marino's	Mama Della's **23**	Columbia Restaurant
Town Tavern **10**	Manuel's on the 28th **18**	Universal Studios CityWalk **24**
Delfino Riviera **23**	McDonald's **27**	Bob Marley's
Denny's **2**	Mel's Drive-In **25**	Emeril's
Dux **9**	Morton's of Chicago **3**	Latin Quarter
Giraffe Tavern **30**	Numero Uno **20**	Margaritaville
Goodings Supermarket **29**	Olympia **14**	Motown Cafe
Islands of Adventure **26**	Pebbles **13, 19, 31**	NASCAR Cafe
Blondie's	Pointe*Orlando **12**	NBA City
Confisco Café	Johnny Rockets	Pat O'Brien's
Croissant Moon	Monty's Couch Harbor	White Wolf Cafe **15**
Enchanted Oak	De Player's Grill	Wild Jack's **1**

Walt Disney World Dining

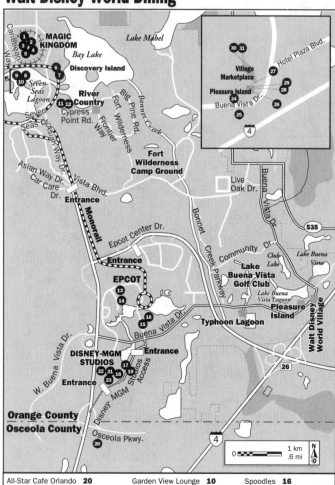

All-Star Cafe Orlando **20**
Artist Point **11**
Beaches and Cream Soda Shop **13**
Bongos Cuban Cafe **24**
California Grill **7**
Chef Mickey's Buffet **6**
Cinderella's Royal Table **2**
Cosmic Ray's Starlight Cafe **4**
Crystal Palace **1**
50's Prime-Time Cafe/
 Tune In Lounge **23**
Flying Fish Cafe **15**
Fulton's Crab House **26**

Garden View Lounge **10**
Gourmet Pantry **31**
Hollywood Brown Derby **18**
House of Blues **29**
Main Street Bakery **5**
Mama Melrose's
 Ristorante **22**
1900 Park Fare **8**
Portobello Yacht Club **27**
Rainforest Cafe **30**
Sci-Fi Dine-In Theater
 Restaurant **21**
Soundstage Rest. **19**

Spoodles **16**
Sunset Ranch Market **17**
Turkey Leg Wagon **3**
Victoria & Albert's **9**
Whispering Canyon Cafe **12**
Wildhorse Saloon **28**
Wolfgang Puck Café **25**
Yachtsman's
 Steakhouse **14**

Dining at Epcot

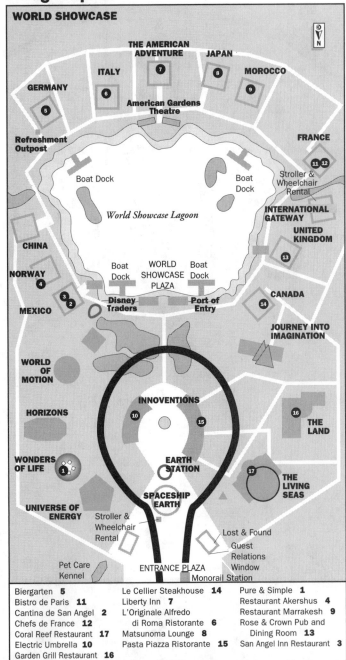

WORLD SHOWCASE

N

GERMANY

ITALY

THE AMERICAN ADVENTURE

JAPAN

MOROCCO

American Gardens Theatre

Refreshment Outpost

Boat Dock

Boat Dock

World Showcase Lagoon

FRANCE

Stroller & Wheelchair Rental

INTERNATIONAL GATEWAY

UNITED KINGDOM

CHINA

NORWAY

Boat Dock

WORLD SHOWCASE PLAZA

Boat Dock

MEXICO

Disney Traders

Port of Entry

CANADA

JOURNEY INTO IMAGINATION

WORLD OF MOTION

HORIZONS

INNOVENTIONS

THE LAND

WONDERS OF LIFE

EARTH STATION

THE LIVING SEAS

UNIVERSE OF ENERGY

SPACESHIP EARTH

Stroller & Wheelchair Rental

Lost & Found

Guest Relations Window

Pet Care Kennel

ENTRANCE PLAZA

Monorail Station

Biergarten **5**	Le Cellier Steakhouse **14**	Pure & Simple **1**
Bistro de Paris **11**	Liberty Inn **7**	Restaurant Akershus **4**
Cantina de San Angel **2**	L'Originale Alfredo	Restaurant Marrakesh **9**
Chefs de France **12**	di Roma Ristorante **6**	Rose & Crown Pub and
Coral Reef Restaurant **17**	Matsunoma Lounge **8**	Dining Room **13**
Electric Umbrella **10**	Pasta Piazza Ristorante **15**	San Angel Inn Restaurant **3**
Garden Grill Restaurant **16**		

3

sions

However you feel
about the Disney
empire, a visit to
its theme parks
will show you
what this
company does

best: create an environment where no detail is overlooked, where "cast members" (don't ever call them employees) are perennially Prozac-perky, where every scrap of litter is whisked away the moment it's dropped. Eventually, Disney's 27,000-acre spread will offer every form of entertainment known to man, neatly packaged and perfected and plasticized. Even now, it could take you a week just to do Disney once over lightly, what with all the golf courses, horseback rides, water sports, and myriad other offerings that most day guests are too overwhelmed to scope out.

If you're a tourist, the insidious ease and self-containment of Walt Disney World, along with its reliability—always clean, always friendly, always scrupulously maintained—can suck you in like quicksand. If you're a traveler, though, you might be tempted to break out beyond the gates of Walt Disney World. Not that there's anything particularly rustic or authentic out there; Orlando's theme parks and attractions number 60-plus (as of this writing), but if you make enough passes along I-4 you'll swear there are more, what with all the high-tech billboards grabbing your attention.

The parks themselves run the gamut. At one end, there's turbo-charged Universal Studios Escape, which is the most-visited attraction in the country after the Disney theme parks. It's instructive to take a look at what's happening here: Once upon a time there was one park, Universal Studios. Today, Universal Studios Escape has mushroomed into a complete destination resort, including two major amusement parks, Universal Studios and Islands of Adventure (with plans for more already on the drawing board); the CityWalk entertainment complex, featuring a mix of restaurants and cafes, live music, nightclubs, theaters and specialty shops; and a cluster of themed hotels and resorts. At the other end of the spectrum, there's homespun Gatorland, where one of the featured shows presents live alligators jumping up to snatch dead chickens.

Getting Your Bearings

Here's the drill: I-4 officially runs east and west, no matter what it looks like on the map, and the exit numbers go higher as you head east. Other major highways, all of which intersect with I-4, are the Florida Turnpike, Highway 528 (the Bee Line Expressway), and U.S. 192 (Irlo Bronson Memorial Highway), where all the low-rent motels and fast-food chains are lined up. Walt Disney World straddles the I-4/U.S. 192 intersection, about 17 miles south of downtown Orlando.

Orlando proper melts imperceptibly into Kissimmee and Lake Buena Vista at this point; don't even bother trying to tell them apart.

Finding your way around Walt Disney World itself is more complicated. Most newcomers stagger around at first, awestruck by the sheer size and scope of Disney World—which encompasses nearly 50 square miles' worth of theme parks, resort hotels, golf courses, and water parks. For starters, there are the Big Four parks—the Magic Kingdom, Epcot, Disney-MGM Studios, and Disney's Animal Kingdom—and five smaller parks, Pleasure Island (see Nightlife and Entertainment), Blizzard Beach, Typhoon Lagoon, Discovery Island, and River Country (see Getting Outside). Each park is miles from the others, carved into a landscape that once consisted of mangrove swamps and orange groves; guests navigate the property by bus, car, monorail, and ferryboat. To survive, you've got to get map-happy: Stop at Disney's Transportation and Ticket Center, where, along with plunking down loads of money for those essential park passes, you can pick up a good map of the entire property along with route information for Disney's monorail, buses, and boats. Grab another map every time you enter a theme park, and you should have it made in the shade.

Theme Park Strategy

You've gotta have a game plan at the World, or the overwhelming sprawl will leave you dazed and confused, wondering, "Did I leave the kids at Splash Mountain, or was it Big Thunder Mountain? Did I park at the 'Chip' lot, or was it 'Dale'?" A few tips:

• If your time is limited, consider staying at a Disney hotel; you'll spend less time commuting, and thus more time at the parks, and you may also be able to benefit from the special early-admission mornings.

• If you can come during the off-season, that's all the better for avoiding lines.

• Skip the so-so mid-afternoon parades and head for the most popular rides then, when lots of park visitors have been siphoned off to stand on the sidewalks craning their necks at floats and costumed characters.

• If you start to burn out mid-day, take a break (for a late lunch, a swim, or a nap) and return to the park around 5 or 6pm, refreshed and raring to go—when everyone else is heading home. Re-entering the park is allowed, even if you're not a Disney guest, as long as you get your hand stamped on your way out.

DIVERSIONS | INTRODUCTION

• Whatever you do, don't waste your time at the parks' full-service restaurants, except at Epcot, where the restaurants are as much fun as the attractions. Instead, stuff your backpack full of goodies (although this is technically against the rules), and just grab snacks, fruit, and fast food on your theme park days.

Price Tag for the Kingdom and Beyond

When it comes to Disney admission prices, there are just about as many ticket options as there are tiny plastic bricks in a Lego pirate ship—and figuring them out takes as much time as putting the ship together. Okay, it's not quite that bad…but just watch the puzzled faces of guests as they gaze at the ticket window. Basically, this is about what it will cost you: one-day, one-park ticket, $48.76 (adults), $39.22 (children 3–9); four-day park hopper pass (one-day admission at Magic Kingdom, Animal Kingdom, Epcot, and MGM Studios), $186.56 (adults), $150.52 (children 3–9); six-day park hopper plus pass (admission to all Disney parks, including water parks, Pleasure Island, and Discovery Island), $281.99 (adults), $230.03 (children 3–9). On the non-Disney front, one-day admission to Universal Studios Florida or Sea World Adventure Park is $48.76 for adults and around $35 for children 3–9. The Orlando FlexTicket offers unlimited admission to Universal Studios, Islands of Adventure, Sea World Adventure Park, and Wet 'n' Wild Orlando. A four-park, seven-day ticket is $169.55 for adults and $127.95 for children 3–9. (For an extra thirty-odd dollars, you can also purchase a five-park, ten-day pass that includes Busch Gardens in Tampa, as well, for $209.95.)

The Lowdown

Best rides for adrenaline junkies… Seems like being scared silly is a much-sought-after state of being these days, and both Disney and Universal do a kick-butt job at providing it. We'll give the nod to Universal, though, for its over-the-top attractions, which their spin masters call the "most thrilling and technologically advanced rides and attractions ever made…." Who's to argue after taking a ride (let's call it a trip) on the **Amazing Adventures of Spider-Man?** This ride combines the sensory tricks of the famed Back to the Future attraction and the 3-D accomplishments of Terminator 2.

Spider-Man is with you all the way, seemingly within touch, as your car hurtles through New York street scenes, past spewing water pipes and raging fires, smashing into vehicles as you go. The ride culminates when Doc Ock takes aim at you with his anti-gravity gun, sending you into a 400-foot sensory plunge. It's not to be missed, though you'll have to be prepared to stand in line for the thrill; waits of 60 to 90 minutes are not uncommon. Surprisingly, three heart-thumping Disney attractions can be found in the sweet little **Magic Kingdom: Buzz Lightyear's Space Ranger Spin, Alien Encounter,** and **Space Mountain.** The Buzz Lightyear ride is a real hoot for folks of all ages. You'll climb aboard a space shuttle and travel the galaxy. The thrill is not so much in the speed or the effects—instead, the object is to fire laser gun pistols at fast-moving interplanetary objects along the way; you get points for every target you hit. Plan on doing this ride over and over, as most people get caught up in their scores and want to try to up them on the next ride. It's sort of an arcade/pinball-type thrill, with the accompanying addiction. Space Mountain set the standard for Disney thrill rides years ago, when this coaster first plunged into the black hole of space. You can't miss it: a 180-foot concrete-and-steel structure, with a line at its entrance about as long as the distance to the moon. (When the doors open at the Kingdom in the morning, watch where everyone sprints to.) The ride hurtles you through the cosmos in almost complete darkness, with flashing comets, shooting stars, and a good amount of twists, turns, and plunges. It's a long wait for a three-minute ride (that's the Disney way— deal with it or be miserable). Still, you haven't done Disney, some say, until you've done Space Mountain. Alien Encounter is worse for many guests, we fear, because you feel a little trapped, strapped into your chair, with your head and neck supported. They really play up the suspense, building and building to a gross-out finale. Less gutsy types may prefer the Magic Kingdom's Splash Mountain, Big Thunder Mountain Railroad, and the Haunted Mansion. The best of the Disney thrill rides, however, is the **Twilight Zone of Terror at Disney-MGM Studios,** which plays on that classic nightmare theme, the free-falling elevator. Every last detail is designed to bring you to another level (sorry) of fear: the dilapidated look of the hotel, the guest book (where

DIVERSIONS | THE LOWDOWN

nobody has ever signed out), the "ghost family" that disappeared forever on that fateful night, the sepulchral tones of narrator Rod Serling—and then, that horrifying moment when you plunge past the open window, 13 stories above the park, and realize this is no illusion. Think you weren't all that scared? Wait'll you see the picture of you they took via hidden camera. At **Epcot, Honey, I Shrunk the Audience** cranks up the thrill level of 3-D movies, thanks to some unexpected special effects like the feel of mice scurrying at your feet (and doffing those 3-D glasses won't help a bit); **Body Wars,** also at Epcot, is fun while it lasts but not as unique or memorable as Disney's other thrill rides (unless, of course, the looping movement makes you vomit; then you won't forget it). The **Countdown to Extinction at Animal Kingdom** takes riders back 65 million years, in order to rescue the last dinosaur before a meteor slams into Earth. You'll encounter the requisite robotic dinos along the way, experience the herky-jerky when you encounter meteor showers, and spend a good amount of time in the dark. If you've done Universal's Back to the Future ride, this one will be old hat. You're likely to find the sweet-sounding **It's Tough to Be a Bug!** show significantly more thrilling. This 3-D experience sends giant bugs into the audience with plenty of surprises. (We won't ruin it for you, but it's best not to take the little ones to this particular entertainment.) The multimillion-dollar **Twister** has been a winner since it first touched down at **Universal Studios**. Only in America would we take a natural disaster and turn it into a rip-roaring attraction. (In fact, the show was originally included in the plans for Universal Studios in Japan, then was canceled when locals cautioned against it. Guess they don't think twisters are all that funny.) But hold on to your hats—you're going to love it. You'll stand and watch as a giant funnel, some five stories tall, advances, throwing out gale-force winds and rain as it comes. Power lines fall, fires ignite, roofs tumble, trucks and cows fly....Then it's over, and you can breathe again. Universal also offers **Terminator 2 3-D,** a live-action and special-effects spectacular that is one outrageous outing. (No way would we bring little kids to this one, unless we covered their eyes for the duration; it's very intense.) Also at Universal, you can cruise along in the

Jaws boat, waiting for that 3-ton, latex-covered shark to emerge from the ocean. And waiting, and waiting....The anticipation builds, and—fake or not—the payoff is still guaranteed to make you jump.

Where the wild things are... Is it a theme park? A zoo? A nature preserve? **Disney's Animal Kingdom** tries to be all of these things, and doesn't quite hit the mark on any. Try as we might, we can't seem to love Disney's newest park. Basically, if it's thrills you seek, you're better off sticking to the tried-and-true theme parks—and if it's animals you want, there are lots of zoos that do a better job. We'll concede that the magnificent **Tree of Life,** the park's looming centerpiece, is truly stunning. The giant tree, measuring more than 50 feet at its base and towering to 145 feet high, features more than 300 hand-carved animal creatures. You could spend a good deal of time just gazing at it, or playing How many animals can you find? (not a bad exercise while you'll waiting in line). The Tree of Life is surrounded by four areas: **Africa, Camp Minnie-Mickey, Dinoland,** and the newly-opened **Asia.** Most guests flock to Africa for a trip on the much-touted **Kilimanjaro Safaris,** where you'll board oversized jeeps and travel through Disney's make-believe African savannah. The animals are real, and you're likely to see elephants, giraffes, hippos, maybe a sleeping lion or two, and tons of birds. Of course, along the way, SOMETHING GOES TERRIBLY WRONG...a bridge almost collapses, poachers are spotted....All turns out well, of course. Generally, however, you'll have more up-close encounters with critters at a large, well-run zoo than on this escapade.

You can pretty much cover all of Animal Kingdom in a short day: For a good rush and decent show, see **It's Tough to Be a Bug!,** nicely located in the Tree of Life. For a quick and cheap thrill, hit the **Countdown to Extinction** in Dinoland. For the requisite water ride, take a trip down the **Kali River Rapids** in Asia. Little kids will like both the playground in Dinoland and Camp Minnie-Mickey for their hurt-your-teeth-it's-so-sweet shows, like **Pocahontas and her Forest Friends.** The Camp *is* a good place to see Mickey, Minnie, Goofy, Pluto, and other Disney characters, though. Skip the train trip to oh-so-boring

Conservation Station, and the equally slow-moving boat rides around the village.

For some bona fide critter-watching, we suggest taking a boat to Disney's **Discovery Island** (tel 407/824–4321). This is the antithesis of the rest of Disney: It's small, old-fashioned, low-tech, and there are real animals! The lush 11-acre nature preserve, in the middle of Bay Lake, is the perfect escape from the theme-park madness. It's an accredited zoo filled with exotic birds and reptiles and a handful of low-key animal shows (no special effects, no drum rolls, no animated displays—hooray!). You can see Discovery in a couple of hours; walk along the winding, three-quarter-mile path to see laughing kookaburras from Australia, black-necked swans, fishing cats from Southeast Asia, giant Galapagos tortoises, alligators, toucans, and some 250 other species of birds.

Fright shows... When it comes to haunted houses, they don't get much worse (or better, depending on your point of view) than **Skull Kingdom** and **Terror on Church Street.** Both are independent attractions, located outside Orlando's major theme parks. In a town with plenty of candidates for the post, these take honors as the trashiest attraction (and we say that with the deepest respect for the art form). For local teens, it's a way to weed out the wusses, but tourists who dare to be scared make up a big part of the audiences at these high-tech spook houses. Skull Kingdom is very, very scary. You'll be sent off into pitch-dark corridors, feeling your way around as sinister and spooky characters—sometimes live and sometimes animated robots—jump out at you at every corner. Special effects, like blasted air, falling spiderwebs, opening doors, and loud noises will keep you jumping each step of the way. Nicely done. Terror on Church Street is also a hit in Europe, where it's called "Pasaje del Terror," proving that bad taste knows no geographic bounds. The concept, however, remains the same, with "remains" being the operative word. You'll join a group of other daredevils, hold hands, and journey forth through 23 spine-chilling theatrical sets. Don't expect witches and bats. Scenes are based on people's most horrifying nightmare visions (no, this does not include the line outside Universal's T2 3-D). Horrible and gross (wait'll you visit the morgue, where corpses on hooks start moving toward you), these vignettes combine live actors, special effects, and sound effects. Think Madame Tussaud's on acid. If you freak out midway (and many people do), there are plenty of escape exits.

Best places to lose your lunch... The great parks of Orlando were long devoid of top-notch roller-coaster thrills. Not anymore. Universal's **Islands of Adventure,** coined as the world's "most technologically advanced theme park," offers some of the best stomach-lurching thrills we've ever encountered. The **Dueling Dragons** ride, a mass of intertwining metal, hurls dragon-shaped racing cars at each other for a high-speed, near-miss nightmare. The cars travel up to 60 mph and come within (what seems like) less than 12 inches of each other. The Hulk Coaster shoots riders up 10 stories with G-force power, then turns them upside down, and sends them into a maze of tracks, plunging them under a bridge, and into underground trenches. You can't miss the 200-foot steel tower that houses **Doctor Doom's Fearfall.** As you get strapped into your seat, feet dangling, you'll learn that Doctor Doom has created a machine designed to drain the fear from you. It will basically drain everything from you (including color, and possibly stomach contents), as you fire up to the top of the structure and then plummet to the ground at an unreasonably speedy rate. Disney has countered Universal's entries with the new **Rock 'n' Roller Coaster starring Aerosmith** at **Disney-MGM Studios,** its first high-speed launch (0–60 mph in 2.8 seconds), upside-down roller coaster ride. On this ride, you'll be fastened into a mock "stretch limo" and thrown into a mangled maze of twists and turns, including three upside-down segments. Along the way, there are familiar Tinseltown scenes (though who's paying attention?) and a loud (there are 120 onboard speakers in each coaster train) Aerosmith soundtrack. We're told the music was synchronized with every twist and turn (but, again, who has time to notice?). On the other hand, **Big Thunder Mountain** at the **Magic Kingdom** is not really all that scary—it's basically a rickety ride on a runaway mine train, with cool props like skeletons that you may not notice as you're whipping around. Kids 40 inches tall can ride this one; for the other two, you must be at least 44 inches tall. A few sudden plummets and high-speed curves will give young ones (though not many adults) some thrills as they travel through old-mining-town

DIVERSIONS | THE LOWDOWN

scenery of faux rocks, fake chickens, and rushing water-falls. Note: This one's better at night.

At **Universal Studios,** the **Back to the Future** simulator ride does an incredibly convincing job of hurtling you, herky-jerky, through space (and nearly down a dinosaur's throat) in a souped-up DeLorean. **Sea World,** determined not to be left behind in the thrill category, has introduced **Kracken,** touted as the longest, tallest, fastest coaster in the land. Coaster afi-cionados—go for it! You'll also want to try the **Wild Arctic** ride, a lurching helicopter "flight" through the heart of a glacier.

Thrills and chills... Water rides (read, be prepared to get soaked): Either you love them or hate them. If you're in the former group, you won't find a better drive-and-drench ride than the **Jurassic Park River Adventure** at Universal's **Islands of Adventure.** Riders travel through a prehistoric land inhabited by fierce, unbelievably real-looking dinosaurs. Five-story creatures growl and bear teeth, some within inches of your face. The ride speeds up as you try to escape from a Tyrannosaurus rex, ending in a stomach-flopping, 85-foot plunge into water. A bit tamer, but just as wet, is the **Dudley Do-Right's Ripsaw Falls** ride. This water flume ride sends riders plummeting 75 feet down beneath the surface of the water. Disney's **Splash Mountain** at the **Magic Kingdom** is a 12-minute log flume ride featuring the characters and music from Disney's *Song of the South*. Riders travel through Brer Rabbit's land of gardens, swamps and caves, before a thrilling 87-foot, 40-mph drop at the end that will leave you completely drenched if you're seated in the first log. This is the best part of the ride, and it's the section which people see when they pass by or stand waiting in line. (Typically shrewd placement on Disney's part.) At **Disney's Animal Kingdom,** you can cool down on the popular **Kali River Rapids.** The faux setting is the turbu-lent Chakrandi River. Along the way you'll be bumped, dipped, rolled, and properly drenched. It's only fitting that **Sea World** should have its own water-coaster thrill ride. On **Journey to Atlantis,** riders are plunged eight at a time into a battle for the lost city of Atlantis (which has myste-riously risen to the surface of a Greek harbor, and is the subject of a media frenzy) via a swirling vortex, with blast-ing fountains and sprays of water along the way. You know

DIVERSIONS | THE LOWDOWN

the first plunge is coming (you can see this one from the queue line), but just when you think it's over, you'll get your second dip-and-drench. Special effects include evil sirens, morphing sets (a golden sea horse turns into Hermes, who doubles as guide and fighter for the forces of good), and maelstroms that threaten to swamp the boats—sort of like doing the Magic Kingdom's Splash Mountain on hallucinogenics. The ride, which was unveiled in 1998 and is Sea World's costliest expansion to date, covers an area of six football fields, and reaches speeds of 50 mph. (Of course if it's really steamy, you can always head to a nearby water park; see Getting Outside.)

For Mario Andretti wanna-bes... Think you can handle a few laps of white-knuckled, heart-pounding speed? Then don a crash helmet and your rookie stripes, and hop into the shotgun seat of a stock car at the **Richard Petty Driving Experience** (tel 800/BE–PETTY). This fantasy experience costs $89.99 for a three-lap simulated Winston Cup qualifying run. The car, driven by one of Richard Petty's professional instructors, travels up to 145 mph. If you'd like to get your own hands on the wheel and your foot on the gas, sign up for the three-hour Rookie Experience. The racetrack is in the Magic Kingdom parking lot. Drive to the entrance of the Magic Kingdom and you'll hear the engines roar. Tip: Tell the attendants you're going to Richard Petty, and you won't have to pay for parking. Disney's long-awaited **Test Track at Epcot** (it was three years late when it finally opened in 1998) sends drivers screeching through hairpin turns and spins at speeds of up to 65 mph. It's the longest, fastest ride in Disney history. So what if you're not actually doing the driving?

The Kingdom for kids... Tiny tots are the Magic Kingdom's biggest fans—and Disney's bread and butter—so it comes as no surprise that they've added more to please them in recent years. At **Mickey's Toon Town Fair,** little ones get to visit Mickey and Minnie's houses (they have separate abodes, of course), cool off in a mini water park, and ride **Goofy's Barnstormer,** a tame, just-for-kids roller coaster. The biggest draw is meeting Mickey and his friends. Stand in line (oh, yes, there will be a wait) and you'll get a one-on-one meeting with the big cheese himself. **The Many Adventures of Winnie**

the Pooh in Fantasyland takes you through Hundred Acre Wood on a very "Blustery Day." A bit of bounce and twirl adds to the whimsical journey. Expect long waits, however, for a ride that ends way too soon. The heaviest nostalgia trip for parents can be found at Fantasyland, where preschoolers gape in wide-eyed wonder at **Cinderella's Golden Carousel** and **Dumbo the Flying Elephant.** To the adult eye these are really glorified carnival rides, but small fry don't seem to care. Perhaps the most imaginative ride in Fantasyland is **Peter Pan's Flight,** a four-minute excursion in which you soar over London and journey to Neverland. **Snow White's Adventures** used to give every six-year-old nightmares; that nasty old witch seemed to pop out at every turn as you rode the tram car through the storybook world. Now the ride has been made more child-friendly, retuned so that the focus is on lovely Snow White, not the poisoned apple–bearing meanie. A similar ride, **Mr. Toad's Wild Ride,** is better still—funny, mildly thrilling, and snappily paced. Meanwhile, over in Adventureland, those randy, rummy **Pirates of the Caribbean** are still sailing—even blasé 12-year-olds may crack a smile watching them pillage, plunder, and chase women in good-natured debauchery. And the **Jungle Cruise** river ride is worth a trip provided the line's not out of sight (warning: just when you think you're in, you suddenly realize the line snakes around several times before you're anywhere near a boat). The boat captain's cornball puns and the animatronic wild animals have a certain retro charm that even adults may succumb to. In Liberty Square, the best thing going is the **Haunted Mansion,** a G-rated fun house with friendly ghosts and lots of special effects. This one's fine for the apprehensive—nothing reaches out and grabs you.

Best place to find Mickey in person... Three little words, spoken in a whisper, have enough power to ripple through a crowd and clear the lines at Space Mountain: *"Look, there's Mickey."* (Tempting, huh?) If you think the line was long at the teacups, wait till you wait for the Big Cheese's paw print. Our first suggestion: Sign up for at least one character meal (see Dining). Some folks we know make reservations for two or three "meet and eat" sessions (featuring different characters at each meal) during their stay. This guarantees that the kids will get to hug their favorite friends, and fill their autograph books (these are sold for about $6 at nearly every Disney shop). You'll avoid disappointment and save more time for the park's rides and attractions, instead of spending your precious hours hunting down Winnie and friends. That said, Disney has improved matters for young paparazzi. At Magic Kingdom, head for **Mickey's Toon Town Fair:** You'll find two separate lines, one waiting to greet Mickey, the other featuring Mickey's pals (Minnie, Pluto, and others). You'll wait in line, but the payoff is a sure shot at a one-on-one encounter with the world's most famous mouse. At **MGM Studios,** Disney characters like Mickey Mouse and Belle and the Beast hang out in **Animation Courtyard.** Several characters can also be found along Mickey and Tigger avenues. At Disney's Animal Kingdom, you'll want to make a beeline for **Camp Minnie-Mickey.** The character-greeting trails feature top stars such as Mickey, Minnie, Pluto, Goofy, Winnie, Tigger, and more. Rafiki (of *The Lion King* fame) and Pocahontas hang at Animal Kingdom's **Conservation Station.** Chip 'n' Dale are often found greeting tykes along the boulevard leading to Africa. Character greetings at Epcot tend to be more serendipitous. Some characters can be spotted in the country from which their story originated: Aladdin in Morocco, Snow White in Germany, and so on....But don't count on it.

By the way, Disney doesn't have the lock on character friends. At Sea World, you're bound to meet Baby Shamu, and at Universal's Islands of Adventure you can hardly get away from the cartoon and movie characters wandering about: Betty Boop, Popeye, the Cat in the Hat, Woody Woodpecker, Yogi Bear....There's an animated favorite around every corner. Kids, of course, love it—though we've seen a lot of grown-up arms around Ms. Boop, too.

The Kingdom for adults... If your last Disney World trip was back in the 1970s, you'll be pleasantly surprised by a stroll around **New Tomorrowland** (where Space Mountain is situated). With the help of creative types like George Lucas, Tomorrowland has a zippy, sci-fi Jetsons-type thing going on, architecturally speaking. Very cool. And the attractions—long overdue for a rehab—

DIVERSIONS | THE LOWDOWN

have recently been updated. Don't miss the new **Buzz Lightyear's Space Ranger Spin.** Climb aboard your space mobile for a trip through the galaxy. The object is to fire laser-beam pistols at targets along the way. A lever allows you to move the car in a 360-degree radius for better positioning. Bright, fast, action-packed, and competitive (a computerized counter keeps track of your hits)—what more could a vacationing adult ask for? And, given all the crowds and hype, you'll have a hard time resisting **The ExtraTERRORestrial Alien Encounter.** Somebody in line will tell you (and you'll probably have plenty of time to chat) that Disney chairman Michael Eisner deemed the original incarnation of this attraction "not scary enough," and sent creators back to the drawing boards. Well, they nailed it this time. The theme is teletransportation run amok; you get strapped into something suspiciously resembling an electric chair, the lights short-circuit, and the fun begins. We won't spoil the climax for you, but we have to warn you, it's kinda gross (you'll overhear adolescents squealing "Ee-*yew!*"). If you find yourself in New Tomorrowland after dark, take the **Skyway to Fantasyland** for aerial views of Cinderella's Castle all aglow.

Only if the lines are too long elsewhere in the Magic Kingdom... The Tomorrowland Speedway, featuring motorized, slow-moving go-carts that are confined to a narrow track, is definitely a bore unless you're five years old and really think you're driving. Zzzz. **Astro-Orbiter** is also a bit of a snooze; better to pop over to **Dreamflight,** a pleasant ride that takes you through the history of aviation. (This is a good place to hide out if you can't stomach another go at Alien Encounter.) We're not too enchanted by the **Swiss Family Robinson Treehouse** (in nearby Adventureland), either—it always seems to have a long, noisy line, and it doesn't seem worth the agony just to see a man-made tree (covered with vinyl leaves) housing a giant tree house. If the kids really need to stretch their legs and you need to sit for a spell, take the raft trip to **Tom Sawyer Island** (in Frontierland), where kids can explore a cave, a fort, and a secret passageway. Simba, schmimba—the long lines at **Legend of the Lion King** are a drag (over in Fantasyland), and the show is a rather dull retread of the movie (which you watch while you wait to get inside the main theater). Unless your kids are absolute fanatics, we'd pass. Can you tolerate cute, cuddly, and corny? Take in the **Country Bear Jamboree,** where audio-animated bears sing, dance, and tell silly jokes. **The Enchanted Tiki Birds,** now updated with characters from *The Lion King,* falls into the same category, with more than 200 birds, plants, and statues chirping and chatting in a tropical serenade. It seems to strike a chord with toddlers and nostalgia buffs—this was Disney's first audio-animated attraction—but considering what else Orlando has to offer in the way of special effects these days, why bother?

Epcot's greatest hits... After the Magic Kingdom, **Epcot** is a letdown for the six-and-under set; maybe you have to be school-aged or older to swallow the earnest sugar-coated educational stuff here. The first thing you'll see at Epcot is the massive silver geosphere called **Spaceship Earth.** Most guests stop right here and take the ride through the history of communication. It's a trip you shouldn't miss, but don't do it first. Instead, circle to the right, behind the Innoventions pavilion, to the **Journey into Imagination Pavilion** and the wild 'n' crazy **Honey, I Shrunk the Audience**—definitely a wake-up call if you've arrived at Epcot bleary-eyed. This is the wackiest attraction at Epcot, a 3-D film featuring Rick Moranis from *Honey, I Shrunk the Kids,* and the special effects are terrific for adults as well as kids. You'll jump out of your seat— literally. We wouldn't hang around this pavilion afterward though; instead, cut through **Innoventions Plaza,** lingering for a moment to enjoy the **Fountain of Nations Water Ballet** (a fountain synchronized with music that is pure Disney), and then go directly to the **Wonders of Life Pavilion.**

Never have the human body's inner workings been explored in such an intriguing way (unless you count that Raquel Welch flick, *Fantastic Voyage,*) than in the Wonders of Life Pavilion. In fact, Body Wars reminds us of that movie—it's a motion-simulation ride that takes you through the human body (whoa! look out for that corpuscle) aboard a miniaturized "inner space" ship. Our invisible man doll was never like this. Next, take in Cranium Command, a theater show that aims to explore the workings of a 12-year-old boy's brain. Of course, this is Disney, so the kid's head is devoid of heavy metal posters and Victoria's Secret lingerie ads, but, realistic or not, it's very funny. In the same pavilion is The Making of Me, the sweetest, most sensitive show you'll ever see on The Subject. Don't worry about telling your kids about the facts of life; this dandy little film explains it all without so much as a bird, a bee, or a snicker. Adults, however, tend to be less drawn to all these Future World attractions than to the architectural wonders of the World Showcase. As you stroll from "country" to "country" with nary a customs official to search your luggage or sternly eyeball your passport photo, you might as well stay for the travelogue films in each nation's pavilion, especially *The Wonders of China*. This Epcot perennial is well worth seeing, even if you have to stand (leaning against rails) to watch it on the panoramic 360-degree movie screen (one Disney cinematic innovation that, fortunately, never made it to your local movie house). The France and Canada pavilions also offer movies that are worth catching if you have the time. The biggest lines are found at *The American Adventure,* an unabashedly patriotic show featuring audio-animatronics characters in a journey through American history. It's a feel-good history lesson that can make some viewers get teary, while others drift off. Perhaps one of its best features is its length: 30 minutes, long enough for babies to sneak in a nap. The kids won't sleep through The Maelstrom, however—the boat ride at the Norway pavilion is much too exciting—the closest Epcot gets to a true thrill ride. You board a Viking ship and navigate a North Sea storm, with trolls peering at you from behind the rocks. There's a mellower ride waiting in Mexico, El Rio del Tiempo (River of Time), in which a boat cruise takes you through the history of Mexico, past a smoldering volcano. Perfect for couples, it's darkly lit, even romantic, and peopled with dolls who appear to have escaped from It's a Small World.

Also-rans at Epcot... There's lots of hands-on stuff to do at the **Innoventions** pavilion in Future World, which features the highest-tech playthings, video games, and virtual-reality gizmos—sort of a game arcade sobered up for adults. It's great—great for the sponsoring companies, that is, who get lots of PR mileage out of this space. In fact, the pavilion feels a bit like a high-tech trade show.

Still want to play? Note that this exposition is split into two parts, one on each side of the fountain, so if one side is crowded, try the other. The Land, a pavilion focused on agriculture and the environment, which may not exactly strike passion in your heart, is a little too 4-H-ish for our tastes, but if you're a gardener, the Living with the Land boat ride might pique your interest, especially the examples of hydroponic gardening. Revamped in 1994, this attraction is more interesting than it sounds. If your kid's (or your partner's) idea of healthful cuisine is a Fruit Roll-Up, drag 'em to Food Rocks, a "tasteful" concert show featuring fruits and veggies cavorting to classic rock tunes. Geared to kids school-age and younger, this lively romp features the likes of Chubby "Cheddar" and "Pita" Gabriel singing about nutrition. The Living Seas' man-made coral reef is intriguing, but we'd skip the droning tour and simply eat at the Coral Reef restaurant (see Dining), making sure to snag a table near the (under) water. Last and definitely least, there's the Kodak-sponsored Journey Into Imagination, which might click with a few more visitors if only it had a little pizazz.

What not to miss at Universal... So you did pretty well in your last 10K road race? It'll serve you well at **Universal Studios Florida.** It's nearly impossible to cram all the rides here into one day, but it can be done. Just get plenty of sleep the night before, wear comfortable shoes, and be ready to hustle, big time. Arrive an hour before opening time with admission pass in hand (you bought this ahead of time at the Visitor Center, right? and at a discount price, we hope), then line up at the turnstile. Pick up a map and daily entertainment schedule, and circle the rides and shows on your "must-see" list. Then as soon as you're through the gate, run like hell to **Terminator 2 3-D,** the *Terminator* movie featuring a rebuilt Terminator (yes, he died at the end of the last one) out on a mission to destroy android foes. If you're not yet fully awake, you soon will be: This ride features the creepy-steely T-1,000,000, and live-action doubles of Arnold Schwarzenegger and Edward Furlong who roar onto the stage on Harleys and then into a giant movie screen, a very cool trick you absolutely must see. To tell you more would spoil the fun—see this one for yourself. Next, in order of importance, are the **Back to the Future** simulation ride—

a fast-paced hurtle through space and time in a mock DeLorean; **Twister; Earthquake: The Big One** (a cable-car ride through the San Francisco earthquake); a cruise in the **Jaws** boat, where everybody can be shark bait for a day; **The Funtastic World of Hanna-Barbera,** a motion-simulated ride through cartoonland; **E.T.,** a swooping bike ride through the sky that ends with a personal thank you from E.T. himself, and **Kongfrontation,** you'll encounter a giant-size robotic King Kong in nighttime New York.

The thing we love about Universal Studios is that adults get as much of a kick out of all these attractions as the youngsters do, and vice versa; once a kid's old enough not to be scared of a roller coaster, the park is your oyster. King Kong, the San Francisco earthquake cable-car ride, and Terminator 2 3-D all feature special effects that are simply unparalleled. If you manage to get them all in, you're doing great. This aggressive touring plan won't allow you time for a long, leisurely lunch—but hey, you can eat anytime, but how often can you be attacked by a giant rubber shark? For a quick bite, grab a chowder (served in hollowed-out sourdough bread) at Chez Alcatraz in San Francisco. Later, if you're not so exhausted you collapse on the nearest park bench, start hitting the shows, or stroll around the various street scenes, notably the **Bates Motel** we all know and love from the movie *Psycho.* If (and only if) you've got younger kids, try to squeeze in both **Nickelodeon Studios,** an homage to this all-kids network, and the very cute **Animal Actors Stage.**

Best and worst of Islands of Adventure... The endless lines say it all: At the Islands, thrill rides are the thing. Like carnival rides on steroids, the **Hulk** and **Dueling Dragons** roller coasters are truly gut-twisting, while **Spider-Man** is the ultimate high-tech adventure (it's only slightly less intense if you whip off the 3-D glasses). **Doctor Doom's Fearfall** is like Disney-MGM's Tower of Terror run amok (not to mention a shameless rip-off of same). Meanwhile, at the replicant version of Jurassic Park (Steven Spielberg was a creative consultant on this attraction, which first debuted in Universal Studios Hollywood), you'll be scared witless on the dia-bolical **Jurassic Park River Adventure.** Don't confuse this with **Triceratops Encounter,** where you'll walk and walk and walk, all for the dubious pleasure of watching a (very) lifelike dinosaur urinate. Skip it, and board the charming **Pteranodon Flyers,** but only if you've got a small child in tow, or at least very short adult—somebody in your pair has to be 52 inches tall or less to "glide" in the two-person gondalas, which hang suspended from a curving track. Also fun for small fry is **The Cat in the Hat** ride at Seuss Landing, something of a trip through the storybook. We wouldn't waste our time on the live shows, which have lotsa lasers and pyrotechnics, but skimp on the story lines. The new **Men in Black Alien Attack** is a ramped-up version of laser tag, where players step into the movie and fire laser zappers at aliens. The aliens shoot back until, of course, Something Goes Terribly Wrong....

Boffo productions from Disney-MGM Studios... If

you found the Magic Kingdom so sweet it made your teeth ache, and Epcot a bit too heavy in the dining-and-shopping category, here's your reward. **Disney-MGM Studios** has action aplenty. Impromptu fires, rainstorms, explosions, and gunplay are among the predominant themes at this amusement-park-cum-movie-and-TV-studio. Only a few attractions are geared solely toward little kids: the Bear in the Blue House, the Honey, I Shrunk the Kids Movie Set Adventure (not to be confused with Honey, I Shrunk the Audience at Epcot), the Goosebumps Fright Show, and the parade. Most everything else can be equally enjoyable for adults, school-age kids, and hard-to-please teens. Warning: Only do **Doug Live!** at Disney MGM-Studios if your kids are rabid fans of the TV show. It's an audience-participation thang—cute enough, but unless you know who Skeeter Valentine, Quail Man, and Patti Mayonnaise are (the show's characters, played by real people here), you'll find this a snooze-o-rama. (That'll change fast, though, if you're cast as one of the Beets or your kid is picked to guest star as Quail Kid.) Thrill seekers will want to bolt to the new **Rock 'n' Roller Coaster Starring Aerosmith.** An original Aerosmith soundtrack, created exclusively for the ride, blasts into your "limo" as it travels at breakneck speed through Tinseltown. Try to hit this ride *before* lunch. There's lots of twists and turns, and three upside-down inversions. The **Twilight Zone Tower of Terror** is the—*ahem*—towering achievement of Walt Disney Imagineering. You'll see it as you drive into the park; the structure looms as a delightfully Gothic presence

DIVERSIONS | THE LOWDOWN

at the end of Sunset Boulevard, all cracked pink stucco with a sparking electric sign and gaping hole in the wall. This one's got all the goodies that have made TZ a cult favorite for decades: levitating eyeball, "doo-doo-doo-doo" theme, Rod Serling, even holographic ghosts. Then there's the moment you enter the you-know-what and free-fall 13 stories in the out-of-control service elevator, only to do the whole thing all over again. At the end, you may want to spring for the souvenir photo of yourself, mouth agape, taken as the plunge begins. You'll be glad you—heh, heh—dropped in. For a study in contrasts, make your next stop the **Beauty and the Beast Stage Show.** It's your typical beast-meets-girl love story, performed by live actors, and the music is terrific. How romantic is it? Notice how many couples are holding hands as they leave the theater. Or maybe they just don't want to get separated as they make a mad dash for **Star Tours,** a vastly popular motion-simulation ride—get there early or late to avoid long lines. Too young or too old to remember the *Star Wars* trilogy? It doesn't matter; with this ride, the story's beside the point. The real thrill is lurching through time and space (while dodging in-your-face planets) in a runaway "Starspeeder" (read: mechanized subway seat). Everybody knows the real stars in action flicks are the stunt doubles. See them in action— minus the boring retakes and makeup sessions—at the **Indiana Jones Epic Stunt Spectacular.** Special effects, razzle-dazzle stunts, and pyrotechnics make this show worth the (incredibly long) wait. Wear a bright-colored shirt, wave your arms spastically, and you might be called up on stage as an extra. (Warning: If you sit in the front row, you'll be so close to the action your eyeballs will sizzle.) Had enough mechanized action? Now's the time to sprint up New York Street and head to the Backlot Theater to catch Disney's **The Hunchback of Notre Dame—A Musical Adventure.** This one is rousing good fun, even if you didn't see the Disney flick, or read the Dumas novel. The costumes are great, the hunchback sympathetic, the gypsy appropriately fiery, and the song lyrics amusing, if not exactly Rodgers and Hammerstein. More proof that Disney does shows like nobody else. Tops in the gee-whiz techno category is, believe it or not, **Voyage of the Little Mermaid.** People without kids in tow might bypass this "sleeper" attraction—but if they do, well, it's their loss. This stage show combines animation, puppetry, lasers, and live performers in a mini-version of the Disney movie. No, you're not just getting misty at this story of boy meets fish, you're actually getting wet.

By now, your hair's soaked and your clothes reek of propane, signs you're having a swell time at Disney-MGM. Seems you're ready for a visit to **Catastrophe Canyon,** on Disney-MGM's Backstage Studio Tour. An innocent-looking shuttle bus takes you through the back lot, past hulks of old movie props, then—uh oh!—it's an earthquake! Fires erupt and (in a common refrain at Disney-MGM) your tour guide says, "Something's wrong, folks!" Eventually (none too soon), it's all over as you pass, fittingly, by the giant propane tanks used to keep Disney-MGM's home fires burning. And shame on you if you don't make it to **The Great Movie Ride,** Disney-MGM's homage to the magic of the movies. After watching a delightful montage of movie clips in a pre-staging area, you'll take a train ride through re-created movie sets enhanced by audio-animatronics. And just when you think you know what this ride is about, the tour guide announces—you've got it—"Something's wrong, folks!"

Disney-MGM flops… Maybe we're too old for this, or maybe we're just Muppeted out, but we weren't all that charmed by **Jim Henson's MuppetVision 4-D.** Perhaps it's that fourth D that's tripping us up. Whatever. See it if you're touring with small fry; otherwise, hold off at least till there's no waiting in line. And even if you do have kids, stay away from the **Honey, I Shrunk the Kids Movie Set Adventure,** unless your parental radar is exquisitely tuned to your child's unique wail of "Momm-mmy! Dadd-dddy!" This maze of giant Froot Loops and humongous ants is wall-to-wall kids, with tunnels leading to slides that dump out the little darlings who knows where. A migraine in the making.…We had high hopes for the new **Goosebumps Fright Show** (based on the hit book series by R. L. Stine), however. And after sitting on a 100-degree concrete sidewalk waiting for the show to begin, we figured it had *better* be good. We were wrong. "Dopey," pronounced our middle-schooler companion on the way out, and she wasn't referring to the Dwarf. The whole point of this exercise seems to be to sell Goosebumps books in the adjacent gift shop.

Best of show... And the prize goes to...Indiana Jones and his stuntmen and women, stars of the **Indiana Jones Epic Stunt Spectacular** at **Disney-MGM Studios**. It's a not-to-be-missed live-action show full of out-of-control vehicles, real explosions, falling rocks, flying spears, crumbling buildings, and amazing movie stunts. You'll recognize some of the settings from the movies, and you'll get a peek at the secrets behind the scenes. The misty, watery **Voyage of the Little Mermaid,** also at MGM, ranks at the top of the list, too. Though a bit on the schmaltzy side, this stage show combines live performances, animation, and special effects. The underwater (not real) grotto theater, complete with floating bubbles (real), rippling water (not real), and mist (real), is a great refuge from the crowds and from Florida's sweltering sun. **SuperStar Television** is an audience-participation show that melds real people with TV shows and movies; if you have exhibitionist tendencies, get in on the "tryouts" held 20 minutes prior to SuperStar Television—a cameo role may well turn out to be the highlight of your visit to Disney-MGM.

At the rival studio park, **Universal Studios,** the shows are equally wonderful, with dazzling special effects and sophisticated humor. Our favorite here is the **Wild, Wild, Wild West Stunt Show,** followed by the rest of the Universal lineup of shows, based on your interest (the titles tell it all): Hitchcock; Beetlejuice; the Gory, Gruesome Make-Up Show; and, a distant runner-up, the Dynamite Stunt Show. Not even a whale-watching cruise gets you as up close and personal with a killer whale as does **Sea World**'s headline attraction, **Shamu: Close Up.** Watching a Sea World trainer "ride" one of these black-and-white gentle giants is quite a sight. Also compelling is Sea World's **Cirque de la Mer (Circus of the Sea).** We didn't quite get the theme—a retelling of the South American tale "The Flight of the Condor"—but no matter; the acrobats, fire-eater, dancers, and comic host (Peruvian actor Cesar Aedo) make this an entertaining, high-energy show. **Pets on Stage** is Sea World's entry into the animal-show arena, featuring silly skits (the emcee seems totally embarrassed to be there) with a menagerie of dogs, cats, birds, rats, even potbelly pigs. The warm, fuzzy side of this is that most of these animals were rescued from shelters. Young children adore this show, and storm the stage to pet the stars at the end.

Ho-hum shows... There are a number of places throughout the parks offering a changing lineup of live entertainment and shows. Generally, if you happen to be passing by and need a place to rest, then consider stopping; otherwise, head to the rides. The **American Gardens Stage,** an outdoor amphitheater in front of the U.S.A. pavilion at **Epcot's World Showcase**, features performers from around the world with music, dance, and native costumery. The shows at the **Theater of the Stars,** on Sunset Boulevard at **Disney-MGM Studios,** feature more elaborate sets and are generally more entertaining. This outdoor theater—a reproduction of the Hollywood Bowl—is a good, shady resting spot. Live productions, usually based on the latest Disney hit, are held at **MGM's Backlot Theater,** which features an animated set, fanciful costumes, and special effects. For some reason this show is popular, but take our advice: Consider it only if there's a short wait, and it's a somewhat cool day (this location gets hot, hot, hot). The **Magic Kingdom** has several live performance locations; none are all that spectacular. The crowds at the **Diamond Horseshoe Saloon Revue** can only be explained by the fact that they're simply aching for a place to sit down—visitors collapse at table seats, or around the bar, and try to endure the too lively Gay Nineties music and way-too-energetic dancers. The supposed-to-be-futuristic dance routine at the **Galaxy Palace Theater at Rocket Tower Plaza** misses the mark completely, and the very amateurish musical shows at the **Castle Forecourt Stage,** in front of Cinderella's Castle, are mainly performed to keep the crowds from mutinying as they wait and wander.

To sea or not to see... Anheuser-Busch, the owner of **SeaWorld of Florida** Adventure Park, has pumped a ton of money into this park to make it a player. Notice the name change? There's a lot more to this place than Shamu these days, including thrill rides, new shows, and a stomach-lurching roller coaster. Still, Shamu rules, charming the most jaded of us, especially kids (who insist upon sitting close to the action so that everybody in the party gets drenched). Even if you've seen the Shamu show before—and they change it regularly, to keep things interesting—you'll still "ooh" and "ahh" as the sleek, black-and-white killer whale shoots out of the water, straddled by a trainer.

Beyond Shamu and the resident dolphins, seal lions, and otters, this park packs some exciting surprises. For instance, there's **Kracken** and **Wild Arctic,** thrill rides that compare with the best of the bunch over at Universal and Disney. Hint: Pay attention to the motion sickness warnings. The Kracken roller coaster is a must-do for coaster aficionados. Sea World calls it the longest, tallest, fastest in the country....You'll hurl; you'll twirl; your stomach will lunge and your heart will plunge....Are we having fun yet? It features a floorless design—this means your feet will dangle—and you also have nothing in front of you to wrap those white-knuckled fingers around.... The coaster exceeds 65 mph with seven inversions, including a cobra roll, zero-gravity roll, and vertical loops and spins. The **Wild Arctic** is a simulated helicopter ride (you can also do this without the jostling motion) through a glacier. Strapped in your seat, you dodge icebergs and zigzag through a frozen landscape, then walk through re-created polar settings to view real polar bears and walruses. (Hint: Don't do this immediately after the Shamu show, when you're soaking wet, because the thermostat is set to chilly.) Then there's the new **Journey to Atlantis,** Sea World's ambitious water-coaster thrill attraction, which combines cool special effects (they call them "aqualusions") with a hair-raising boat ride. Other new features at Sea World include a Key West–themed area and a pyrotechnics-and-waterskiing show based on the world's favorite TV jiggle show, *Baywatch* (the plot's a tad lame, which makes the tie-in all the more fitting). The action at Sea World centers around the shows; you plan your itinerary around them, and spend the rest of your time touring walk-through exhibits like **Penguin Encounter.** Another of Sea World's virtues is its **Terrors of the Deep** aquarium, a walk-through tunnel populated with the scarier denizens of the deep, such as moray eels, barracudas, rays, scorpion fish, and sharks. Way cooler than the Living Seas at Epcot. We'd also make it a point to take a peek at the sea lions at **Pacific Point Preserve** and the so-ugly-they're-cute manatees at **Manatees: The Last Generation?** These walruslike creatures, sometimes called sea cows, are a Florida treasure, currently threatened by red tide and motorboat propellers. We'd give lower priority to the **"Clyde and Seamore" Sea Lion and Otter Show** (little kids like it, but adults

fidget like crazy), the Tropical Reef exhibit, and everything else.

Another roadside attraction... So, you've done
Disney and the teens in your brood are moaning the
B-word...what next? **DisneyQuest,** five stories of virtual reality, will keep them busy for hours. Its four
worlds include the Explore Zone, a trip to exotic lands;
Score Zone, with competition games galore; Create
Zone, the place for self-expression; and Replay Zone,
featuring a retro-futuristic spin on classic rides and
games. The cost seems steep at first ($27 adults; $21
for kids ages 3–9), but imagine how many quarters
you've dropped in an hour at the local arcade. If you
want to see wild animals (in non-Disney habitats),
head out to **Gatorland.** The fact that this 50-year-old
park struggles against entertainment giants like Disney
and Universal is endearing, and one can only hope that
these old-fashioned, Florida-flavored attractions will
survive. You enter Gatorland through a giant, tooth-
filled gator's jaw, and plan your day (three hours should
do it) around shows featuring gator wrestling, snakes of
Florida, and gator jumparoo (wherein gators leap high
out of the water to be hand-fed a snack of dead chickens). Gatorland is a commercial alligator farm covering
some 110 acres, whose gators have been featured in
myriad TV commercials and movies, including
Indiana Jones and the Temple of Doom. Try not to think
about the fact that their cousins end up as belts in the
boutique and as gator chowder in Pearl's Smoke
House restaurant. Nice features of the park include its
natural Florida setting, a cypress swamp, and its role
as a wading bird sanctuary and rookery. From
February through summer, snowy egrets, American
egrets, herons, and other shorebirds build hundreds of
nests and care for their young amid the alligators' 10-
acre breeding marsh. The gator wranglers and snake
handlers also share a lot of information about their
charges in a down-home, folksy manner, along the
lines of "Never insult an alligator until you've crossed
the river," and this bit of advice on how to recognize
a deadly coral snake: "If the nose is black, that's bad
for Jack." You'll leave the park with a healthy respect
for these toothy reptiles, especially since *they* emerge

from the gator wrestling nonsense with their dignity intact.

Meanwhile, *Titanic* fever lives on at **Titanic: Ship of Dreams** at the **Mercado** (see Nightlife and Entertainment). This permanent exhibition combines the historic (*Titanic* dinnerware and other artifacts), the dramatic (actors pretending to be ship's passengers and survivors), and the weird (a chess table made from wood floating around the *Titanic* wreck site). Ultimately, it's both sad and chilling. Of course, you're snapped back to reality when you see Leo's costume from the James Cameron *Titanic* flick, and copies of the famous necklace in the gift shop. **Ripley's Believe It or Not!** doesn't even pretend to take itself seriously. Even the building is a joke: It's set into the ground at an angle, enough so that the exit is dizzying, as though the whole thing were being sucked into a giant sinkhole. Among the bizarre exhibits on display are replicas of the world's tallest man and the world's fattest man (so far, it sounds like typical talk-show fare), the man with two pupils in each eye, an actual shrunken head, and a 1907 Rolls Royce crafted from matchsticks. If you're drawn to carnival freak shows and Diane Arbus photographs, you'll love the place. As if all this weren't enough, a new attraction based on **The Guiness Book of World Records** (and owned by the same folks who brought you Ripley's Believe It or Not!) is on its way to Orlando. Apparently the market for this sort of high-brow amusement has not yet been fully tapped. Finally, if you'd like to add a little educational value to your entertainment, check out the wacky new **WonderWorks** at Pointe*Orlando on International Drive. This interactive entertainment center, housed in a zany, upside-down building, features a variety of unusual activities. Sit in an electric chair, experience the sensation of an earthquake or hurricane, play computer-simulated basketball, make giant bubbles, see what you'll look like 25 years from now...and more.

For those who'd rather be paraffined and pampered... You know you deserve it—big time! After hours spent trekking through theme parks, waiting in line, and fighting the crowds, what could be finer than a few hours at a luscious spa? Our first choice: the lush and lovely **Portofino Bay Hotel spa** (see Accomodations). Universal Studio's European-style, full-service spa offers a full scale of luxury treatments. Try a soothing herbal body wrap, or, maybe one of their mud therapies, followed by a shiatsu massage. The staff at the **Wyndham Palace Resort & Spa** perform a special theme-park foot massage that leaves weary feet feeling refreshed and baby's-bottom soft. This spa offers a number of other deliciously pampering procedures, including aromatherapy massage, European facials, and an herbal eye-lift treatment that eliminates (at least temporarily) those tiny furrows that develop from waking up at 4am to beat the crowds at the Magic Kingdom. Or better yet, send the rest of your group to Magic Kingdom while you treat yourself to the three-hour Spa Relaxer treatment at the **Celebrity Spa,** located at the deluxe Star Island Resort and Country Club. The spa is just minutes from the main entrance to Disney, but inside it's worlds away. The special includes a half-hour facial and body treatment, shampoo and style, plus a manicure and pedicure, all for about $100 (not much more than you'd end up spending at the park in a day). The spa offers a variety of à la carte services, too; pick from a menu of nearly 50 different treatments. **The Disney Institute** boasts a luxurious full-service spa, complete with lap pools, exercise equipment, fitness classes, and a host of beauty treatments. One of the best parts of this experience is sitting in the pedicure chair with your grateful feet immersed in hot, bubbly water and your neck embraced by a warm, herb-filled pillow. This could well be the most pleasurable part of your Disney experience, especially if you've been jerked around by one too many motion-simulation rides. Similar spa treatments are offered at Disney's **Grand Floridian** resort's small day-spas, perfect for that much-needed massage or manicure (see Accomodations).

Join the parade... NOT. Unless you have a child who absolutely insists on attending Disney's overcrowded street displays, your best bet is to avoid them like the plague. Instead, take advantage of the chance to hit the more popular rides while the lines are shorter. Check the schedule for parade times, or just watch as folks begin to claim their space on the streets, sometimes an hour before the show begins. At the **Magic Kingdom,** the **Mickey Mania Parade** is held at 3pm daily, and mania it is, with elbow-to-elbow, stroller-to-stroller crowds lining Main Street to watch the daily extravaganza of floats, giant inflated Disney characters, live dancers, clowns, and more. Parents heft little ones on their shoulders and shove bigger ones forward for a better viewing spot, employing tactics that would impress a New York cabbie angling for a fare. As we said, skip it if you can. The same holds true for Magic Kingdom's nighttime **Main Street Electrical Parade.** The parade returns home after a stint in Europe, spruced up with shimmering lights and costumes. The 26-unit procession walks the 3.4-mile Main Street parade route, and includes a host of giant Disney characters outlined in glittery lights. Problem is, folks start lining up for the event a full one to two hours beforehand! Can you imagine telling your three-year-old, "Just wait, honey; it'll only be another 60 minutes or so...." Yeah, right. Definitely not worth the trouble. Ditto for **Disney-MGM Studios' Feature Parade.** The theme of this one changes frequently to reflect the latest Disney movie, but the scene is always depressingly the same: sweat-drenched, irritable crowds waiting for the floats, costumed performers, and music to arrive. Better to attend your hometown parade, and spend your time here at the park's rides and attractions. The new **Fantasmic! Show at Disney-MGM Studios** is a nightly spectacular of lights, lasers, and water. The extravaganza, which features music and characters from Disney classics (what else?) lasts about 25 minutes, but (and this is a big but), you'll usually need to get in line at least an hour ahead of time to snag a seat (it's inside an amphitheater, so, alas, you can't see it from outside). We say, go back to the hotel instead, pour a glass of wine, and relax poolside.

For a look at Orlando before Mickey arrived...

Long before there were theme parks, there was Central Florida, a hot, isolated wilderness that was home to cattle ranchers, orange growers, and those looking for a tropical paradise far from civilization. Take a look at Orlando's pioneer past at the **Orange County Historical Museum**, a quiet oasis in Loch Haven Park, the cultural center of Orlando and Central Florida. While much of this small museum consists of archival materials, there's an old (1926—that's old for Florida) fire station and a re-created pioneer kitchen, newspaper press room, and Victorian parlor. Also in the Loch Haven Park complex is the **Orlando Museum of Art,** one of the best museums in the South. Its permanent collections feature 19th- and 20th-century American, pre-Columbian, and African art; artists represented include Childe Hassam and Judy Pfaff. This smallish but user-friendly museum is in the midst of a major expansion program that will enable it to host "block-buster" shows such as *Imperial Tombs of China,* considered the most important exhibition to leave China. Finally, also in the same complex, there's the **Orlando Science Center,** a hands-on science museum geared toward children, that is a great favorite with local grade-school groups.

Behind the scenes... Did you realize that more than 10,000 rosebushes decorate the World Showcase grounds? Or that the Morocco pavilion was a gift from the Kingdom of Morocco, and is made up of more than 9 tons of handcrafted tile? Bet you didn't know that the Swiss Family Treehouse has 600 branches and 800,000 vinyl leaves. If you have a passion for detail (or maybe you're boning up to compete on *Jeopardy,*) check into one of the many backstage tours offered at the parks. The **Hidden Treasures of the World Showcase** is a two-hour walking tour that concentrates on the architecture and construction techniques of **Epcot**'s individual country pavilions. Don't even consider it if you have kids along, but if you like design and detail and have some child-free time on your hands, sign up. The **Gardens of the World** tour is a must for plant and flower lovers who have an extra three hours to walk around studying the designs of several World Showcase gardens. On the **D.E.E.P.: Dolphin Exploration and Education Program,** you get to participate in a scientific study at the Living Seas pavilion in Epcot. The tour (cost: about $45) includes tidbits on dolphin behavior, and explains how researchers interact with them. It's okay for young marine-biologist wanna-bes, but if you're really into this sort of thing, consider a visit to **Sea World's Dolphin Interaction Program (D.I.P.)** With this one, kids ages 10 and up (and grown-ups, if they want) actually don a wetsuit and get into the pool with dolphins and trainers. After a lengthy briefing

DIVERSIONS | THE LOWDOWN

about dolphins and their behavior, participants learn the trainers' tricks of the trade, and can try their hand at summoning dolphin behaviors (we made ours, Scarlet, tail-walk the length of the pool—too cool!). This three-hour adventure will cost you—it runs around 150 bucks, not including optional souvenir photo—but it may well be the highlight of your visit to Sea World. Plan ahead, though—these programs book up months in advance. The park also offers some less-pricey behind-the-scenes tours, each lasting about an hour (cost: just $4.95), which include a shark encounter and a manatee visit. These can be arranged at the last minute.

You have to have an extraordinary interest in Disney to endure, much less enjoy, the **World's Backstage Magic** tour, which takes guests behind the scenes to see how Disney does it. You'll explore the "utilidor" system beneath the **Magic Kingdom** and travel backstage to all three Disney theme parks. The good news is that you'll skip the lines; the bad news is that the tour lasts seven hours, and sometimes feels like a day at school. The four-hour **Keys to the Kingdom** tour is similar to Backstage Magic—you'll see the utilidors and production center—but you'll have to wait in line at the attractions. This one is open to guests as young as 10 years old (though we can't imagine too many 10-year-olds who'd enjoy this full-of-facts walk-about). The two-plus-hour **Inside Animation** tour is a look at how Disney creates the classics, and includes an opportunity to make your own Mickey Mouse cel. For availability and reservations for all these tours, call 407/WDW–TOUR. If none of these sound like your kind of pleasure, you can always sign up for a **Disney VIP** tour (cost: $65 an hour, with a four-hour minimum), a custom-designed program tailored to your individual interests; it might include a shopper's tour of the Kingdom, a behind-the-scenes look at one or all of the theme parks, or whatever else you might have in mind. (How about a no-waiting-in-lines tour?) To book, call 407/560–6233 up to 24 hours in advance (not available December 25–31). As far as tots and teens are concerned, parents looking for a little free time will be glad to know they can dump their kids into **Camp Disney** without stifling their children's urge to explore. Supervised day programs at the camp include field trips for 7- to 10-year-olds (like Broadway Bound, Face Magic, and a variety of animal study programs). Eleven-to-15-year-olds can attend similar programs, geared toward older ages. Call 407/WDW–TOUR for information.

For type-A, guilt-ridden adults... What?!! Spend all this vacation time without stretching yourself personally or improving your golf/tennis/(fill in the blank) game? If your psyche just won't let you have that much socially unredeeming fun without suffering major guilt pangs, you're the perfect candidate for **The Disney Institute.** Cashing in on the growing popularity of learning vacations, the Institute offers more than 60 programs in eight interest areas. Sign up for one-hour, half-day, full-day, or multi-day programs, and take your pick from a variety of subjects: animation, video production, photography, rock climbing, golf, tennis, culinary arts, bird watching, gardening, storytelling. If you really want to learn how to make the perfect sauce or scale a mountain, there are better places to do it. But if you happen to be here anyway, feeling guilty, well....Note: Rumor has it that in the near future, the Institute may be open to private, corporate-type groups. Check ahead.

Bright lights and Disney nights... Forget about spotting the Big Dipper in this town: No fewer than six nightly fireworks finales pepper the skies over Disney World. The impressive **Electrical Water Pageant** is the kind of presentation Disney does best: A come-to-life cartoon character travels the Seven Seas to the strains of music and light. Watch as King Neptune slithers through the water, leading an array of animated sea life (okay, it's actually a 1,000-foot barge, transporting an imaginative maze of lights and music, weaving through the Seven Seas Lagoon and Bay Lake). Combine this with dining at a Disney resort—you can see the show from the Polynesian (where it begins at about 9pm), and the Grand Floridian, Wilderness Lodge, Fort Wilderness, and Contemporary resorts. Some nights, the show makes it to the Magic Kingdom as well (check the schedule). As mentioned above, the **Original Electric Parade** has also returned to the Magic Kingdom, after playing overseas. The 26-unit procession includes more than 575,000 lights, adorning giant-sized Disney characters. The nightly parade lights up Main Street, and creates massive pedestrian traffic jams! Skip it; unless you snag a seat some one to two hours ahead of time, you won't see much of it anyway. We have to ask: What's all the fuss about the "spectacular" **IllumiNations show at Epcot?** Your kids will probably give this one a big thumbs-down: not enough noise, not enough flash, where's the finale? Fireworks and laser lights are set off over the **World Showcase Lagoon,** to classic musical scores. We suspect this is Disney's attempt to keep you eating and drinking at Showcase restaurants and pubs. Finally, it's New Year's Eve every night at **Pleasure Island,** as a laser-and-light show, fireworks, and professional dancers help ring in a hectic, ever-recurring new year. The Pleasure Island cast tries hard to make you have fun; party-hearty tourists line the streets, throw confetti, and pretend.

The Index

Celebrity Spa. Offering nearly 50 different treatments, this full-service, European-style spa is the perfect cure to theme park madness.... *Tel 407/396–8300. Star Island Resort and Country Club, 5000 Ave. of the Stars, Kissimmee.*
(see p. 139)

Discovery Island. This Disney zoo is not to be confused with Disney's giant new Animal Kingdom. You'll get a lot closer to the animals at this small, low-key park; it's full of gators, flamingoes, giant turtles, and lots of birds.... *Tel 407/824–4321. www.disneyworld.com. Discovery Island, Lake Buena Vista. Open daily 9:30am–6pm.* **(see p. 120)**

Disney's Animal Kingdom. Disney's latest theme park takes you through jam-packed trails littered with natural barrier cages that serve as the homes for everything from moles to gorillas.... *Tel 407/824–4321. www.disneyworld.com. 551 North Rainforest Road, Bay Lake.*

(see pp. 118, 119, 122, 125)

The Disney Institute. Somewhat earnest learning vacations, with one notable bonus: use of a state-of-the-art fitness center. Beauty treatments are available at the spa, even to non-Disney guests, at an extra charge.... *Tel 407/827– 7049. www.disneyworld.com. Walt Disney World.*

(see pp. 139, 143)

Disney-MGM Studios. One hundred thirty-five acres of TV and movie magic, featuring the awesome Twilight Zone Tower of Terror.... *Tel 407/824–4321. www.disneyworld.com. Walt Disney World. Hours vary according to season.*

(see pp. 117, 121, 125, 131, 133, 134, 135, 140)

DisneyQuest. This giant modern day arcade features five floors of virtual reality fun. Great for older kids who've outgrown the Mouse scene.... Tel 407/828–4600. www.dis-neyquest.com. Downtown Disney, 1486 East Buena Vista Dr., Lake Buena Vista. Open daily 10:30am–midnight.

(see p. 137)

Epcot. Walt Disney's visionary community comes across as an edu-cational toy store-cum-faux United Nations.... *Tel 407/824– 4321. www.disneyworld.com. Walt Disney World. Hours vary according to season.*

(see pp. 118, 123, 127, 128, 135, 141, 144)

Gatorland. Florida's largest alligator farm, housing 5,000 gators and crocs, and also a rookery for thousands of shorebirds. Learn all about 'em, see gator wrestling and gator jumparoo.... *Tel 407/855–5496, 800/393–5297. 14501 S. Orange Blossom Trail, Orlando. Open daily 8am–dusk.* **(see p. 137)**

Guinness Book of World Records. By the same folks that brought you Ripley's Believe It or Not! It should be open by press time. For information, contact the Orlando Visitor Center.... *Tel 800/551–0181. 8723 International Dr., Suite 101, Orlando. Open daily 8am–7pm.* **(see p. 138)**

Islands of Adventure. Universal Studios' fantastic new theme park had Steven Spielberg as its creative consultant—and it

DIVERSIONS | THE INDEX

shows. The park features state-of-the-art thrills-and-chills roller coasters, 3-D film, live-action and simulator rides, and water flumes.... *Tel 407/363–8000. www.uescape.com. Universal Islands of Adventure, 1000 Universal Studios Plaza, Orlando. Open daily; hours vary.* **(see pp. 121, 122, 130)**

Magic Kingdom. Disney's first Florida theme park, the 100-acre Magic Kingdom is the sugarcoated heart of Walt Disney World.... *Tel 407/824–4321. www.disneyworld.com. Walt Disney World.*
(see pp. 117, 121, 122, 123, 125, 126, 135, 140, 142)

Orange County Historical Museum. Explore Orlando's pioneer past through old photographs, re-created settings, and a 1926 firehouse with antique fire trucks.... *Tel 407/897–6350. Loch Haven Park, 812 E. Rollins St., Orlando. Open Mon–Sat 9am–5pm, Sun noon–5pm.*
(see p. 140)

Orlando Museum of Art. Permanent collections feature 19th- and 20th-century American art, pre-Columbian and African art, and a hands-on exhibit for children.... *Tel 407/896–4231. Loch Haven Park, 2416 N. Mills Ave., Orlando. Open Tue–Sat 9am–5pm, Sun noon–5pm.* **(see p. 141)**

Orlando Science Center. Small and child-friendly, this museum features interactive science exhibits and a planetarium.... *Tel 407/897–6350; fax 407/514–2149. 777 E. Princeton St., Orlando. Open Mon–Thur 9am–5pm, Fri–Sat 9am–9pm, Sun noon–5pm.* **(see p. 141)**

Pleasure Island. A popular place where laser shows and dancers bring in the New Year (every night).... *Tel 407/934–7781. www.disneyworld.com. Pleasure Island, Lake Buena Vista.*
(see p. 144)

Richard Petty Driving Experience. If driving at breakneck speeds in a two-seater stock car is your kind of thrill, save your pennies and head to this one-of-a-kind attraction. No reservation is needed—just sign your life away on the release form, and hop in for three laps around the race track with a professional driver at the wheel. Located in the Magic Kingdom parking lot.... *Tel 407/939–0130, 800/237–3889. www.rpde.com. 3450 North World Dr., Lake Buena Vista. Open daily 9am–5pm.* **(see p. 123)**

Ripley's Believe It or Not! "Truth is stranger than fiction," Robert Ripley believed, and the oddities and exhibits displayed at this museum are mighty strange, indeed.... *Tel 407/363–4418. 8201 International Dr., Orlando. Open daily 9am–11pm.* **(see p. 138)**

Sea World of Florida. What's black and white and wet all over? Shamu, naturally. See Shamu and crew, collide with an avalanche, and take a side trip to Key West at the world's most popular marine-life park.... *Tel 407/363–2200, 404/327–2727. www.seaworld.com. 7007 Sea World Dr., Orlando. Open daily 9am–7pm; extended seasonal hours.* **(see pp. 122, 134, 135, 141)**

Skull Kingdom. Very, very spooky attraction, full of dark corners, special effects, and live characters. If you like haunted houses, don't miss it.... *Tel 407/354–1564. 5933 American Way, Orlando. Open daily noon–11pm.* **(see p. 120)**

Terror on Church Street. These dark passageways take you deep into nightmare land, with the help of creepy actors, scary music, and ghastly special effects.... *Tel 407/422–2434. www.churchstreetstation.com. 135 S. Orange Ave., Orlando. Open Mon–Thur 7pm–midnight (1am in summer); Fri–Sat 7pm–1am.* **(see p. 120)**

Titanic: Ship of Dreams. This permanent exhibit combines authentic artifacts, movie memorabilia, and costumed actors. Only for true *Titanic* buffs.... *Tel 407/248–1166. Mercado Shopping Center, 8445 International Dr., Orlando.* **(see p. 138)**

Universal Studios Florida. Just when you thought Universal's rides couldn't get any hairier, they open Terminator 2 3-D, featuring a custom-made movie (he said he'd be back) and live action. This proves why Universal is still tops in the thrills department.... *Tel 407/363–8000. www.universalstudios. com. 1000 Universal Studios Plaza, Orlando. Opens daily at 9am; closing times vary according to season.* **(see pp. 118, 122, 129, 134)**

WonderWorks. This attraction is full of amusing interactive exhibits like the bubble machine, sound tunnels, virtual reality sports, and computer games. Kids might even learn something along the way.... *Tel 407/351–8800. 9067*

DIVERSIONS | THE INDEX

International Dr. (at Pointe*Orlando), Orlando. Open daily 10am-11pm. **(see p. 138)**

Wyndham Palace Resort & Spa. Treat your dawgs to a pampering "theme-park foot massage" or choose from among a range of luxurious and aromatic treatments at this European-style spa.... *Tel 800/327–2906. www.wyndham.com. Walt Disney World Hotel Plaza, Lake Buena Vista.*
(see p. 139)

Orlando/Walt Disney World Area Diversions

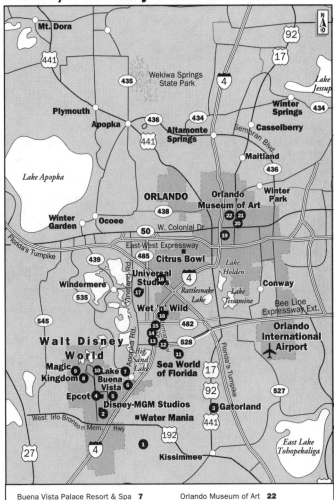

Buena Vista Palace Resort & Spa **7**	Orlando Museum of Art **22**
Celebrity Spa **1**	Orlando Science Center **20**
Discovery Island **10**	Richard Petty Driving Experience **8**
The Disney Institute **6**	Ripley's Believe It or Not! **15**
Disney-MGM Studios **2**	Sea World of Florida **11**
DisneyQuest **5**	Skull Kingdom **16**
Epcot **4**	Terror on Church Street **19**
Gatorland **3**	Titanic: Ship of Dreams **14**
Guinness Book of Records **12**	Universal Studios Florida **17**
Islands of Adventure **18**	WonderWorks **13**
Magic Kingdom **17**	
Orange County Historical Museum **21**	

getting

4

outside

Ask Orlandoans
what they like
best about living
in Orlando and
most will tell you
"the weather."
They'll boast

about an average annual temperature of a very pleasant 72 degrees, with plenty of sunshine and soft breezes. But, we ask, what about the hot and humid summer months, when all of central Florida turns into one giant buggy sweatbox? No matter; frequent afternoon thunderstorms sweep through to cool things down; there's always air-conditioning; plus you get used to it. What humidity? The weather, it seems, is what keeps Orlandoans in Orlando and gets them outdoors to play.

Of course, the area's appeal is more suited to some activities than it is to others. Suffice it to say that this ex-swamp-turned-tourist-mecca will never pass muster with the rugged, gorp-chomping crowd. Try as they might, even Disney's wild imagineers and gigantic budgets can't turn Orlando into a scenic paradise. Face it: Thunder Mountain is not the Tetons. The Wilderness Lodge hot springs do not compare to Old Faithful. And no matter how many sangrias you drink, the grounds surrounding the new Coronado Springs Resort will never look like the Mojave Desert. Not surprisingly, recreation in Central Florida centers around water, courts, and courses. There are more than 300 lakes in the greater Orlando area, and hundreds of elaborate hotel pools. Golfers will think they've died and gone to heaven, with more than 125 courses located within a 45-minute drive of downtown Orlando. Sure, it gets hot out on the course during the summer, but the plummet in greens fees (sometimes as low as half price, starting in May) makes up for the rise in temperature.

Golf, tennis, boating, fishing, and waterskiing are all offered at Disney, mostly in pristine, man-made environments, sans mosquitoes and flies. (We don't even want to know how they get rid of the buggers.) Outside the parks, you'll find even more activities to choose from. You could spend a day at the recently opened Discovery Cove, swimming with bottlenose dolphins and snorkeling in a coral-reef lagoon. Grab a rubber mat and zip down a wet slide or tube the whitewater rapids at one of five water parks in the area. Canoe the scenic Wekiva River; take a guided horseback tour through the woods; float in a hot air balloon above Cinderella's Castle; or, hop in an airboat to go gator hunting. All that and more is here to be tried—without ever stepping into an amusement park. Just be sure to bring your sunscreen.

Resources

Duffers, write down this number: 800/374–8633. It's for **Advanced Tee Times U.S.A.,** Florida's central reservation service for golf. This free information and tee-time reservation service is designed to make golfing easier for the tourist. Use it to book free advance tee times or to sign up for an all-inclusive package. The network provides access to public, semiprivate, and private courses across the state, and can offer advice on where to play. You can reserve tee times up to three months in advance, or just give them a call when you wake up to a gorgeous-day-for-golf morning. If you plan to golf on your Orlando/Disney vacation, you'll want to request a free copy of the *Greater Orlando/Daytona Beach and Central Florida Golfer's Guide*. Not all courses are listed—just the advertisers, we suspect—but it's a good source of information, addresses, and phone numbers for most of the biggies. Call 800/864–6101. All golf courses offer high- and low-season rates. Most courses give big price breaks in the early morning and mid-afternoon, and it's usually cheaper to golf midweek than on the weekends. Disney resort guests get a discount at WDW courses. But check with your hotel, too; many offer coupon discounts to a number of local courses. Finally, stop in at the Orlando Visitor Center on International Drive and inquire about discounts. All greens fees listed in this book are for non-guests in high season.

The Lowdown

Thrills and chills... It's 90 degrees Fahrenheit and about 100 percent humidity; where do you want to be? It's no surprise that water parks are big attractions here. Walt Disney World alone has three—Blizzard Beach, Typhoon Lagoon, and River Country. The independent players are Wet 'n' Wild and Water Mania. How to choose really depends on what your favorite water park feature is, since you'll be handing over a chunk of change ($20 or more per person for adults) for the privilege of getting soaked.

If you like stomach-lurching plunges—the steeper the better—try **Wet 'n' Wild** (tel 407/351–1800; 6200 International Dr., Orlando), the water park that claims to be the world's first and the nation's best-attended. Those who are experts on these places—teens—label this one "awesome." The park's Hydra Fighter is a hit, combining favorite kid-pleasing ingredients for summer fun—swings, water, and squirt guns. How can it miss? You'll grab a seat in one of the back-to-back high-powered swings equipped with its own personal water cannon. Want to go higher? Faster? Keep firing that cannon to keep the water pressure rising. Wet 'n' Wild's Water Wars attraction carries the fun of a classic water balloon fight to the limit. You'll stand on a launching platform facing your opponent (someone whom you know and love??!), position water bombs… aim…pull back…and FIRE! Unfortunately, the attraction is not included in the ticket price; you have to shell out more change for the pleasure of bombarding your family and friends. The Black Hole is a wet version of Disney's Space Mountain; you ride a two-person raft through a pitch-black corkscrew, propelled by a 1,000-gallon-a-minute blast of water. Other rides include the Surge, a five-person tube ride that careers along twisted, banked curves, and the Fuji Flyer, a toboggan ride that sends squealing riders plunging down six curving stories. And, of course, there's the ever-popular vertical free-fall slide, Bomb Bay, which hurtles you through the air in a capsule before splashdown. On the thrill-o-meter, this water park rates at the top. (The runner-up in the Best Slides department is Disney's Blizzard Beach; see next page.) Other good features about Wet 'n' Wild: It's open till 11pm (the other parks close earlier), making it a great place to hang on sultry Orlando nights; live music is offered at night; and if you arrive after 5pm, prices are slashed 50 percent. By day, prices are comparable to Disney's, but unlike the Disney parks, Wet 'n' Wild runs discount coupons in several visitor magazines.

If the idea of body surfing in a wave pool attracts you, hotfoot it over to **Typhoon Lagoon** (tel 407/824–4321; Walt Disney World). The scene is pure Disney: It's the aftermath of a typhoon. A shipwrecked boat teeters on a mountaintop, and, just below, a surf machine generates knock-your-suit-off tidal waves about every 90 seconds. You hear the roar of the wave approaching; everyone squeals; then, a 6-foot wall of water, shaped like a perfectly crested wave, sends you flying forward or diving for cover. This is rip-roaring good fun, if you can avoid landing in a pileup of bathers. At Shark Reef, you can suit up frog-man-style and snorkel across a pool with tropical fish, sting-rays, and (somehow non-life-threatening) hammered sharks. This can be adventurous, but a bit rush-rush; avoid it if it's super-crowded or you'll spend forever waiting in line, compared to a very short time actually in the water. Then there's Castaway Creek, one of those meandering tube rides. The Disneyized version of this takes you through a grotto and a rainforest. This can be heaven on a hot day, but it, too, is nightmarish when crowded, unless you like the idea of being jammed against concrete riverbanks. The ride can also be ruined by aggressive types who mistake it for a bumper-boat attraction.

Blizzard Beach (tel 407/560–2480; Walt Disney World) wins points for creativity. As the story goes, a freak snowstorm dumped powdery white stuff on Disney World. Ski-resort operators quickly moved in to create Florida's first ski resort on the mountain of snow. But, alas, temperatures quickly climbed to normal levels, leaving behind slush, bobsled rides, and slalom courses—and the makings of a wild and woolly water park. A landscape of dripping icicles and patches of snow (you'll touch them to make sure they're not real), melting ice caves (complete with freezing water), a ski lodge, even a working chair lift, carry the theme to its limits. Tops with teens and daring adults is the Summit Plummet slide. You take the chair lift to the "ski jump" on top of Mount Gushmore, then free-fall more than 100 feet into a pool at the bottom. Then you wait in line another hour or so and do it again. The usual water-park mix of inner-tube rides, rafts, and wave pools is also offered. This place gets crowded, and often closes due to capacity limits shortly after the doors open. Get here early. Don't even *think* about going to **River Country** (tel 407/824–4321; Walt Disney World) during peak vacation times. This is the smallest of the parks, and its tame slides and gentle "watering hole" atmosphere attract families with young ones. What you'll find is not the quiet nature escape you may have been expecting. Instead, it's full of toddlers throwing temper tantrums because they're not quite tall enough to go on the slides. (Those who are quickly tire of them.) Save your money and the aggravation, and stick around the hotel pool; you'll have more fun. **Water Mania** (tel 407/396–2626; 6073 W. Irlo Bronson Hwy./U.S. 192, Kissimmee) is the area's second, and trying hard to be the first water park—mostly concrete, with loud pop music providing the atmosphere—but it's also less expensive and less crowded than the rest. The Wipe Out surfing simulator here is a decent rival to the similar one at Typhoon Lagoon, minus the stagy setting....

Golfers' first resorts... There are as many golf packages as there are ways to get a hamburger in this town; golf-and-room packages abound, and many resorts offer free transportation and preferred access to otherwise private courses.

While the rest of your group is meeting the

GETTING OUTSIDE | THE LOWDOWN

Terminator, you can try to straighten out that slice at the **Arnold Palmer Golf Academy** (tel 407/876–5362, 800/523–5999). Golfers from all over the country come to the academy, located at the Arnold Palmer Bay Hill Club and Lodge (see Accommodations). Check into one of the lodge rooms or suites (about $80 to $160 a night), and you'll have a 27-hole championship course right outside your door. Just walking the fairways of the **Poinciana Golf and Racquet Resort** (tel 407/933–5300) is bound to give your game a lift. This 18-hole, par-72 semiprivate course was sculpted by Robert Von Hagge and Bruce Devlin out of an old cypress forest. Don't let the short-ness of the course fool you, the staff pros will tell you; there are lots of bunkers, and water comes into play on 12 holes. Nonguests should call five days in advance for tee times; greens fees run $35 to $50.

Golf clubs: the A-list... A number of top area courses welcome nonmembers, which is good news for all Orlando-bound golfers. The top-notch **Mission Inn Golf and Tennis Resort** (see Accommodations), about 35 minutes northwest of Orlando, offers two champi-onship courses and attracts a loyal following of return players. El Campeon (The Champion), designed in 1926 by C. E. Clarke of Troon, Scotland, is consistently voted one of Florida's top 25 courses by *Golfweek* magazine. Rolling hills, towering pines, and tee boxes that put you up to 85 feet in elevation will make you think you've been transported to Scotland. Rates include a cart and run about $50 to $85; the public is welcome. At the **Grenelefe Golf and Tennis Resort** (see Accommo-dations), you can play three championship courses and never have to leave home. Guests stay in fairway villas and can spend every waking hour, if they wish, driving and putting. Yeah, yeah, there's fishing and tennis and boating as well. Who cares? The course at **Kissimmee Bay Country Club** (tel 407/348–4653; 2801 Kissimmee Bay Blvd., Kissimmee), designed by architect Lloyd Clifton around century-old oak trees and lush foliage, has been nominated by *Golf Digest* as one of America's Best New Courses. Tee times for nonmembers must be reserved seven days in advance; greens fees are $59 to $69. Six lakes weave through wide fairways lined by ancient oaks and cypress trees at the **International Golf Club** (tel 407/239–6909; 6351 International Dr.,

Orlando). Friendly greens and soft bunkers keep frustration levels here to a minimum. Non-member tee-time policy varies; call ahead for details. Greens fees run about $85 to $95. **Orange Lake Country Club** (tel 407/239–1050; 8505 Irlo Bronson Hwy./U.S. 192, Kissimmee) boasts a 27-hole Joe Lee–designed championship course with lots of woods, water, and sand. Tee-time reservations can be made 24 or 48 hours in advance; the general public will pay about $80 in season, but resort guests get a price break. Ask about their afternoon specials; they run around $35, including cart and greens fee.

The Oaks (tel 407/933–4055; 3232 S. Bermuda Ave., Kissimmee) remains a standout for beauty and challenge. They don't call it "The Oaks" for nothing: You'll walk through great stands of the mighty trees, trying to stay on course. Greens fees are modest, around $29 to $39. It's the greens themselves that'll keep bringing you back to the **Eastwood Golf Club** (tel 407/281–4653; 13950 Golf Blvd., Orlando), an 18-hole championship layout by Lloyd Clifton that's widely known in the area as having the best Bermuda greens in Central Florida. Tee times are available seven days in advance. Greens fees are $27 to $43.

Disney for duffers... If you're not incredibly sick of cartoon cuteness by the time you hit the golf course, you surely will be when you round the sixth hole at the Magnolia Golf Course and find a sand trap shaped like Mickey. (We suggest investing in an overpriced set of balls with the big mouse's face printed on them, then whacking the crap out of them. It's a great stress reliever.) Disney has five PGA courses in all, plus a par-36 practice course. These courses are popular with both resort guests and day visitors. Greens fees run about $100 to $130 for resort guests (nonguests pay about $10 more), but you'll get a big break—more than a 50 percent discount—if you wait to play late in the afternoon, generally after 3pm. Disney resort guests get preferred tee times and, often, free transportation from the resort to the course.

The **Osprey Ridge** course, located at the Bonnet Creek Golf Club (tel 407/824–2675, greens fees around $150), is the toughest and most interesting corner of Disney linkdom. Lots of work and dollars went into turning swampland into this very manicured rolling terrain, now dotted with lakes and streams. Disney guilt (after its major alteration of the natural order of things) must have prompted the placement of nesting platforms for local ospreys throughout the course, hence the name. The **Eagle Pines** course, also at Bonnet Creek, is lined with pine needles and sand, giving it a beachlike look. It offers less of a challenge than most other Disney courses (greens fees run around $150).

The **Palm** and **Magnolia** golf courses (tel 407/824–2288; both at the Shades of Green resort, greens fees $100–130) are great examples of what can be done with landscaping when money is no object. They're best for duffers who prefer long, narrow, and tight challenges. The **Oak Trail** course (tel 407/824–2270), located across from the Polynesian Resort, features nine holes, a combination of par-5s, par-3s, and par-4s. It's an inexpensive (about $25 for one round) walking course, mainly used by duffers to brush up on their games. We'd stay away from the **Lake Buena Vista Golf Course** (tel 407/828–3741). This short, uninteresting course at the Disney Institute attracts tons of tourists and weekend hackers, and is not worth the high price tag. Finally, what town would be perfect without its own golf course? Celebration, Disney's eerie attempt at the perfect planned community, boasts the **Celebration Golf Club,** an 18-hole course designed by Robert Trent Jones, Sr.

More birdies and bogeys... Some duffers fork out the big bucks for a room at the **Hyatt Regency Grand Cypress** (tel 407/239–1234, 800/233–1234; 1 Grand Cypress Blvd., Orlando; see Accommodations) just to get onto its golf course. What's not to like? Here you'll find 45 holes of Jack Nicklaus–designed golf, a nine-hole pitch-and-putt course, and a staff willing to please. Greens fees are about $140. **Marriott's Orlando World Center** (tel 407/239–4200, 800/621–0638; 1 World Center Dr., Orlando; see Accommodations), where guests can play an 18-hole Joe Lee–designed championship course, is also popular. Woods, water, bridges, and grass-sloped bunkers attract weekend duffers and serious golfers alike, who pay about $85 for a round.

Rollin' on the river... You've done Splash Mountain; you've floated River Country. They don't count. If you want to call it sport, you're going to have to lift a paddle and hit a real river. For a look at natural Florida, sign up for one of the Sanford canoe trips at **Katie's Wekiva River Landing** (tel 407/628–1482; 190 Katie's Cove). Located in Sanford, Florida, about a half-hour drive from Orlando, the scenic Wekiva River is perfect for day trips. The upper portion of the Wekiva is an aquatic preserve, and its entire 16 miles is a Florida State Canoe Trail. You'll see lots of little critters and birds as you float along. Several guided trips are available: The 9-mile Little Wekiva River Run is the most popular—it's quiet and pristine before it opens into a busy, boat-filled scene. The Rock Springs Run is a 19-mile, all-day adventure for the more experienced paddler. If you're here during the winter and early spring months, consider the company's 12-mile Blue Springs Run, a canoe trip on the St. John's River that ends at the Crystal River wildlife preserve, famous for its wintering manatees (see "Under the seas," p. 165). This run is for experienced paddlers only.

Cruisin' Disney... Fun, fun, fun; will it ever end? Stop by **Sammy Duvall's Water Sports Centre,** located at **Disney's Contemporary Resort Marina,** to select your on-the-water pleasure...wakeboarding, parasailing, skiing, kneeboarding, innertubing, and more. As the name implies, this is water sports central. Several Disney resorts also rent watercraft, including Fort Wilderness, Polynesian, Grand Floridian, Wilderness Lodge, Yacht and Beach Club, and the Swan and Dolphin hotels; the marinas at Dixie Landings, Port Orleans, Old Key West, and Disney Village Marketplace offer them as well. Rentals are available to non-resort guests, too. Unfortunately, you'll share the waters with zillions of others, including jet-skiers and Disney shuttle launches. Not a real nature lover's getaway. Rentals out of the Fort Wilderness Campground offer the best opportunity for solitude and peace.

Away from it all... Slow the internal clock down with an excursion to nearby Winter Park, about 5 miles north of Orlando. This affluent and historic area in Central Florida is laced with lakes and waterways, ancient trees, and elegant homes and gardens. The best way to see the scenery is to take a **Winter Park Boat Tour** (tel 407/644–4056; 312 E. Morse Blvd., Winter Park), a relaxing pontoon-boat ride that's been a tradition in Winter Park for more than 50 years. The one-hour narrated cruise takes you through a chain of lakes and canals lined with giant cypress trees and ancient oaks dripping with Spanish moss. The narrated tour passes Rollins College, Kraft Azalea Gardens, and historic mansions.

Hook, line, and sinker... There's some of the best fishing in the state to be had in the lakes and streams surrounding the greater Orlando area. Bass fishing is big here, and you'll find lots of guide services to show you where to cast your line—for about $200 a day. Go out with Shiner King—the number-one-world-record holder in the Fishing Hall of Fame, and listed in *Florida Sportman*'s list of Top Ten Biggest Bass Certified—on one of his "Bass Blastin'" guided trips. Shiner's **Bass Blastin' Guide Service** (tel 800/882–8333; PO Box 422707, Kissimmee) says it specializes in bass over 10 pounds, and they've caught more than 1,000 trophy bass to prove it. Don't expect anything fancy; this is old-fashioned fishing with live shiners and lures—catch and mount. If you need a ride, no problem; they'll pick you up and drop you back off at your resort. **Pro Bass Guide Service** (tel 407/877–9676, 800/771–9676; 398 Grove Court, Winter Garden) is so sure of their angling expertise that they have a "no bass—no pay" policy on their all-day trips, guaranteeing you'll hook 'em. Captain Paul Solomon operates out of nearby Winter Garden and runs a big, nasty bass boat on the Butler Chain of Lakes.

If these catch-'em-and-eat-'em outfits offend your sensibilities, check out the more politically correct **Bass Challenger Guide Service** (tel 407/273–8045, 800/241–5314; PO Box 679155, Orlando). "Catch a Memory" is its very sweet slogan; they practice CPR—catch, photograph, and release.

For a real backwoods excursion, try **Backcountry Charter Service** (tel 407/668–5516, 800/932–7335; 31 Cunningham Rd., DeBary). You'll travel about an hour and a half to the world famous (at least among anglers) Indian River Lagoon, near the Kennedy Space Center, where you'll go after inshore saltwater game fish. Watch as manatees, dolphins, and stingrays circle the boat. If you prefer big-game fishing, connect with **Atlantic White Water Sport Fishing** (tel 407/783–0268; PO Box 2145, Melbourne). Captain Mike Kane will take you out for some serious deep-sea sport fishing off the shores near the Kennedy Space Center.

Disney dunks... The heaviest large-mouth bass caught and recorded at WDW was 14 pounds, 6 ounces. Don't count on landing one that size, but the odds of snagging one weighing, say, 6 or 7 pounds are pretty good. Seems that back in the '60s, the Disney folk stocked **Bay Lake** with 70,000 bass. Bay Lake, by the way, is the largest lake in the World (Disney World, that is). This is where you're likely to head if you sign up for one of Disney's two-hour guided excursions. Disney's **Buena Vista Lagoon** is another popular choice. No fishing license is needed to fish Disney waters, by the way. **Dixie Landings** offers a stocked fishing hole. Guided excursions are also available at a number of Disney resorts, including the Fort Wilderness Campground, the Grand Floridian, Contemporary, Wilderness Lodge, Polynesian, and Yacht and Beach Club, as well as at the Disney Village Marketplace. If you're interested in a guided trip, be sure to call ahead for reservations. For Bay Lake excursions, call 407/824–2621; for Buena Vista Lagoon trips, call 407/828–2461; for Crescent Lake fishing, call 407/934–3256; and for Sassagoula River trips, call 407/934–5409.

Flying on water... If you've just gotta get out on the water and feel the wind in your hair, then hop on an airboat. Zipping through swamps at roller-coaster speeds is a uniquely Floridian experience. You'll get the speed you crave and a nice look at Florida's natural side at **Boggy Creek Airboat Rides** (tel 407/344–9550; 3702 Big Bass Rd., Kissimmee). Their 30-minute tours offer a scenic view of East Lake Toho as you travel to five different wetland areas. The leisurely idle down a natural creek ends in a high-speed, 50-mile-an-hour race across the swampy lake ($16 adults, half-price for kids 8 and under; one-hour night tours run $25).

Tennis, anyone?... Orlando has more than 800 tennis courts for visitors. You'll find courts in most of the larger hotels and resorts; many of them will rent equipment, arrange lessons, or even set up matches for you. If you're looking to improve your game, check into the **Poinciana Golf and Racquet Resort** in Kissimmee (see Accommodations). Be warned, though: you'll rub tennis elbows with lots of golfers at this fairway villa resort and country club. Courts are also available to visitors at the pretty **Mission Inn Golf and Tennis Resort** (see Accommodations), about 35 minutes northwest of Orlando. Play a few games, and then drink in the views of rolling countryside and lush grounds. The **Grand Cypress Racquet Club** (at the Hyatt Regency Grand Cypress; see Accommodations) in Orlando is a full-service facility that draws some names to its courts. You'll get state-of-the-art lessons, video analysis, hard-court play, and lots of court-time instruction.

Disney courts... Disney answers with 30 courts in its World, including the 11-court tennis center at the **Disney Wide World of Sports** complex. (Tennis buffs may want to plan their visit for April, when the complex hosts the U.S. Clay Court Tennis Championship.) Clay courts are also available at the Contemporary, Grand Floridian, and for guests only at the Disney Institute resorts. Day visitors are welcome at the **Racquet Club at the Contemporary** resort, the **Tennis Club at the Dolphin,** and **Fort Wilderness Campground**. Court time at the Contemporary costs about $15 an hour (for both day visitors and Disney-resort guests); the eight courts at the Dolphin also run about $15, but you can get on for free after 6pm. Courts are free at Fort Wilderness. At **The Disney Institute**, **Key West Vacation Club**, and **Yacht and Beach Club**, complimentary courts are available only to resort guests. The two courts at the **Grand Floridian** are open to resort guests only, and cost $15 an hour. Private lessons are offered for $40 an hour at the Contemporary (tel 407/824–3578) and the Grand Floridian (tel 407/824–2134). Finally, The Disney Institute (tel 800/496–6337) offers several courses on tennis, including a three-day program.

Going public... Not all the courts in Orlando are corporate assets. Public courts are located at **Godwin Park** in St. Cloud (tel 407/957–7243; 4th St. between Delaware and Wyoming Aves.); **Oak Street Park** in Kissimmee (tel 407/932–4050; 1500 Oak St.); **Osceola County YMCA** in Kissimmee (tel 407/847–7413; 2117 W. Mabbette St.); **O. P. Johnson Park** in St. Cloud (tel

407/957–7243; 4th St. between Georgia and Louisiana Aves.); and the **Partin Triangle Park** in St. Cloud (tel 407/344–2939; 2830 Neptune St.). These are all free on a first-come, first-served basis.

Skimming the surface... Feel like a little waterskiing? For about $85 an hour, instructors at Disney will take up to four guests out (you don't have to be a Disney resort guest) on **Bay Lake.** They will pick you up at the Contemporary, Fort Wilderness, Polynesian, Wilderness Lodge, or Grand Floridian marina at scheduled times throughout the day. Reservations are required, though (tel 407/824–2621); during peak season times they may be tough to get. (For those bucks, you better be a fast learner. Or take a friend—the fee is per boat, not per person.) **Ski World** (tel 407/894–5012, 800/238–4631; 1415 N. Orange Ave.) in Orlando will also take you out. They use a variety of local lakes, depending on where the waters are calmest that day.

Alligator games... Gator hunting is a bona fide Florida pastime, even if the only hunting you'll do is with a flash-light or camera. (Gator *spotting* is more like it.) **Boggy Creek Airboat Rides** (tel 407/344–9550; 3702 Big Bass Rd., Kissimmee) will take you on an eerie, hour-long nighttime safari, hunting the low waters for alligators—it's almost as creepy as Terror on Church Street. Daytime rides are great to see Florida *au naturale.* One-hour tours cost $25.

Mini-golf... Take a quick drive down International Drive in Orlando or U.S. 192 in Kissimmee, and you'd swear that putt-putt golf is the official sport of Orlando. There are adventure/mini-golf courses around every corner, and all of them seem to be full of rambunctious kids swinging for the hole-in-one prizes. If this is your kind of fun, you'll be delirious with pleasure. Take your pick. Naturally, Disney jumped on this bandwagon in a large way, with three courses: **Fantasia Gardens Miniature Golf** (tel 407/824–4321), located just southwest of the Swan and Dolphin resorts, sprawls over 11 acres with 36 holes of putting pleasure—gardens, fountains, topiary statues, the works. Brand new is Disney's **Winter Summerland,** a mini-golf complex, with two themed courses—one is fun in the sun, the other a winter wonderland. Santa and his elves play at both. Of course, Disney does mini-golf bigger and better than local entrepreneurs, but it'll mean waiting in line and paying more, too. Putting at Fantasia costs up to $7.50, while Orlando/Kissimmee mini-golf usually runs about $5. Since most kids could not care less about fancy greenery (and adults will get plenty tired of cartoon characters seen in every imaginable shape, form, and texture), why pay more? You'll have just as much fun at **Pirate's Cove Adventure Golf** in Kissimmee (tel 407/396–7484; Lake Buena Vista), or their Orlando location (tel 407/351–7378; 8601 International Dr.). These both feature all the windmills and waterfalls, mazes and traps that make mini-golf a hoot with the younger set. Add soft-serve cones and rock-and-roll music and you've got a sure winner with the kids.

Who wants to be an animal trainer?... If your final answer is "me," sign up for **Sea World D.I.P.** That's Dolphin Interaction Program, for you city slickers. Rise and shine early for this activity: DIP participants arrive before 7am, don wetsuits, and hop in the water for a close encounter with a Sea World bottlenose dolphin. Trainers reveal their secrets, and then it's your turn to try. Before long you'll wave your arm and...wow! Your new friend will return the greeting with its own fin wave. Sea World bends over backwards to teach respect for these lovable creatures—partly to counteract criticism from animal rights and ecological groups. We thought it was a kind and gentle rendezvous, and the dolphin didn't seem to mind at all. In fact, we got the distinct impression that she was sorry to see us go. To take the DIP, you have to be at least 10 years old and 52 inches tall. The two-hour program costs $148 per person; this includes admission into the park for the day. You'll need to make reservations way in advance, though; the program can sell out up to six months ahead. Call 800/327–2424 and they'll mail you a brochure and registration form.

Wet, wild, and wonderful... You've already had breakfast with Mickey and lunch with Pooh—how about a day swimming with Flipper? Okay, the critter isn't really Flipper, but it *is* the real thing. At recently opened **Discovery Cove,** located adjacent to Sea World, you'll spend the day swimming with dolphins, snorkeling with manta rays, and floating among tropical fish and sea animals. This beachy oasis features acres of sugar-white sand, thatched-roof huts, cabanas, robin's-egg-blue lagoons, and winding rivers. Coached by professional animal trainers, guests can swim and play with dolphins in three lagoons. How about a high-speed dorsal fin ride? Adventurous snorkelers can also swim among rays, some up to 4 feet in diameter, and go nose-to-nose with sharks and barracudas (safely separated by clear underwater partitions). There are coral reefs and underwater ruins to explore, then swim under a waterfall into a tropical aviary. Admission to Discovery Cove is limited, so you won't be fighting crowds or spending much time waiting for the fun to begin. Cost is $179 plus tax for the day, and includes all gear, a personal guide, the dolphin swim encounter, and lunch. Sign up now (tel 877/4–DISCOVERY, www.discovery cove.com).

Under the seas... Granted, central Florida is not a diving mecca, but if you want to get under the water and swim with the fish, you can do it here. It's no surprise that the most talked-about dive is one manufactured by Disney. Daily scuba dives are available in the 6-million-gallon aquarium at **The Living Seas Pavilion** at Epcot. Each day at 4:30 and 5:30pm, all certified divers (with proof) can take the Disney plunge. The program includes an orientation to The Living Seas, a 30-minute dive, and (what else?) a T-shirt. All this for about $140. Reservations are required; call 407/939–8687. For a more true-to-life diving excursion, take a safari/ecology trip to central Florida's **Crystal River,** where from November through March you can swim among the giant manatees. Manatees flee the cold ocean waters in the winter and gather in the warm, freshwater springs of Crystal River. This is a rare opportunity to come into contact (you can actually pet them—and they like it!) with one of the world's most endangered marine mammals. For information on when, where, and how to do it, contact the **U.S. Fish and Wildlife Service** office in Crystal River National Wildlife Reserve (tel 352/563–2088).

Back in the saddle again... No one would ever mistake Florida for the Wild West, no matter how often residents

GETTING OUTSIDE | THE LOWDOWN

here remind you that this was once cowboy country. That was a long time ago; today, the grasslands are gone and the cows are on the dinner plates, but horseback riding is still here. At the world-class **Grand Cypress Equestrian Center** (tel 407/239–1938, 800/835–7377; 1 Equestrian Dr.) in Orlando, three different guided riding tours are offered, depending on your abilities. Beginners can hop in the saddle for a walking tour; intermediates can walk and trot; and experienced English saddle riders can canter on the trails surrounding the Grand Cypress Golf Course. Trips run about $30 to $45 and last 50 minutes. The **Fort Wilderness Campground** (tel 407/824–2832) offers beginner trail riding. You can take a 45-minute guided tour (a slow-paced, often hot and buggy, walk) through woods and along waterways. Kids must be at least nine years old; rides cost about $23. Younger tykes (aged two to eight) can hop in the saddle at the campground's petting farm for a $2 pony ride. At **Horse World Poinciana Riding Stables** (tel 407/847–4343; 3705 S. Poinciana Blvd.) in Kissimmee, you can ride on 750 acres of wooded trails. Guided nature and private trail rides are available. Kids five years old and under can ride with an adult. It costs about $30 to $40 for adults, $15 for children.

In the air... We understand the appeal of hovering aloft over Vermont's fall foliage, or the Grand Canyon, but over Race Rock restaurant and Wet 'n' Wild? Somehow, Orlando's pancake-flat topography doesn't seem dramatic enough to warrant a flyover. If you want to see Orlando's attractions from on high, you could simply go up to the 27th-floor bar at the Wyndham Palace Resort and Spa and have a drink. Or ask for a window seat on the plane flight home. But, then again, a hot air balloon flight over the distinctly Orlando skyscape (read: neon globes, futuristic balls, towers of terror, and castles...) may be an experience you won't soon forget. If so, you can sign up for one with **Orange Blossom Balloons** in Lake Buena Vista (tel 407/239–7677).

A walk in the park... You've had it, right? Too much noise, too much concrete, too much whizbang. What you need is a nice, quiet stroll. The Orlando area has a number of pockets of green peace where you can slow down and smell the flowers. Venture downtown to pretty **Lake Eola Park**, a tiny oasis in the center of Orlando, and walk around the flower-lined brick paths that circle the lake. If you're feeling romantic, rent one of the whimsical swan boats and paddle around the lake. Or try **Big Tree Park** (tel 407/788–0405) in Altamonte Springs, home to one of the oldest and largest trees in America. The 3,500-year-old, 138-foot bald cypress tree is named "The Senator" after Senator H. G. Overstreet, who donated the tree and land to Seminole County. Who says there's no history in Orlando? **Blue Springs State Park**, located in Orange City (tel 904/775–3663), has a warm-water spring where you can see wintering manatees.

Turkey Lake Park (tel 407/299–5594), off I Drive in Orlando, is a popular daytime picnic area. You'll find biking and hiking trails, a swimming pool, a wooden fishing pier, canoe rentals, and a petting zoo on its 300 acres. Not exactly wilderness, but a nice getaway. Another good spot to go on a very hot day is **Wekiva Springs State Park** (tel 407/884–2009). The river spouts a cool spring, the closest thing central Florida has to a Vermont swimming hole. There are lots of recreational activities, including canoeing, boating, camping, fishing, hiking, and tubing. Contact **Marvelous Adventures** (tel 800/430–2774; www.marvelousadventures.com/Tours/wekiva.html) for canoeing and hiking tours.

Cypress Island in Kissimmee's Lake Tohopekaliga (tel 407/935–9202; 1541 Scotty's Rd.) bills itself as the "real Florida island adventure," but don't believe it. Yep, the Florida swamp is here—and so are exotic animals, airboat rides, Jet Ski rentals, golf-cart tours, pony rides, and a snack bar. You'll travel on an airboat out to the island, leaving from the Cypress Island Country Store in Kissimmee. You can come to picnic on the 200 acres of meadows and forest and walk the trails, spotting the roaming wildlife. More people come to be Joe Tourist—rent a waverunner, or hop aboard the swamp buggy tractor or golf cart for a tour of the island. Too bad the state, or a nature conservancy, didn't buy the island to keep it in its natural state. Instead, a corporation has moved in and has to pay attention to the bottom line. Thus the ice cream stand, the waverunners, the upcoming gator wrestling show.... Our advice: Stay away.

Walks around the World... As if you'll need to do any more walking than the gazillion miles you'll put in at the theme parks....But say you've opted to stay out of the parks for the day and need a little exercise, you could always stroll the 1.4-mile walk around the lake at the **Disney Caribbean Beach** resort. **Disney Dixie Landings** also has a number of walkways and promenades spread throughout the resort. The **Fort Wilderness Campground** (tel 407/824–2900; 4510 N. Fort Wilderness Trail) offers a relatively peaceful oasis in the World; more than 700 acres of cypress and pine woods surround the resort, with lots of biking and walking paths. There's no charge for day guests. Bike rentals are available as well, or take out a canoe and explore the maze of waterways. There's also a 2.3-mile fitness course with exercise stations.

Garden strolls... Sunshine every day and subtropical weather make this region prime growing territory for lush gardens and magnificent flowers. It's hard to top the flower displays at **Epcot.** If you're a garden lover, you can spend days roaming the grounds, strolling the paths, and, well, smelling the flowers—some 3 million plants and annuals and 10,000 roses. Green thumbers might consider the special behind-the-scenes **Gardens of the World** tour (sign up at The Land pavilion at Epcot; see Diversions). This three-hour walking tour studies the special effects and design concepts of several World Showcase gardens. You've got to really be into plants to enjoy this tour, though; kids (and most adults) will consider it a big yawn. If you time your visit for the month of May, you can catch E**pcot's International Flower & Garden Festival,** a celebration of horticulture featuring millions of blossoms, topiary designs, demonstrations, workshops, guest speakers, guided tours, how-to sessions, and world-class horticulture displays.

In Orlando, the **Harry P. Leu Gardens** (tel 407/246–2620; 1920 N. Forest Ave., Orlando) boasts the largest camellia collection and formal rose garden in the South. Guided tours of the 50-acre property and restored house museum are offered. The **Bok Tower Gardens** (tel 813/676–1408; 1151 Tower Blvd., in nearby Lake Wales) features a 255-foot Singing Tower with 57 bronze bells in the center of the sanctuary, set among reflecting pools and winding pathways. The 128-acre gardens are located on Iron Mountain—a whopping 298 feet above sea level. Both of these gardens are a waste of time for most tourists, however, who will have enough trouble finding time to see the major theme park attractions.

On the rocks... Yes, Virginia, there is tall granite in the flat-as-a-pancake state of Florida, and it is possible to get vertical at **The Disney Institute** (tel 800/ 496–6337). Picture yourself as a rugged mountain climber; if you can dream it, you can do it, the Disney folk tell us. Okay, the rock mountains were probably manufactured at some Disney granite factory, but the techniques (and sore muscles) will be the same as if you're scaling the Tetons of Wyoming. The institute offers a variety of rock-climbing courses, including a four-session, beginner-to-intermediate class.

On the edge... If there's someone willing to pay for an adrenaline rush, there's someone in the Orlando area who will provide it. Have you ever fantasized about being a fighter pilot engaging in aerial combat, taking down the enemy? Here's your chance: For about $750 (fantasies don't come cheap, you know) you can take the controls of a Marchetti SF260 fighter trainer at **Fighter Pilots U.S.A.** (tel 407/931–4333, 800/568–6748; 3033 W. Patrick St.) in Kissimmee. This is not a simulator: You go up in the air in a real fighter plane, sitting next to a retired fighter pilot, who has a matching set of controls. Another plane goes up at the same time, and you fight! You'll go after each other, shoot bullets (don't worry, they're not real), and practice tactics and maneuvers, all in a haze of riveting war noise and smoke (the planes are equipped with smoke and simulated kill systems). You don't need a pilot's license or previous flying experience; just bring your money and a raging sense of adventure.

If battles and war get your juices flowing, you can always join forces at **Paintball World** (tel 407/396– 4199; 2701 Holiday Trail) in Kissimmee. Bring the whole family (kids must be at least 10 years old); you'll divide up into teams and pit your skills against the others. For about $25 you get to run around plastering the other warriors with CO_2-powered semiautomatic paintball guns in a rollicking game of "Capture the Flag." Not exactly a politically correct way to spend an evening, but we'll bet you a Mickey autograph your teenager loves it.

shop

ping

5

Star-struck?
Mouse-obsessed?
Bargain-mad?
Orlando is the
place to buy all
those things—like
the rasta cap with

attached dreadlocks, or the designer leather Mickey Mouse armchair—that you didn't know you needed till you saw 'em. Orlando may not be a shopping mecca on the scale of, say, Milan or Paris, but when it comes to kitsch, it has no peers.

Need it be said that this isn't the place to stock up on Harris tweeds and snappy skirted suits? While you can certainly purchase designer names at the outlet malls, and even at Disney character stores (Nicole Miller lends her cachet to Mickey tote bags, for example), the real finds are those things you'd never buy at home: the *Pulp Fiction* poster, signed by John Travolta, Quentin Tarantino, and Samuel L. Jackson ($695 at Sid Cahuenga's One-of-a-Kind), or the autographed Courtney Love equivalent (also $695 at Starbilia); the floor lamp shaded with a froth of lime-green hair ($140 at Hoypoloi); or the hand-blown glass replica of Cinderella's Castle (yours for the princely sum of $25 grand at the Magic Kingdom's Crystal Arts shop). The area can lay claim to seven shopping malls, six outlet centers, two giant flea markets, and a shop at the end of each ride (sung to the tune of "The Twelve Days of Christmas"). With a lineup like this, is it any wonder that Orlando reigns as the fastest-growing retail market in the country? Now is the time to snag those delicious little glow-in-the-dark bikini panties ($6.95, Glow) and that cunning aviator cap ($24, Rocky & Bullwinkle Shop, Universal Islands of Adventure). On a budget? You can have a grand time sleuthing out tacky-and-terrific trinkets, whether you go uptown (the Disney shops) or downtown (Flea World, billed as "America's largest flea market under one roof").

As if all this wasn't enough, two new shopping centers will have joined the mix by the time you read this. Coming to Belz (a complex of outlet stores) is **Festival Bay,** a 1.1 million-square-foot shopping/dining/entertainment complex (most interesting tenant: Ron Jon's Surf Shop). Also new on the block is **Orlando Premium Outlets,** off exit 27 near Sea World Orlando, which promises savings of 25 to 65 percent on such high-profile names as Louis Feraud, Kenneth Cole, Oilily, Tod's, and Versace. Vacationers, pray for a rainy day.

And you thought you'd be stuck with another "Honk if you love Florida" T-shirt.

What to Buy

Well, that should be obvious: souvenirs, and plenty of 'em. Orlando is more than happy to oblige. Within Walt Disney World itself, you'll find more souvenir shops than we can name (though we've made a valiant effort in the Index). While the lowly T-shirt is by far the biggest seller of all Disney-character merchandise, you could, in fact, create a whole wardrobe around Mickey, starting with Mickey-face silk briefs or cotton bikinis and the ever-wholesome Mickey bra, and topped with a Mickey sundress, shorts, sweater, shirt, vest, tie, blazer, socks, a cap, and fanny pack or tote bag. But why stop there? Why, you could outfit your entire home in Mickey lamps, wallpaper borders, glassware, sculpture, and designer leather furniture. If Martha Stweart can do it, why not Mickey? And for that Mickey Mouse operation you call a business, how about a Mickey mousepad, desk blotter, and date book? You could get this carried away; we wouldn't. But, if you want a little something Disney as a memento of your trip—something a bit more sentimental than a Visa bill—you won't have a lick of trouble finding it at any of the Disney theme parks, not to mention every hotel gift shop, convenience store, and gas station.

For those with a taste for tack, Orlando is Shangri-la reincarnated. The stores lining U.S. 192 on the way into town feature some of the cheesiest mementos ever made: iridescent sand-sculpture alligators, varnished cedar clocks, souvenirs made from shells, Florida snow globes. Best of all, every store carries pretty much the same tacky merchandise, so there's no need to shop around. If you're looking to outfit a shrine to bad taste, have at it.

Target Zones

Personally, we wouldn't waste our time ducking into the shops at the theme parks when there's so much else to do (and we've paid so dearly to do it). But some of the shops are so cute it's tough to resist them. Hard-core shoppers may want to troll Main Street at the **Magic Kingdom,** a villagey strip where you can buy all things Disney. Elsewhere in the Magic Kingdom, shops tie in with their surrounding areas: nautical and pirate gear at Adventureland, Americana at Liberty Square, country crafts at Frontierland, and so on. **Epcot** has nearly 70 shops; the most interesting are among the re-created foreign villages at World Showcase, where you can find unusual souvenirs and playthings like sheepskin drums from Morocco, wild-animal masks fashioned from wood, and pots of assorted silver beads, waiting to be selected and strung for a one-of-a-kind keepsake. (Skip the shops at Future World; there's nothing futuristic about them.) **Disney's Animal Kingdom** is the place to outfit your kids in an *Out of Africa* motif. Dress 'em up as the hunter (safari vests and pith helmets) or the hunted (leopard-print shirts and shorts sets) at Wonders of the Wild, in Safari Village. Check out Mombasa Marketplace/Ziwani Traders for authentic African gifts. This shop stocks cool drums, wooden animal sets, Nigerian straw baskets (great for carrying your other souvenirs, and a buy at $20) and our most fabulous find: carved wooden salad tongs with a zebra motif ($8). The shops scattered around at **Disney-MGM Studios** carry the typical character merchandise, but also some fun stuff for movie buffs. Check out Sid Cahuenga's One-of-a-Kind for vintage movie posters, celebrity-autographed black-and-white publicity stills, and movie props. At **Universal Studios Florida** and **Islands of Adventure**, the shops fit so seamlessly into the motifs that you might miss them. Be assured, though, there's themed shopping available outside every attraction. Look for that "Pet Tornado" kit at Aftermath, the *Twister* store, those Terminator 2–style wraparound shades at Cyber Image (the shop outside T2 3-D), and so on.

Downtown Disney is a restaurant and retail complex apart from the theme parks, near the main entrance to Walt Disney World. Connected via footbridge, Downtown Disney West Side, Downtown Disney Marketplace, and Pleasure Island are home to several shops, including the Largest Disney Shop on Earth!—**World of Disney.** It's a bit like Bloomie's, but if you look closely, you'll realize that everything is MMonogrammed or otherwise Mickeyfied, from evening bags to undies. Sounds positively Goofy, but some of this stuff is awesome, if you can get past the fact it celebrates a rodent. Would you believe a bejeweled evening bag, featuring Mickey's likeness in Austrian crystals? It's fabulous! Two other standout shops here are **LEGO Imagination Center** and **Starbilias.** You can have a grand time at the LEGO store without actually setting foot inside the place; outside are 75 incredible LEGO creations and LEGO play stations for small fry. (Nobody frisks the little tykes when they leave, but it's considered good form to leave the LEGO pieces behind when you depart.) Check out the LEGO sea monster in Lake Buena Vista (the birds in the water are LEGO-ed, not feathered, as well), the snoring grandpop, and best of all, the tourists who peer back at you with little LEGO eyes. Starbilias is the place to go for Coca-Cola collectibles (the big seller here; we don't get it, either), vintage license plates, and an autographed photo of Nirvana, signed by the late Kurt Cobain. Hours are generally 9:30am to 11pm. A short stroll away is **Pleasure Island,**

the nightclub/entertainment complex that is Disney's foray into cooldom. Pleasure Island aims for "hip" with a few shops that try to be trendy but don't quite make it. You can shop Pleasure Island's stores until 7pm without paying to get in; after that, when the clubs open, you pay a cover charge. **Crossroads at Lake Buena Vista** benefits from a great location—this strip shopping center is just a hop and a skip from the entrance to Walt Disney World Village and all the hotels at the junction of I-4 and State Road 535. Disney-maintained, this center offers one-stop shopping for vacationers, with all the necessary services and stores: a good bookstore/gift shop, a post office, clothing stores, a liquor store, a swimsuit shop, even a 24-hour supermarket with a pharmacy and one-hour photo lab on premises. There's also a Disney character shop, in case you missed the other one million opportunities (is there some sort of Orlando ordinance requiring a character shop every 200 feet?). Crossroads also has a good selection of restaurants, operating at a much more relaxed pace than their theme park counterparts.

Right across from the convention center is a glorified shopping mall called **Pointe*Orlando.** It's just a quick hop (or trolley ride) from the hotels on International Drive. The humongous, overturned toy box and 32-foot Raggedy Ann mark the spot of the ultimate toy store, **FAO Schwarz.** Qualifying as a tourist attraction in its own right, this store features a full-scale talking Darth Vader (in the Star Wars shop), a wing devoted to Barbie (the original Material Girl), and a plethora of puppies and kitties (realistic-looking Pomeranians and Siamese among them) to adopt. (Keep in mind you may have to buy a seat on the plane for that life-size $500 stuffed St. Bernard.) Also at Pointe*Orlando: **Disney Worldport.** Here's where you can pick up that MM propeller beanie and the silk double-M boxer shorts you passed up at World of Disney at Downtown Disney Marketplace. Same stuff, different store. (Getting sick of those mouse ears yet?) Other shops here include **Dapy,** where you can buy that must-have giggling Mona Lisa pillow; and **Florida Wild,** which features stuff made in the Sunshine State, like those dreadful glittery T-shirts, and a Florida version of that old standby, Monopoly. Then there are the usual suspects: **A/X Armani Exchange, Abercrombie & Fitch,** and **Victoria's Secret.** You might as well tie in a visit to Muvico Cinema's IMAX 3-D theater while you're here, or pop across the street to WonderWorks, since you're already paying for parking.

Church Street Station Exchange, in the block-long Church Street Station dining and entertainment complex in downtown Orlando, houses more than 45 specialty shops and restaurants in a turn-of-the-century setting. The **Mercado** has a built-in clientele; it's within walking distance of the numerous hotels on International Drive. The intent here was to create a Mediterranean village atmosphere, with shops in little alleyways centered on an open-air courtyard. Despite the fact that some of the merchandise is fairly high end (and some is very cheesy), the Mercado has kind of a low-rent feel. Maybe it's because displays tend to tumble out into the walkways, and the small shops are crammed with merchandise.

Then there are the traditional retail malls. The Orlando area has, count 'em, seven. Together, they offer—would you believe it—1,000 stores. Scary. Mall-wise, the **Florida Mall** seems like the place to go these days, with the recent addition of A-list tenants like Saks Fifth Avenue, Burdine's, J.Crew, Pottery Barn, Restoration Hardware, and even an Abercrombie & Fitch for kids, offering mini-versions of their must-have sportswear for label-conscious tykes.

Bargain Hunting

You can't consider yourself a bona fide shopaholic unless you include an outlet mall on your vacation itinerary. Orlando makes it easy; there are two outlet pods on the north end of International Drive: **Belz Factory Outlet World** and **Belz Designer Outlet Centre.** Belz has 170 outlet stores, spread over two enclosed malls and four strip centers (or annexes, as they call them). Naturally, the good stuff is spread around: Head to Mall 1 for shoes (Bally, Bruno Magli, Stride-Rite), Mall 2 for upscale kiddie duds (Baby Guess, OshKosh B'gosh, Umbro)—oops! we also found Birkenstock lurking there— and the various annexes for brands like Tommy Hilfiger, Timberland, Calvin Klein, and Reebok. Because you buy directly from the manufacturers, Belz lets you save up to 75 percent on first-quality goods—overstocks as well as the occasional irregular pieces and odd sizes, and last year's fashions. Belz Designer Outlet Centre is skewed toward the high end, with 45 outlets offering discounts of 30 to 60 percent off full retail. The prices aren't rock bottom, but if you have an educated eye and can discern what this stuff is really worth (perhaps that DKNY tunic really is a steal at $149), you're likely to come away with some great deals. Names include Ann Taylor, Coach Leather Goods, Fitz & Floyd, Donna Karan, Cole Haan, and Fossil. Some of the same names crop up at **Orlando Premium Outlets,** the newcomer to Orlando's outlet shopping scene, plus the added cachet of Versace, Bottega Veneta, and Louis

Feraud. Look for savings of 25 to 65 percent off full retail. If you're big into Disney character duds, check out Character Warehouse—you might find that $30 Animal Kingdom sweatshirt you've been looking for marked down to $9.99. **Lake Buena Vista Factory Stores** offer direct-from-the-manufacturer savings of up to 75 percent on over-run products and last season's merchandise.

But you haven't really shopped Orlando-style until you've had the Flea Market Experience. If you've cut your teeth on yard sales, tag sales, rummage sales, church bazaars, even Greek agoras and Moroccan souks, you may be ready for the ultimate shopper's challenge: finding the gems among the junk at **Flea World,** the largest open-air flea market in the country. More than 1,700 dealers sell their wares here. We've all read the stories: *Art Dealer Finds Priceless Painting; Housewife Pays $15 for Fabergé Egg.* Of course, what you'll probably go home with is a 12-pack of tube socks or a potbellied pig, so you'd better enjoy the entertainment value of all this, the hunt and the haggling over price. Where else can you get tattooed and body-pierced, buy an adult video, adopt a cockatiel, and hire a lawyer, all in the same afternoon? Come to think of it, if you buy all that stuff, you'll probably need a divorce attorney.

Every other store along U.S. 192 sports big signs shrieking "Bargain!" and "Five T-shirts, $10!!" Many of the stores have the word "bargain"—or some variation thereof—right in their names. Beware: Just because a store looks like a discounter doesn't mean it has discount prices. These places carry a lot of Disney and Universal Studio apparel and souvenirs, some licensed and some not, as well as anything and everything with the word "Florida" imprinted on it. We compared prices of identical items at two of the biggie discount stores, **Bargain World** and **Smart Department Store,** and found them to be about the same. These stores also carry discounted brand-name items from Nike, Reebok, and L.A. Gear, as well as licensed sports apparel.

Hours of Business

Most stores open at 10am and close at 9 or 10pm. Some stay open longer, including Pointe*Orlando (10am–11pm), Church Street Station Exchange (11am–11pm), the Mercado (10am–11pm), Disney Downtown Marketplace (9:30am–11pm), and Pleasure Island (10am–1am; you pay a cover charge beginning at 7pm). Factory outlet malls and traditional retail malls are usually open from 11am to 6pm on Sundays. Hours may be extended in high season. With stand-alone stores, it's always wise to check first, especially if you're making a bit of a trip (and with Orlando traffic, it's *always* a bit of a trip). Most are open seven days a week; the Index notes if they're not.

Sales Tax

Tax rates are determined by county. Orange County has a 6 percent tax rate; Seminole County has a 7 percent tax rate. All prepared food is taxable.

The Lowdown

For the hard-core Disney fan... If your love of Mickey knows no bounds (including good taste) and price is no object, head to **Art of Disney** and **Disney at Home,** both at Downtown Disney Marketplace. Among the treasures that await you: a really good-looking Mickey leather chair—complete with ears and shoes—by Paddy Gordon, priced at (better sit down for this) $3,400. What better place to sit and sip some bubbly, from an MM Waterford flute ($95–150 per set), natch? This is also the place to find limited-edition Disney figurines, original animation cels of Disney cartoons, and production cels of Disney cartoons and movies. Pull the whole look together with the must-have Mickey armoire, crafted of curly maple with Mickey feet and little brass Mickey knobs ($4,000), complemented by the Mickey designer bed featuring cut-out Mickeys ($595 twin to $995 king). And then there's the ultimate souvenir for fans of the Gloved One: a limited-edition, 60-inch-tall replica of Mickey Mouse, hand outstretched in that charming way of his, made of solid California pine. For just $8,000, you'll own a piece of art that truly complements any decor (but goes particularly well with Baumaus). If you don't want to go to those extremes but want just a touch of Disneyana in your decor, we suggest **Disney's Days of Christmas** in Downtown Disney Marketplace. There you can find baubles, balls for your tree celebrating such hallowed figures as Goofy and Donald Duck, and collectible Seven Dwarfs ornaments made by Christopher Radko. Then there's the all-important Santa Hat with Mouse Ears, and the "Mickey Angel" tree-topper—a concept we find just plain scary.

Funky finds... If all that MM gear sends you reaching for the MMaalox, seek out a store with less mouse and more attitude. At **Hoypoloi** (Downtown Disney West Side), you'll discover floor lamps shaded with Day-Glo green or pink wigs ($140), desk lamps shaped like martinis, and a great alternative to the hotel wake-up call, the Zen Alarm Clock, which rouses you with gradually increasing chimes ($140). Cheaper, tackier, and even more fun are the goods at **Dapy** (Pointe*Orlando and Universal Studios CityWalk), where accent pieces include the Giggling Mona Lisa pillow (press her belly and she titters) for $24.99, a life-size cardboard cutout of Austin Powers's Dr. Evil, black-light art and lava lamps, and everything Elvis. For one-of-a-kind items made by Orlandoans much handier than you are, plan a shopping expedition to the **Arts Market,** held the first Saturday of every month at Church Street Station. You never know what you'll find— the quality ranges from great to god-awful—but we promise it'll be more intriguing than a made-in-China Mickey snowglobe.

For the Minnie wanna-be... Alas, she can't actually grow up to be Minnie or Mickey ("After all, there's only one Mickey and Minnie," a WDW public relations type told us, with a perfectly straight face), but she can look the part. **World of Disney,** at Downtown Disney Marketplace, has an assortment of totally cute costumes, including Snow White, Cinderella (post-makeover), Ariel the Mermaid, Tinkerbell, Jasmine, and of course, Minnie. If she's a junior fashionista, indulge her with the Disney gang– embroidered baseball jacket ($62, Disney Worldport).

And for that Civil War Nurse Barbie she's always dreamed of... Sure, you can find Barbie dolls at any Toys 'R' Us, but if you're in the market for Colonial Barbie, or Kenyan Barbie, or Netherlands Barbie, or Civil War Nurse Barbie, the local toy store isn't your best bet. **Toys Fantastic** at Disney Downtown Marketplace has every Barbie you could imagine, not to mention her pals, cousins, chums, sisters, and all the Pepto Bismol–pink accoutrements (hot tub, convertible, RV) it takes to be

Barbie. No wonder we spotted a bumper sticker in the parking lot that read: "I wanna be Barbie. That bitch has everything!" Even more over-the-top is **Barbie's Street of Dreams** at **FAO Schwarz** (Pointe*Orlando), where collectible Barbies reign. Alongside the typical beach bunny Barbies are George Washington Barbie (dashing in a fuchsia waistcoat), Monet's Water Lily Barbie (making quite an Impression at $82), even Chinese Empress Barbie, truly the cat's Mao. No matter how fancy the Barbie, though, your little darling won't be able to resist giving Babs a haircut and ballpoint-pen freckles.

For the Jimmy Buffett wanna-be... Maybe it's the heat, but there's something about O-Town that can turn even Brooks Brothers types into Bubbas and Bubbettes. One minute you're checking your e-mail, the next you're buying a T-shirt that reads "Life is short—drink faster!" Might as well look the part: Pick up a baseball cap that sports its own curly gray ponytail from **Dapy** and a cigar-box print shirt or minidress from **Captain Crackers** (both at Universal Studios CityWalk). Cover those not-ready-for-primetime gams—please—with a pair of longish surfer shorts from **Boardwalk Surf and Sport** (Pointe*Orlando). Never mind that the nearest ocean is hours away—we be jammin'.

His 'n' hers... What's with all the boudoir gear at the theme park shops? Someone in Marketing obviously caught on to the fact that not all of us are into wispy black lace and peek-a-boo panels. Get a load of the cute-and-comfy Grumpy-wear pj's at **Disney Worldport** (Pointe*Orlando.) And we're suckers for the his-and-hers matching Mickey silk underwear—for her, a silk chemise; for him, sexy boxers—available at Disney Worldport and **World of Disney** at Downtown Disney Marketplace. If your significant other spends a bit too much time hunched over the newspaper, grab his or her attention in your snappy little Sunday Funnies printed silk pajamas ($55 on sale) or boxers ($20) at **Photo Funnies,** in Universal's Islands of Adventure. S/he'll have to get *real* close to read that last panel of Hagar the Horrible. If that doesn't work wonders for your love life, try a princess hat and some well-placed body glitter from **Shop of Wonders** (also at Universal). Great gifts for gals, too. For the truly desperate, they even stock "love spell" kits.

We can't imagine what kind of twisted soul would want a *Titanic*-logoed bathrobe, but somebody must; they're available at the gift shop at **Titanic: Ship of Dreams.** Far more tasteful, we think, is Rose's heart-shaped sapphire necklace, as seen on Kate Winslet's neck in the James Cameron movie. The loveliest—and alas, priciest—version of this little trinket sells for $750 at the Titanic shop.

Love gone wrong? Promise us you'll stay away from the high-tech temptations at **Spy U.S.A.** (the Mercado), where they take dead aim at the lovelorn with low-priced lockpick sets ($9.95), phone bugging devices, and other tools for the tormented (or criminally insane).

For the Warren Buffet wanna-be... Everybody knows somebody who just can't leave the office behind. What to buy for the workaholic type who checks stock quotes while in line for the Shamu show? How about a milk chocolate laptop from **B.B. Sweets Homemade Ice Cream and Chocolate** at Church Street Station? Or a Mickey-themed desk set or daily planner, with a tastefully embossed Mickey on black leather? Might bring a breath of fresh air to the office! These can be found at **World of Disney** at Downtown Disney Marketplace and **Disney Worldport** at Pointe*Orlando.

Incredible edibles... Not even the scary witch dunking (poisoned?) apples into caramel will keep the kids away from **Disney's Candy Cauldron** (Downtown Disney West Side). Buy 'em a bag of gummi gators, then treat yourself to the *good stuff* at **Ghirardelli Soda Fountain & Chocolate Shop.** ("Like sex, kids are too young to appreciate good chocolate," whispered the gal at the counter. Who's gonna argue?) For a serious sugar rush (or potent PMS antidote), try the World's Largest Chocolate Bar, a 5-pound, foil-wrapped hunk of heaven. They also serve outrageously expensive—and delicious—ice cream concoctions. Figure it this way: Even at five bucks a scoop, it's cheaper than Prozac. Nobody beats the French when it comes to luscious pastry, so indulge in sublime tartlets, brioches, and éclairs at **Boulangerie Patisserie** at Epcot's World Showcase France. We can't guarantee the bakers were all born in France, but their recipes and methods are all properly Gallic. Prefer hot-and-spicy to sticky-sweet? **Buffalo Trading Co.,** at Church Street Station, offers the full line of "Ass Kickin' Food" products, including chili fixins,

Buffalo wing sauce, and the Bloody Mary from Hell, complemented by make-your-own beer bread. Now, *that's* a meal. More firepower can be found at the **Tabasco Country Store** at CityWalk, stocked with gifts inspired by the legendary pepper sauce. And don't say we didn't warn you about Mickey Roni & Cheese, available all over WDW. Talk about your shameless hucksterism! Once the little ones have scarfed down these cunning little cheese-covered Mickeys at $2.95 a box, they'll never again be happy with Kraft's (25¢) version of same.

To bring out the Nicklaus in you... You may have discovered Orlando's world-class golf courses, and the fact that golf legends Arnold Palmer and Gary Player own developments here. If all this only intimidates you because your game is strictly bush league, maybe your equipment's to blame. **Special Tee Golf and Tennis** carries links equipment and apparel by more than 100 manufacturers. Then again, maybe the problem is your swing. Each Special Tee shop (there are two on I Drive) offers a fitting range so you can analyze your swing and try out a variety of clubs. Walt Disney World also has several golf shops, including the **Lake Buena Vista Pro Shop** at the Villas at The Disney Institute.

To bring out the Nicholson in you... Ya gotta have shades. Even if you're not interested in creating an aura of mystery and raw sexual power, sunglasses are de rigueur in Orlando, where eyes need protection from the searing tropical sun. You can find cheapo models at every convenience store and supermarket, but you'll find the best selection of stylin' shades at **Sunglass Hut Outlet** in Lake Buena Vista Factory Stores, where they carry lines such as Revo, Oakley, and polarized Maui Gem at 20 to 30 percent off.

Fun finds for small fry... First, a word of warning: Even if you're not a shopper, you'll end up in more gift shops than you thought possible during your Orlando stay. Theme park engineers are now craftily designing rides that disgorge passengers directly into gift shops. You could blindfold the kids at this juncture, or hustle them right on through the place before their little eyes have time to focus on, say, that giant stuffed Shamu. We say: Good luck. You might as well bite the bullet and steer them toward the really fun (read: less pricey) finds. At Sea World Adventure Park's **Wild Arctic Gift Shop,** there are piles and piles of adoptable plush, including some unusual creatures like stuffed manatees and narwhals, in a range of prices. Meanwhile, at **Shamu's Emporium** (the Sea World shop with the widest selection of merchandise), you'll find irresistible shark-shaped squirt guns and inflatable, ride-on Shamu water toys. You can't go wrong with the squeaky Shamu puppet, a natural for backseat puppet shows. At Universal Studios Florida, check out the **Universal Studios Store** for cool stuff aimed at the preteen set, like the Pet Tornado ($24.95) and other *Twister*-themed gear, as well as the classic, 24-inch E.T. figure, a "Bates Motel, the Final Cut" T-shirt, and the DeLorean car (of *Back to the Future* fame) that drives in circles. Tip: Don't waste your time in the post-ride shops at Universal's Islands of Adventure. They've put all the goods from every Island under the same roof at **Adventure Trading Company** (near the park entrance/exit). Look for huggable plush like E.T., the Cat in the Hat, and the Grinch, and cool Spider-Man backpacks. Also worth a visit if your kids are small: **Dr. Seuss' All the Books You Can Read,** chock-full of Seuss classics like *One Fish, Two Fish...*, videos, and software. Bonus: Seuss characters show up here in person for a meet-and-greet at 11am, 2pm, and 4pm. The most interesting shops at Epcot's World Showcase are **Village Traders,** where stock includes animal masks and sets of tiny wooden animals from Kenya; and **Medina Arts,** in the Moroccan souk, where you'll find authentic-looking sheepskin drums and, at the pushcart outside, unusual brass beads. The shops at the Magic Kingdom are heavy on character merchandise, but you can find some cute items in Frontierland at **Frontier Trading Post,** including Daniel Boone–style coonskin caps and woven leather bracelets. At Disney-MGM, the **"Indy Truck"** pushcart has giant rubber snakes, humongous fake cockroaches (or Palmetto bugs, as they're genteelly known in Florida)— perfect for sending Grandma into cardiac arrest when you scatter them around her kitchen—as well as politically incorrect cap guns. Even upscale **FAO Schwarz** has some goodies priced for the allowance crowd, including a huge bin of marbles in myriad colors and styles, priced individually from 20¢ to $1.50. Both **World of Disney** and **Disney Worldport** have their share of trinkets, such as plush character key chains ($6), wraparound Winnie-the-Pooh sunglasses ($9), and the irresistible Mickey Mouse propeller beanie ($11).

Best cheapie souvenir that we can't identify... "Nobody knows what they are, but everbody wants one" is how the gal at the counter put it: We're talking about tubular, gel-filled sacs, perfect for lobbing at siblings. Universal's shops have bins of these, at $4 a pop...you tell us what they are.

For the pint-size road warrior... For the tot who's graduated from teething rings to burning rubber (and wouldn't be caught dead in anything Disney), may we suggest the perfect gift? A miniature black leather H-D biker jacket ($49), available at **Biker's Image,** in Pointe*Orlando.

Character duds at a discount... For cut-rate Disney clothing (remainders, close-outs, and past-season stock, but who cares?) try **Character Warehouse** at Belz Factory Outlet World, Mall 2. The stock changes from day to day, but we found "Twilight Zone Tower of Terror" T-shirts for a realistic $4.99, and silk-screened Mickey sweatshirts for $9.99 (similar shirts inside the park sell for around $30). Adorable little infant "onesies" printed with Disney pals were priced at $4.99 and up. Generally, stuff crops up here a few months after it debuts in the Disney stores. Items include toys and garments tied in with Walt Disney Co. animated films, as well as Mickey and friends merchandise. **Character Corner,** at Lake Buena Vista Factory Stores, also sells over-runs and past-season character clothing, toys, and accessories, at savings of up to 75 percent. You won't find the range of merchandise you'll find at the shops in Disney, but at these prices, so what? Universal Studios Florida has its own discount store within the park, **Second Hand Rose.** Located near the Kongfrontation attraction, this one offers discounted merchandise from the other shops throughout the park.

Fashion, Florida-style... Everybody's done it: bought something that looked great on vacation, brought it home and unpacked it, then shrieked, "What was I thinking?!" and exiled it to the back of the closet where it won't offend anybody. **Pointe*Orlando,** on the other hand, offers relatively risk-free shopping with the likes of **A/X Armani Exchange, Abercrombie & Fitch, Banana Republic,** and **Chico's.** Guys who favor that just-stepped-off-the-yacht look may go for the preppy duds at **Harrington Bay Clothiers** in Downtown Disney Marketplace, where the racks feature names like Boston Traders, Nautica, and Tommy Hilfiger. And of course, several other well-known names are represented at the outlets, where you may strike it lucky (or you may be faced with a lot of stuff that didn't sell at full retail for good reason). Très preppy kiddie clothes—mini-versions of lines from Hilfiger, Guess, and so on—fill the racks at **Little People's Place,** Pointe*Orlando.

Glass act... What little girl wouldn't be dazzled by her very own Cinderella-style glass slipper (to be displayed on a bureau top, not worn)? **European Crystal Arts** at the Downtown Disney Marketplace features the requisite crystal characters along with lots of twinkling glass creations—vases, bowls, goblets, lamps, jewelry—from all over the world. Glassblowers work on the premises to create tiny, multicolored glass figurines of animals, clowns, and the like. And check out the truly mind-blowing replica of Cinderella's castle, made of hand-blown glass and selling for a mere $8,500. (Teensier versions go for $14.50 and up.)

These boots are made for stalking... At **Reel Finds,** Pleasure Island, you can paw through celebrity castoffs like gold ankle boots "from the personal collection of Cher" ($210) and fetching black leather pumps from the wardrobe of Elizabeth Taylor (they fetch $150). Oh, and look at those tiny leather cowboy boots worn by late actor Hervé Villechaize, for $155. There's also lots of memorabilia from *Gone With the Wind* at this eminently browsable shop. The stuff is priced high enough that only the truly celeb-obsessed would actually purchase anything here, giving the shop more of a museum feel than a retail-store atmosphere. Perhaps that's the intention. **Sid Cahuenga's One-of-a-Kind** reigns as the coolest shop at Disney-MGM, not that there's much competition. The cluttery front porch has bins full of movie posters, like cult fave *The Matrix* (Spanish version) and oldies like *The Love Bug* and *Chitty Chitty*

SHOPPING | THE LOWDOWN

Bang Bang. Many of these are unframed and cheap, perfect for adding that touch of whimsy to a dorm room or home office. Inside the shop is a collection of stuff that proves even stars make fashion faux pas. Witness the earth-toned pantsuit and worn-down flats from Jaclyn Smith, and a dowdy Donna Karan supposedly worn by Cher. Drew Barrymore is so cool that even the stuff worn *near her* has cachet; how else to explain why anyone would want a (dreadful) sweater worn by an extra in one of her movies? Sid's also carries signed publicity pix from flavors-of-the-month like Jennifer Love Hewitt, Ricky Martin, and Britney Spears. The stock changes frequently, depending on what treasures their "L.A. source" can find, we're told. Meanwhile, **Starbilias** at Downtown Disney West Side, seems to have cornered the market in dead-celeb mementos. Autographed items from River Phoenix, Grateful Dead, Kurt Cobain, and the Carpenters were on display during a recent visit, all priced above a thousand bucks. Cool finds include a guitar used and autographed by Pink Floyd for $6,995, John and Yoko's *Double Fantasy* album cover and glossy pic (signed by the couple) for $2,795, and a framed publicity photo signed by the cast of *Friends.* (It sells for $995, approximately the amount the stars get paid *per minute* on the show.) Of course, all of these might have been snapped up by well-heeled fans by the time you visit. If you feel guilty about ogling this stuff and not buying, spring for an Oscar-statuette key chain bearing your name—if your name is a common one, that is. If the only thing that will do is your own mantlepiece-worthy Oscar (and you'd rather not hijack a delivery truck), visit **Universal Studios Store,** where you'll find a bunch of authentic-looking "Best Actor" and "Best Actress" awards.

The good, the bad, and the ghastly... It's not all sweetness and light in the town that Mickey Mouse made famous: Witness the gruesome goods at the **Terror on Church Street gift shop.** Anybody who comes near this place knows what they're getting into—this spook-house attraction is a major gross-o-rama—but in case you wander past unawares, be warned: They stock severed legs, sawed-off hands, bloodied fingers, and oh-so-lifelike hanging bats, among other gory goods. Teens who relate better to Marilyn Manson than Mickey Mouse will love this place. Start planning now for that Halloween bash. Of course, you'll need a place to stash these little trinkets. Why not a truly unique carry-all, the "saco de toro"? This handy item, made out of a bull's scrotum, is about the size of a bocce ball and comes in an assortment of "colors, sizes, shapes, and textures," we are told. Get one of your own for $32.95 (they also sell a desktop version for $44.95). A great gift item, if you've got the…nerve. **Buffalo Trading Co.** at Church Street Station, a store that celebrates the cracker cowboy in all of us, features items like ultra-short cutoffs, Civil War play sets (complete with cannons), and "Ass Kickin" food products.

For the 11th-hour shopper… Oops. You spent all your time riding and re-riding Buzz Lightyear and now you're going home empty-handed? In your dreams. This is Orlando, remember? Even the airport has a mall, of sorts. The main terminal of **Orlando International Airport** has more shops than most Main Streets, including boutiques and theme stores run by Universal, Sea World, Walt Disney World, and the Orlando Magic. Price-wise? Whadda you care? You're desperate. So you didn't spend hours sleuthing out that perfect souvenir…. Nobody will be the wiser.

The Index

Abercrombie & Fitch. Goof-proof shopping for the teen- and pre-teen set, featuring parachute pants and garment-dyed T's with that lived-in look…. *Tel 407/370–4899. Point*Orlando, 9101 International Dr.* **(see p. 185)**

Adventure Trading Co. This huge emporium features souvenirs from each Island, plus some gel-filled squishy cylinders that look like Spider Man's you-know-what…. *Tel 407/363–8000. Port of Entry, Islands of Adventure.* **(see p. 183)**

Art of Disney. Call it nirvana for the hard-core Disneyophile who won't bat an eye at paying, say, $1,000 and up for an original film cel from *Snow White* or *The Lion King*. Production cels can be had for $250 to $300, on average.... *Tel 407/828–3929. www.downtowndisney.com. Disney Village Marketplace.* **(see p. 178)**

Arts Market. Hankering for a hand-made something or other without the MM logo? Local craftsfolk sell their wares at this Church Street fair, on the first Sat. of each month, October–April (or thereabouts.) No mouse crap; they promise.... *Tel 407/246–3278. Church Street, Orlando.*
(see p. 179)

A/X Armani Exchange. The more-affordable side of Italian über-designer Giorgio Armani, a master of understated elegance. You'll never leave this store a fashion victim.... *Tel 407/352–3311. Pointe*Orlando, 9101 International Dr.*
(see p. 185)

Banana Republic. Sure, they're everywhere. But if you need something classic in a pinch, you can't go wrong.... *Tel 407/903–0443. Pointe*Orlando, 9101 International Dr.*
(see p. 185)

B.B. Sweets Homemade Ice Cream and Chocolate. This old-fashioned ice cream fountain and candy shop stocks hand-dipped chocolates and novelty items like white-chocolate cell phones and milk-chocolate computers. Hook 'em up to that marzipan modem you already own.... *Tel 407/423–8379. Church Street Station, 129 W. Church St.* **(see p. 181)**

Belz Designer Outlet Centre. This outlet mall caters to label-conscious shoppers, with tenants like DKNY, Off-5th (Saks Fifth Avenue), Cole Haan, Fila, and Flapdoodles.... *Tel 407/354–0300. www.beltz.com. 5211 International Dr.*
(see p. 176)

Belz Factory Outlet World. For some people, this is a bigger draw than the theme parks. With 170 outlets, you're bound to find something that fits, or comes in a color other than puce. Just follow the tour buses.... *Tel 407/354–0126. www.beltz.com. 5401 W. Oak Ridge Rd. at International Dr. (north end of International Dr.).* **(see p. 176)**

Biker's Image. You *know* Harley's gone mainstream when you find it in an upscale shopping mall. This store carries everything Harley, including steel-toed boots and adorable leathers for small fry.... *Tel 407/352–1826. Pointe*Orlando, 9101 International Dr.* **(see p. 184)**

Boardwalk Surf and Sport. The surf's always up at this shop (check out the blue wave in the window), where the look is pure Moondoggie.... *Tel 407/370–0436. Pointe*Orlando, 9101 International Dr.* **(see p. 180)**

Boulangerie Patisserie. Real butter, cream, and loads of sugar....The French pastries here are worth the indulgence. A true bliss-out.... *Tel 407/824–4321. Epcot's France World Showcase.* **(see p. 181)**

Buffalo Trading Co. This Western-style general store offers a mix of merchandise that runs the gamut from handkerchief-print bandannas to silver-and-turquoise jewelry and $395 men's beaded suede jackets.... *Tel 407/841–5588. Church Street Station, 128 W. Church St.* **(see pp. 181, 187)**

Captain Crackers. Forget the boring button-downs; surely you're the type who can carry off a slinky, hibiscus-print sarong or a Hawaiian-style shirt covered with pink flamingos. These are clothes with attitude. If not here, where?... *Tel 407/363–8320. Universal Studios CityWalk.* **(see p. 180)**

Character Corner. Resist the theme park shops and pushcarts; get your official Disney character clothing here instead, where over-runs and last season's goods are marked down to realistic prices, sometimes up to 75 percent off.... *Tel 407/238–0011. Lake Buena Vista Factory Stores, 15591 Apopka-Vineland Rd. (S.R. 535).* **(see p. 184)**

Character Warehouse. Why pay inflated prices for official Disney character clothing? Remainders and closeouts go here, where they're heavily discounted.... *Tel 407/ 345–5285. Belz Factory Outlet World, Mall 2, 5401 W. Oak Ridge Rd. at International Dr. (north end of International Dr.).* **(see p. 184)**

Chico's. Simple designs and natural colors and fabrics are the trademark at this women's clothing shop.... *Tel*

407/827–1090. *Crossroads at Lake Buena Vista, I-4 at exit 27 (State Rd. 535). Tel 407/352-4780. Pointe*Orlando, 1901 International Dr.* **(see p. 185)**

Dapy. "Daffy" is more like it. It's a little '60s, a little nostalgia, and a lot of bad taste—everything you could possibly want in a store.... *Tel 407/248-1274. Pointe*Orlando, 9101 International Dr. Tel 407/363–8320. Universal Studios CityWalk.* **(see pp. 179, 180)**

Disney at Home. You've heard of Stickley; why not Mickley? From mouse-covered shower curtains to Winnie the Pooh bedding to fabulous MM armoires, this is the place to Disney-fy your decor.... *Tel 407/828–2590. www.down-towndisney.com. Downtown Disney Marketplace.*
(see p. 178)

Disney's Days of Christmas. It's Christmas in July, or whenever, at this shop chock-full of holiday ornaments (many featuring Disney characters, naturally) and decorations. Get your Quasimodo Christmas bauble here.... *Tel 407/ 828-3800. www.downtowndisney.com. Downtown Disney Marketplace.* **(see p. 178)**

Disney Worldport. Is it déjà vu, or did you see this same stuff at World of Disney? Whatever. Here's another chance to pick up that Mickey Mouse propeller beanie you missed it the first time.... *Tel 407/903–5400. Pointe*Orlando, 9101 International Dr.* **(see pp. 179, 180, 181. 183)**

Dr. Seuss' All the Books You Can Read. Seuss-o-rama! Books, videos, software, and guest appearances by the Cat in the Hat, the Grinch (delightfully nasty), and Thing One and Thing Two.... *Tel 407/363–8000. Seuss Landing, Islands of Adventure.* **(see p. 183)**

European Crystal Arts. It's a small (glass) world after all.... *Tel 407/828–3616. Disney Downtown Marketplace.*
(see p. 185)

FAO Schwarz. It's hard to miss this one: A 32-foot Raggedy Ann marks the spot. The "ultimate toy store" is a super rainy-day destination (if you don't mind spilling some cash), with tons of games, a Star Wars shop, everything Barbie, and, of course, the big dancing piano keyboard.... *Tel 407/352–*

9900. www.faoschwarz.com. Pointe* Orlando, 9101 International Dr. **(see pp. 180, 183)**

Festival Bay. Shop till you drop at this new retail venue. Stores include the totally Florida Ron Jon Surf Shop.... Tel 901/ 260–7400. www.belz.com. International Dr. **(see p. 172)**

Flea World. America's largest open-air flea market is some colossal affair, with 1,700-plus dealer booths. It's a crazy scene (sometimes elephants entertain the masses), with everything from Caribbean art to zebra-print slipcovers.... Tel 407/330–1792. U.S. 17–92, Sanford. Open Fri–Sat, 9–6.
(see p. 177)

The Florida Mall. This modern mega-mall features three architectural styles and more than 200 stores.... Tel 407/851–MALL. 8001 S. Orange Blossom Trail. **(see p. 176)**

Florida Wild. This novelty shop features (mainly) made-in-the-Sunshine-State goods, some tasteful, some tacky.... Tel 407/903–1314. Pointe*Orlando, 9101 International Dr.
(see p. 175)

Frontier Trading Post. One of the more interesting shops at the Magic Kingdom, offering fun stuff like cowboy poetry books and cute coonskin caps for the kids.... Tel 407/824–1247. Frontierland, the Magic Kingdom. **(see p. 183)**

Ghirardelli Soda Fountain & Chocolate Shop. Just the smell of this place will add 10 pounds to your girlish/boyish figure, so why not go for broke with the World's Largest Chocolate Bar?... Tel 407/824–4321. Downtown Disney Marketplace.
(see p. 181)

Glow! For those must-have glow-in-the-dark bikini panties, Day-Glo Yo-Yos—you-name-it. You glow, girl!... Tel 407/ 363–8000. Universal Studios CityWalk. **(see p. 172)**

Harrington Bay Clothiers. Perfect for the preppy guy who's lost his luggage, this shop features names like Polo, Nautica, and Tommy Hilfiger.... Tel 407/828–3800. Downtown Disney Marketplace. **(see p. 185)**

Hoypoloi. Supremely artsy for Downtown Disney, this small shop features cool accessories for the home (e.g., lamps shaped like martinis, not Mickeys).... *Tel 407/824– 4321. Downtown Disney West Side.* **(see p. 179)**

"Indy Truck." Rubber snakes (remember the Harrison Ford line in the movie, "Snakes! Anything but snakes!"?), humongous faux cockroaches, and cap guns. Now we're talking souvenirs.... *Tel 407/824–4321. Disney-MGM Studios.*
(see p. 183)

Lake Buena Vista Factory Stores. Find The Gap, Liz Claiborne, Character Corner (Disney duds, discounted), and Sunglass Hut.... Tel 407/238–9801. *www.lbvfactorystores.com. 15591 Apopka-Vineland Rd. (S.R. 535).* **(see p. 177)**

Lake Buena Vista Pro Shop. This shop at Disney's Lake Buena Vista Golf Course stocks rental clubs, shoes, and range balls, and sells golf apparel, gear, and accessories.... *Tel 407/828–3741. The Villas at the Disney Institute.*
(see p. 182)

LEGO Imagination Center. Wow. The things you could make out of LEGOs, if you had about a trillion of 'em (and no life). The incredible LEGO creations outside this shop—including a sea serpent in the lake—should inspire you and yours to buy lots of LEGOs and make your own dazzling creations.... *Tel 407/824–4321. www.downtowndisney.com. Downtown Disney Marketplace.* **(see p. 174)**

Little People's Place. For kids who wouldn't be caught dead in a Mickey Mouse T-shirt, this shop offers miniature versions of designer looks from Tommy Hilfiger, Guess, and other fashion-forward labels.... *Tel 407/370–3032. Pointe*Orlando, 9101 International Dr.* **(see p. 185)**

Medina Arts. Here are some playthings they won't find at Toys 'R' Us—authentic Moroccan musical instruments. Woodcrafts and clothing in a souklike setting.... *Tel 407/ 824–4321. Epcot's World Showcase Morocco.*
(see p. 183)

Orlando International Airport. We're not suggesting you make a trip to the airport strictly for shopping, but if you're heading there anyway, check out the boutiques and theme stores run by Universal Florida, Sea World Adventure Parks, Walt Disney World, even the Orlando Magic. Great for last-minute souvenir shopping; in fact, you could skip the theme parks altogether and just shop here, turn around, and go home.... *Tel 407/825–2001. S.R. 528.* **(see p. 187)**

Photo Funnies. Plop yourself into your favorite comic strip, and get the pic to prove it. Now this is what we call a souvenir.... *Tel 407/363–8000. Toon Lagoon, Islands of Adventure.*
(see p. 180)

Pointe*Orlando. This multilevel complex houses upscale shops and pushcarts, restaurants, and bars, and a 21-screen cinema with an IMAX 3-D theater.... *Tel 407/248– 2838. Near the convention center at 9101 International Dr.*
(see p. 185)

Reel Finds. This place is more fun than a yard sale in Malibu. They've got shoes from the closets of Liz and Cher, hats from Joan Crawford, and more. The prices encourage more gawking than buying, though.... *Tel 407/824–4321. Pleasure Island.*
(see p. 185)

Second Hand Rose. For souvenir shoppers on a budget. This store stocks discounted merchandise (overstocks, past-season stuff) from Universal Studios' theme shops.... *Tel 407/ 363–8320. Near Kongfrontation, Universal Studios Florida.*
(see p. 184)

Shamu's Emporium. Sea World's largest gift shop features everything Shamu (and crew), from tub toys to telescopes.... *Tel 407/351–3600. Located directly inside the front gate, Sea World Florida.* **(see p. 183)**

Shop of Wonders. Charms, amulets, and funky jewelry make this one more than just another schlocky souvenir shop.... *Tel 407/363–8000. Lost Continent, Islands of Adventure.*
(see p. 180)

Sid Cahuenga's One-of-a-Kind. Celebrity autographs, movie props, and signed movie posters are among the goods at Disney-MGM Studios' most interesting shop.... *Tel 407/824–4321. Hollywood Blvd., Disney-MGM Studios*
(see p. 185)

Special Tee Golf and Tennis. This is the largest golf store around, offering equipment and apparel from more than

100 big names, like Nicklaus, Izod, Titleist, Ping, Norman, and Head.... *Tel 407/363–1281. www.specialteegolf. com. 8747 International Dr.* **(see p. 182)**

Spy U.S.A. That just anybody can buy this James Bondian stuff is truly chilling; you'll take a peek out of sheer curiosity.... *Tel 407/351–7774. The Mercado, 8445 International Dr.* **(see p. 181)**

Starbilias. Formerly located in Las Vegas, this shop houses one of the largest collections of celebrity memorabilia in the world. Autographs of Hollywood idols, music legends, and sports greats are among the goods for sale, as are antique barber chairs, Wurlitzer organs, and Coke machines (depending upon when you visit).... *Tel 407/827–0104. Downtown Disney West Side.*
(see p. 186)

Sunglass Hut Outlet. You've seen their stores at the mall. Now see what didn't sell at full retail (maybe the style was simply ahead of its time) at the outlet store.... *Tel 407/ 238–9801. Lake Buena Vista Factory Stores, 15591 Apopka-Vineland Rd. (S.R. 535).* **(see p. 182)**

Tabasco Country Store. Feeling hot under the collar? You will after you sample the goods here, inspired by the legendary, incendiary pepper sauce.... *Tel 407/363–8000. Universal Studios CityWalk.* **(see p. 182)**

Terror on Church Street gift shop. This tiny gift shop is part of the Terror on Church Street attraction. If you're into practical jokes like hanging a body part out the trunk of somebody's car, you'll be in fine form after a visit here. The ghoul behind the counter will be happy to give you a hand.... *Tel 407/649–FEAR. 135 S. Orange Ave. Open Sun–Thur, 7pm–midnight (until 1am mid-June–Aug); Fri–Sat, 7pm–1am.* **(see p. 186)**

Titanic: Ship of Dreams. Get your *Titanic*-logoed bathrobe here or, better yet, a little bauble like the one Kate Winslet wore in the movie. Cool earrings shaped like the doomed luxury liner, too.... *Tel 407/248–1166. www.Titanic ShipOfDreams.com. The Mercado, 8445 International Dr.*
(see p. 181)

Toys Fantastic. This store stocks every Barbie you could imagine, from Kenyan to Colonial, even the original vixenish model in the black striped bathing suit.... *Tel 407/828–3800. www.downtowndisney.com. Downtown Disney Marketplace.* **(see p. 179)**

Universal Studios Store. This is Universal Studios' biggest store, located near the exit (perfect for those who make a last-minute dash to buy souvenirs).... *Tel 407/363–8000. Universal Studios Florida.*

(see pp. 183, 186)

Village Traders. Go for that Indiana Jones mystique in a snappy safari vest, or pick up a carved wood zebra mask or a set of tiny jungle animals at this great shop. Items from Africa, India, and Australia are featured.... *Tel 407/824–4321. Epcot's World Showcase Outpost.* **(see p. 183)**

Wild Arctic Gift Shop. Warm cuddlies from the frozen north are stocked at this Sea World shop, including plush polar bears, walruses, beluga whales, harbor seals, arctic foxes, and narwhals.... *Tel 407/351–3600. Located inside the Wild Arctic attraction, Sea World Florida.* **(see p. 183)**

World of Disney. The world's largest shop devoted to Disney character merchandise. From shot glasses to shoes, underwear to umbrellas, it's all Mickey, all the time.... *Tel 407/248–4321. www.downtowndisney.com. Downtown Disney Marketplace.* **(see pp. 179, 180, 181, 183)**

SHOPPING | THE INDEX

night
enterta

6
life &
inment

In this less-is-
definitely-not-more
land of options,
you'll find
plenty to do
after the sun sets.
Granted, once the

magic wears off, many folks drag their kicking, screaming overtired tots to bed and then collapse themselves. Who can blame them? Other, hardier souls return to the theme parks to be chased by aliens or saved by Spider-Man. Special firework displays, parades, and light shows also keep folks coming back until closing hours—and sometimes beyond. (If you're a Disney resort guest, special E-tickets, at $10 or so apiece, will get you into the Magic Kingdom after hours to ride some of the more popular rides.) But there's also plenty to do outside the confines of the major parks. Orlando is teeming with luaus, whodunit mystery theaters, Wild West shows, rodeos, comedy clubs, discos, street carnivals, magicians, jugglers, live bands, and more, more, more—all enticing you to do things that you wouldn't be caught dead doing back home, like tearing your chicken apart with your fingers while jeering the king's jousters.

Mostly, this takes the form of childlike vacation fun, rated G, cleaned up and homogenized for the entire family. Here in the great entertainment capital of the world, the nightlife rarely gets as hot as the daytime temperatures. If you want your nightlife saucier, you'll have to venture into downtown Orlando or to nearby Winter Park. There you'll find a burgeoning nightlife scene, including a collection of live-music venues, discos, dance floors, and coffee houses.

One-Night Standouts

When heading out on the town for the night, most visitors head to one of the one-stop entertainment complexes—a distinctly Orlando invention (though, alas, we hear it's starting to catch on in other tourist destinations). Your choices: **Disney's Pleasure Island, Universal's CityWalk,** and Orlando's **Church Street Station.** Each features live-music venues, dance clubs, restaurants, and shops, wrapped up in a single, contained location. You'll pay one fee at the gate, getting you in all the clubs in the complex. Forget about seeking out local color, culture, and ethnicity. At these all-in-one entertainmentplexes, you'll find a variety of clubs and restaurants that are strategically selected to offer something for everyone, but watered down to offend no one.

At **Pleasure Island,** there are 6 acres of entertainment, including nightclubs, full-service restaurants, a variety of boutiques and shops, and a movie-theater complex. During the day the nightclubs are closed, though visitors can still stroll the streets and shop and dine. After 7pm, the gates go up, the lights go on, hands get stamped, and the music begins. Tourists mill in and out of the clubs, consulting their maps and programs as they chart their pilgrimage of fun. There's 8Trax, a seventies-themed club; Wildhorse Saloon, for country-music lovers; Mannequins Dance Palace, a high-energy, contemporary dance club; the Adventurer's Club, a quirky storytelling hangout; the Rock 'n' Roll Beach Club; Comedy Warehouse; the BET Soundstage Club; and the Pleasure Island Jazz Company. Loud music blasts, a few scantily clad dancers gyrate on outdoor stages, and alcohol is served on the streets. Still, the Island scene has a sterilized, fun-for-the-whole-family feel to it, and the entertainment is mediocre at best. (The one exception is the Jazz Company, which consistently brings nationally recognized artists as well as talented unknowns to its stage.) Every evening at Pleasure Island ends with a New Year's Eve celebration—noisemakers, confetti, lights, countdown, the works. It's an appropriate choice; a night at Pleasure Island often leaves you feeling the underlying desperation and forced gaiety of a typical New Year's Eve. Oh yeah, you'll wait in line for the clubs and venues, too.

Universal CityWalk, the newest entry into the resort entertainment-complex market, is closer to the cutting edge, noticeably hipper than its competition. The 30-acre complex of hot-colored buildings, moving sidewalks, streetscapes, and free-form sculptures, all wrapped around a 4-acre harbor, is Universal's answer to Pleasure Island, and they do a much better job with it. Pleasure Island is largely a collection of themed venues, manufactured by Disney. Universal CityWalk sought popular entertainment leaders in different genres, and gathered them under one "roof." The high-energy result is a lot of unabashed fun. CityWalk lets you choose among the world's largest Hard Rock Cafe and Hard Rock Live Orlando (a 2,200-capacity concert hall); Jimmy Buffett's Margaritaville Cafe; Bob Marley—A Tribute to Freedom; Latin Quarter, with music and food offerings from all 21 Latin American nations; CityJazz, a live performance venue; Motown Cafe; Pat O'Brien's; Universal Cineplex; and a number of restaurants and shops.

Church Street Station in Orlando was actually the first on the block to offer an evening entertainment attraction. The old-fashioned, good-time atmosphere seems more authentic than the others, if only because of its downtown location in historic buildings. And Church Street venues are surrounded by other downtown restaurants and pubs, making it feel more like a block party or street festival than an attraction. While Church

Street attracts an older crowd of visitors and vacationing families, you'll also find a lively local contingent hanging out at the nearby bars and clubs. Whether you buy an admission ticket to the Church Street Station venues or not, it's fun to check out the nightly street party, stroll the avenues, dine at one of the many nearby restaurants, and then grab a seat at an outdoor pub for a little people-watching. The Church Street Station clubs are lively and corny. There's **Rosie O'Grady's,** with Dixieland music and can-can girls; Cheyenne Saloon, for country-and-western music; Orchid Garden, for rock-and-roll; and Phineas Phogg's, a dance club for the over-21, young tourist crowd. The entertainment may not impress you, but the settings will: The renovated turn-of-the-century buildings are beautiful—lots of stained glass, balconies, dark wood, chandeliers, and Victorian-era details. Definitely worth a peek. There's also shopping at the Exchange, a three-story Victorian pavilion, plus food and games at Commander Ragtime's Midway, assorted street performers, and a host of restaurants and nightclubs nearby.

Other Nightlife Hot Spots

Can't commit to a one-fee, one-night orgy of entertainment? That's okay, there are a number of other nightlife hot spots to cruise. **Downtown Disney,** adjacent to Pleasure Island, is home to the top-notch House of Blues, the AMC complex of 24 movie theaters (the largest in the Southeast), the Cirque du Soleil (a wonderful circus slash theatrical display), and a host of trendy restaurants and specialty shops. It's also the location of the Virgin Megastore, Richard Branson's gigantic music and video shop. Now here's some cheap entertainment: You could spend most of the evening at Virgin if you wanted, listening to music and viewing videos. The store has 20 video/laser preview stations and more than 300 CD listening stations. The West Side section of Downtown is always hopping, drawing young tourists and a smattering of locals. The Disney **BoardWalk** streetmosphere is a manufactured Eastern Seaboard village, complete with beach cottages, New England–style inn and, yes, a boardwalk—which meanders a quarter of a mile along Crescent Bay. Specialty shops, bakeries, and eateries line the plank walkway. You'll also find the ESPN World sports bar and arcade here, along with Jellyrolls Piano Bar, and the Atlantic Ballroom, a dance hall featuring live music from the forties to the nineties. At **Pointe*Orlando**, you'll also find a cluster of nightclubs, restaurants, a theater complex, and shopping. Most people come here to shop and eat, two of America's favorite nighttime activities. Ditto for the **Mercado,** a lively marketplace on International Drive studded with restaurants, shops, and entertainment. Street musicians, mimes, jugglers, and clowns perform in the open-air courtyard. Street entertainment, free parking, and shopping draw crowds of tourists. **Downtown Orlando,** particularly the nightclubs and bars along Orange Avenue, offers a variety of good choices; this is where savvy twentysomethings (is that an oxymoron?) head to escape the hordes of tourists. Clubs are clustered together, making it easy to sample a number of hangouts in a short span of time.

Covers

A note about cover charges: Orlando's club owners love a promotion. Ladies' nights, happy hours, wear black, wear white, bring a friend....You name it, and they're doing it to get you in the door. If things are slow, watch for no covers, free drafts, and $1.50 house drinks. If you want to start early, say before 9pm, you may get in for free at a number of clubs. Generally, expect to pay a small cover ($3 to $6) at most clubs once the entertainment begins. If there are big names on stage, tickets soar to $15 to $30. Generally, it's best to call ahead.

Resources

You'll find lots of free entertainment guides and brochures cluttering up hotel counters, visitors centers, convenience stores, even gas stations. Pick them up, browse through them, and clip out any discount coupons you think you might use. But for the real scoop on local action, you'll want to pick up the free *Orlando Weekly* (tel 407/645–5888) guide to arts and entertainment. It's available at selected bars, nightclubs, and restaurants. Or get ahold of the monthly *Axis Orlando* publication, a very hip guide to the local scene. (Contact Axis at 407/823–8054, ext. 28; 11875 High Tech Ave., Suite 250, Orlando 32817.) A yearly subscription costs $15, but they'll tell you where you can pick up a single issue for free when you're in town. If you're planning on taking in one of Orlando's cultural activities, like a theater production, ballet, opera, or concert, check out OTIX! first. Half-price tickets for same-day performances are offered at more than 90 activities, including Cirque du Soleil, Orlando Broadway Series, Orlando Philharmonic, and SAK Comedy Lab. OTIX! can be purchased at the Orlando Visitor Center, 8723

NIGHTLIFE & ENTERTAINMENT | INTRODUCTION

International Drive, on the southeast corner of International Drive and Austrian Row.

The Lowdown

Nightlife

Where the stars shine... If you pick just one spot to do your night-crawling, let it be the **Sapphire Supper Club** in downtown Orlando. Housed in an antique building, the Sapphire combines style and substance. It's the strongest venue in town for diverse live music. The club's been around for a long time, though not always under the same ownership. Now, under the Sapphire marquee, the club features a wide range of live performers, from eclectic to alternative, funk to blues to jazz, including some top names. The age range and look of the crowd changes with the featured band. Drop in any night of the week and the house, which seats 300 to 400 people, will be packed wall-to-wall, standing room only. If the music doesn't send you, the martinis will. How 'bout a Super Dag Daddy? This martini, named after The Dag, a band that plays here regularly, tastes like a watermelon-flavored Jolly Rancher. Or try the Dirty Donkey, a knock-your-sandals-off gin concoction. There's the mint-chocolate-chip martini, the lemon drop—more than 25 selections in all. James Bond wouldn't approve of the drink menu, but he'd love the sexy setting. The celebrity-backed **House of Blues** (Dan Aykroyd, Jim Belushi, John Goodman, and Aerosmith were cofounders) has become one of the top music venues in the area. The complex includes a restaurant, bar, and concert hall. Top-name artists like Eric Clapton, Steve Winwood, Aretha Franklin, and L.L. Cool J perform in the 2,000-seat concert hall. There's live music nightly, everything from rock 'n' roll, jazz, and R&B to country, swing, and the blues.

Meat market and mosh pits... Orlando's not on the water, but somehow beach bars feel right at home here. The party-hearty, drink-till-you-drop college crowd gathers nightly at **Zuma Beach Club** on Orange Avenue. Waitresses parade around in bikinis, serving up more beer on a Friday night than they give away in a week at Busch

Garden's hospitality center. If you're in the mood for loud and rambunctious, elbow your way to the dance floor for a little dangerous disco. Somewhat of a meat factory, the **Baja Beach Club** attracts a beer-drinking, just-over-21 crowd looking to connect. The club's top-40 format packs them in, and the outdoor deck, grill, and volleyball court is elbow to elbow. Need we say more? Tourists in newly purchased parrot shirts gather at **Jimmy Buffett's Margaritaville Cafe** at Universal CityWalk, searching for a little fun. Can you possibly stand another rendition of "Margaritaville"? If so, join the sunburned masses and order up that cheeseburger. It's a tourists'-night-out crowd at the **Rock 'n' Roll Beach Club** on Pleasure Island. Live rock-and-roll bands play loud and try hard to get the out-of-towners to loosen up and work their way onto the small dance floor. The young crowd lingers around the billiards table and plays a little pinball until they drink away their inhibitions. It's best to wait until a little later in the evening, say 9:30 or 10pm (not too late, though—remember this is Disney country, and when the clock strikes midnight the carriage turns into a pumpkin), forget about the quality of the music (it's mediocre at best), and just have a little fun on the dance floor.

Rock your world... Tired of trying to remember the name of your kid's new favorite band? Oldsters can always dance to the oldies-but-goodies at the **Orchid Garden Ballroom** at Church Street Station. No surprises here (plan on at least one rendition of "Rollin' on the River") as a live band dishes out popular rock-and-roll hits, dating from the 1950s and beyond. Need some sunshine on a cloudy day? If you love the old Detroit City sounds, head to **Motown Cafe.** The music pays tribute to giant hit-makers like Aretha, Diana, and the Temptations at this new restaurant/bar/museum at Universal CityWalk. Live performances are held on two stages; for a quieter spot, try the third-level retro-style lounge. If you're looking for live, up-to-date performances, on the other hand, check out the schedule at **Hard Rock Live Orlando.** This roomy, 2,200-seat CityWalk performance hall consistently brings in top-name national and international artists.

Dancing fool... You can almost hear the hormones sizzling at the high-energy **Club at Firestone** in downtown Orlando. This former tire store, known for its late night revelries (it's open until 3am), is Orlando's top dance bar for the over-21 crowd. Dress up, arrive late, and forget about getting up early the next day....**Mannequins Dance Palace** on Disney's Pleasure Island was recently named the number-one dance club in the Southeast. We suspect the Disney PR folk worked hard to land that one. The place is interesting enough: two floors filled with eerie life-size mannequins hanging from the rafters and peeping out from corners. The rotating dance floor is lit with state-of-the-art laser lights and the sound system is the best. (Of course—this is Disney, and we expect no less.) But the clientele, though young, is made up mostly of self-conscious tourists who need a lot of liquid courage before they'll venture out to the dance floor (Maybe the mannequins are scaring them away). Still, it's probably the liveliest place on Pleasure Island. **Phineas Phogg's** dance club at Church Street Station is too cute for words—filled with hot air balloon decor and high energy music. Word has it that the club is expected to get a re-do, including a new name and new atmosphere. It's time. Until then, only tourists with a Church Street passport are drawn to the club. If you like to twirl, dip, and swing to Big Band sounds, check out the **Atlantic Ballroom** at Disney's Boardwalk. This 1930s-style dance hall is dressed up in rich blues, reds, and golds, and filled with twinkling lights and retro-swing sounds. Order one of the signature martinis before hitting the parquet dance floor.

Smoking 'gars and martini bars... Ahhh...the good old days when genteel men retired to the smoking room for after-dinner cigars, bourbon, and conversation. Well, they're back. Cigar clubs are popping up everywhere—even in Orlando. The concept is so old-fashioned, it's in again. Proud stogie tokers, enamored of their own habits, can meet at **Art's,** Orlando's trendy new cigar club. The 3,400-square-foot lounge and retail operation has 84 private and 20 corporate cigar lockers for lease. Members (annual fees run $100 to $345) can lounge, drink, and puff in the dark-paneled, smoke-filled Club Room. A nod to the times: Women tokers are welcome, too. The upscale **Ybor's Martini Bar** in Orlando is a fast hit with hipster puffers. Check out the Taste of Cigars event, held from 5 to 8pm on the first and third Wednesdays of each month, and featuring special liquors and complimentary cigars plus a buffet. You're a long, long way from the Hoop-Dee-Doo Revue dinner show.... Smokers with money to burn can stop by **Cigarz** in Winter Park. Feeling Prosperous? How 'bout that $11,000 Avo cigar on sale here? No one's bought it yet, but plenty more pricey 'gars have gone up in smoke in the small but comfy cigar smoking room.

Do the Hustle!... We love to cut a rug as much as the next person, but is it really necessary to relive the disco days? Wasn't one decade of leisure suits, Farrah flips, and shag carpeting enough? Apparently, Disney doesn't think so. At its **8Trax** Pleasure Island club, sunburned tourists dance the night away à la Travolta under disco ball lights, to boogie-oogie hits from the likes of KC and the Sunshine Band, Donna Summer, and the Bee Gees. It's like being stuck in a bad dream that's lasted a quarter of a century....

Jamaicin' me crazy... It's a hot and sultry night and you're on vacation...what better than a little reggae to keep you in the mood? Stop by **Bob Marley—A Tribute to Freedom** at Universal's CityWalk, patterned after Marley's home and garden in Kingston. Live bands play on the courtyard stage, surrounded by lush gardens. Order up a plate of roasted plantains and relax. You'll find less atmosphere but plenty of island tunes at the **International Reggae Club** in Orlando. The local club is usually devoid of tourists but draws a local crowd of reggae enthusiasts.

All that jazz... Rock-and-roll music too "square" for you? The **Sapphire Supper Club** in downtown Orlando hosts a number of top jazz acts throughout the year. Sip on a shaken, not stirred, martini, and wade into the crowd; this place is usually filled to the max. The **House of Blues** at Downtown Disney West Side features a wide range of top-name musicians, but jazz and blues artists—both top-name and anonymous—make up a large part of the line-up. Check out the monthly calendar; there's something going on every night of the week. Look, too, for Universal's **CityJazz** to bring in a lineup of popular artists. You can check out the stories behind jazz greats at the Down Beat Jazz Hall of Fame, as well, or sit in as current musicians like Wynton Marsalis and Herbie Hancock conduct clinics at the Thelonious Monk Academy of Jazz during the day and then perform over at the CityJazz concert hall at night. It's all part of the CityJazz venue....

Disney's **Pleasure Island Jazz Company** has also done a great job of bringing serious jazz acts to town. National artists on tour make the Jazz Company a regular stop; there's lots of good stuff happening in this club. The room carries a traveling-musician theme, with suitcases and steamer trunks for decor and signed photos and memorabilia of famous jazz artists on the walls. Tables are placed in a half circle around the stage—a cozy setup. You'll find that half the crowd are locals who know what's going on, and the other half are tourists who paid admission to Pleasure Island and are making the rounds. **Pinkie Lee's** is a fun place to spend an entire evening. Come early for dinner and chow down on Southern dishes like corn-dusted catfish, fried green tomatoes, and grilled sausage with red beans and rice, then settle back for some live jazz. The quality of the music is unpredictable; this is one of those hit-or-miss venues. But it's easy to forgive, once you've feasted on that authentic Southern cuisine and relaxed in the easy-going setting. If you're so inclined, check out the gospel brunch on Sunday mornings—it beats Sunday school.

Bar essentials... Looking for a cold drink without fanfare, froufrou, or frills? At **Top of the Palace** on the 27th floor of the Wyndham Palace Resort & Spa, you'll have a great view of the Kingdom and its nightly fireworks, plus entertainment and better-than-average drinks (read: strong). For souls craving silence and solitude, meanwhile, **Crew's Cup Lounge,** at Disney's Yacht Club resort, features slip-in, sink-in leather chairs and loads of peace and quiet. Locals crowd into the **Laughing Kookaburra Goodtime Bar,** also located at the Wyndham Palace. The decor and setting are pretty mundane, but the free buffet is a real draw. After a few drinks and a full belly, the music (Top 40 dance music and classic rock-and-roll) starts up and, hey, why not stay? The best belly-up bar is **Wally's,** a longtime downtown Orlando favorite. This down-on-your-luck kind of place draws a mixed clientele, from the neighborhood wino to the city's latest movers and shakers. Count on a crowd (sometimes even at 8 in the morning), good conversation, and stiff drinks.

For those who know a bodhran from a penny-whistle... The best Irish pubs (in fact, the only Irish pubs) in town are found outside the World. We like downtown **Scruffy Murphy's** (who can resist the name?) for its dark and warm-as-a-shot-of-Jameson-whiskey atmosphere. **Kate O'Brien's Irish Pub** offers a livelier ambience and is consistently crowded, especially during its popular happy hour (from 4 to 7pm). Finally, traditional Irish music lovers will want to head to the hugely popular **Mulvaney's Irish Pub** to sample the atmosphere and hear live entertainment, including Irish folk music.

Red hot rhythms and saucy salsa... Latin culture and sounds have arrived in Orlando at last. We'd like to think this development is a nod to Florida's ethnic diversity, but we suspect it's more likely due to the increasing popularity of Latin music and food. Either way, the lively, hip new **Latin Quarter** at Universal CityWalk is a nice addition to the nightlife scene. Universal calls it an "interactive adventure." (Eating, dancing...we suppose that's interactive.) We do agree it's the best Latin club in town. Music from all 21 Latin nations is presented here, including salsa, merengue, and Latin pop, as are costumed dance troupes. At **Bongos Cuban Cafe,** you'll want to grab one of the bongo-shaped bar stools (on hot nights, head for the patio overlooking the Seven Seas Lagoon), order up a mint-drenched *mojito,* and take in the scene. This Downtown Disney Latin-themed restaurant/nightclub, owned by Gloria Estefan and her husband Emilio, is a festive, brightly colored, pineapple-shaped adobe festooned with hand-painted murals of Old Cuba, plenty of tile work, and lots of Latin sounds. It's pretty tame; most folks come in for dinner or a couple of drinks (though after 10pm the place does begin to sizzle a bit). Those inclined to stogies can cross the street afterward to **Sosa Family Cigars,** where they'll find a selection of fine imports to top off the evening.

Ride 'em cowboys... Though now heavily masked by tourist attractions, fast-food joints, and tacky T-shirt shops, there still exists a cowboy/cowgirl subculture here. Don't expect the Cowboy Bar from Jackson Hole, but there are a few places around town where you can do a little two-steppin' and line dancing. Cowgirls (and boys) won't get the blues at the only-in-Orlando **8 Seconds** country-western entertainment center. We're talking wham-bam bull riding, monster mud machine races, out-

NIGHTLIFE & ENTERTAINMENT | THE LOWDOWN

law truck wars....This strange land of pickup trucks, cowboy hats, and beer cans may sometimes seem a bit desperate, as Yankee transplants try hard to emulate John Wayne. But if you're into the country-western scene, this place has it all—dance halls with live bands, two-step and line dance lessons, a pool hall, 12 bars, barbecue dinners, and gambling. Saturday night is the time to go. Crowds hoot and holler as urban cowboys struggle to stay on a 2,000-pound bull. (Up to 40 live bulls are waiting for any would-be riders.) The rider who stays on closest to 8 seconds wins, and paramedics are standing by, just in case the bull is the victor. Oooo, doggie. You'll find tourists aplenty at the **Wildhorse Saloon** on Disney World's Pleasure Island. This restaurant/bar/nightclub, a sister act to the more famous Wildhorse Saloon in Nashville, draws plenty of wanna-be-a-cowboy city slickers. Loud, live foot-stomping, hand-clapping music entices the crowd to hit the dance floor for a bit of two-stepping and body waggling. It's a good idea to down a half-dozen or so longnecks before entering....The best thing going at the **Cheyenne Saloon and Opera House** at Church Street Station is its great atmosphere—housed in a historic Victorian building, the saloon is full of dark wood and brass. Sit at the bar that wraps around the dance floor, and watch the wait staff do double duty performing dance numbers and serving drinks. If you're ready to carry the Western thing even further, spend a Friday night at the local rodeo in the **Kissimmee Sports Arena,** where real cowboys and cowgirls compete in calf roping, bareback riding, steer wrestling, barrel racing, and bull riding. Yah-hoo!

Bar-stool quarterbacks... It doesn't matter who's playing; any night is a good night at Orlando's many sports bars. Even during slow, value-season times, you'll have to wait in line to get into **ESPN World** at Disney's BoardWalk entertainment district. Why miss a game just because you're on vacation? Sports-crazed visitors flock to this lounge and restaurant, where they can watch just about any athletic event that might be going on at the moment—all at once. There's about a gazillion television sets in the restaurant and lounge, all tuned into some sportscast. It's the final minutes of a close game, you've been sucking down brewskis all evening, and nature is screaming?…Not to worry. There are even sets strategic-ally placed above the stalls in the restrooms. Next door, you can try your hand at the ESPN arcade, a fantasyland of vir-tual reality and video-arcade sports games. The **Official All-Star Cafe** at the entrance of the Wide World of Sports complex is Disney's newest sports-themed restaurant. Celebrity sports figures, including Tiger Woods, Shaquille O'Neal, Joe Montana, Wayne Gretzky, Ken Griffey, Jr., Andre Agassi, and Monica Seles, have hopped on the bandwagon with this one. No surprises, here—32 gigantic video screens and baseball mitt–shaped booths highlight the decor, and the food is ho-hum and overpriced. Universal responded to the sports-themed restaurant/bar craze with the recently opened **NBA City** at CityWalk. Hoopster fans can gather here to watch NBA and WNBA action, amid roundball memorabilia. Test your b-ball skills while you down a couple of longnecks. For those who pre-fer the roar of engines to the roar of the crowd, just down the street in CityWalk you'll find the **NASCAR Cafe,** a restaurant that caters to driving fans. Out front, the car dri-ven by the current NASCAR Winston Cup champion is on display, while additional famous racing cars are on view inside, along with a variety of other racing memorabilia. (see Dining) Burgers, beer, and big games are the focus at **JB's Sports Restaurant/All Star Club** in the Universal Studios area off I Drive in Orlando. This casual, hoot-and-holler establishment, voted the number one sports bar in central Florida by locals, shows 17 games at any one time on large-screen televisions. It also stays open until 2am for some late night celebrating, or commiserating, depending on how your team did. Hard-core fans who are into good beer, decent munchies, and sports-loving crowds gather at the **Orlando Ale House & Raw Bar.** You'll find several locations throughout Orlando; it's a local fave. **Devaney's Sports Pub** is another fun place to be during game time. You'll be surrounded by such Magic memorabilia as Shaq's gigantic shoes (certainly increasing in value now that he's gone west), plus autographed jerseys and game balls. Eight big-screen TVs make it tough to miss any of the action, and lots of nightly food and drink specials are offered. It's a party.

Just for laughs… When was the last time you sat through a live stand-up comedy routine without hearing the "F-word"? You'll hear nothing naughty at Disney's **Comedy**

Warehouse on Pleasure Island. This squeaky-clean improv show features house comedians and is usually pretty corny; order a Shirley Temple to get in the mood. Better comedy can be heard at the **SAK Comedy Lab** in downtown Orlando. Guaranteed to make you smile, the award-winning shows feature troupes of actors and boast some of the best in improvisation comedy. Drew Carey could take lessons from these folks.

Painting the town lavender... Suffice it to say that Orlando is no San Francisco. And when it comes to societal norms, Disney World is about as conservative as it gets. (Though to be fair, we should note that the company has hosted Gay Day at Walt Disney World each year since 1991, attracting more than 100,000 participants.) Those looking for same-sex companionship are best off heading into Orlando, where you'll find **Southern Nights** and the **Big Bang,** or over to **Sadie's Tavern** (voted Orlando's best lesbian bar by *Axis Orlando* readers) in Winter Park.

Where to dump the kids... Why should only grown-ups get to have fun when the sun sets? In this made-for-kids vacationland, the good times continue into the night for young as well as old, with a variety of kids' clubs and evening entertainment venues to choose from. This is good news for parents, since it means you can plan a night out—or two—*sans famille.* Note that parents aren't just dropping the kids off—these are Disney sponsored, well supervised kids' programs that take place at the resort— typically in an activity area/room. There's well-trained, grown-up supervision at all times. The **Neverland Club** at Disney's Polynesian Resort goes all-out to please small fry. From 5pm until midnight, kids are entertained with video games, a Disney movie, and a live animal show put on by Disney's Discovery Island cast. The evening begins with a kid-pleasing dinner buffet of PB&J sandwiches, pizza, hot dogs, and chicken strips, and ends with photo-op sessions with Goofy. Kids aged 4 to 12 are welcome. Other Disney kids' clubs are less deluxe: At the **Cub's Den** at the Wilderness Lodge, little ones are entertained with board and video games and arts and crafts. The **SandCastle Club** at the Beach Club Resort and the **Mouseketeer Clubhouse** at the Contemporary and Grand Floridian resorts both offer refreshments, arts-and-crafts activities, and entertainment to their nighttime visitors. The

Campfire Program at the Fort Wilderness campground is free to all Disney resort guests. Held every evening at the Meadow Trading Post, this old-fashioned outdoor event features appearances by Chip 'n' Dale, live entertainment, cartoons, and a movie. Unlike the other venues, however, the children are not supervised here, so if they're not old enough to be left alone, an adult has to stay with them. At **Camp Holiday** at the Holiday Inn Sunspree, kids enjoy games, activities, variety shows, and puppet shows, and take part in kids' karaoke. Dinner is served in the kids-only restaurant. Duck!

Entertainment

Only in Orlando... One look at Orlando's dinner theaters and you'll realize that moderation is a word that's been left out of the local lexicon. Tourists flock to these over-the-top extravaganzas, though, making tickets difficult to come by during peak vacation times. Go figure. (For nitty-gritty details, see Dining.) The **Arabian Nights** dinner attraction, voted number one by *Orlando Sentinel* readers, offers some of the best and most showy and extravagant entertainment—including chariot races (yes, with real horses and manure), thrilling rides, and spectacular horse acts. This over-the-top, Las Vegas–style showmanship will impress even the most jaded among you. The kids will enjoy cheering for their designated knights at the **Medieval Times Dinner & Tournament.** You might even become the princess to be rescued. The audience is divided into teams and encouraged to cheer lustily as their favorites do battle. If you just can't get enough of knightly/Renaissance-style dinner shows, you can also head over to **King Henry's Feast.** The setting is Henry VIII's court, where you'll watch a surprisingly entertaining assemblage of fighting knights, magicians, sword swallowers, fire blowers, aerial ballerinas, and court jesters. An all-time favorite with kids is **Mickey's Tropical Revue** at Disney's Polynesian Resort. The big cheese joins the cast for this luau/dinner show. Consider it suitable for young children only; it's not much fun for adults. Luaus are also big in Orlando. If you don't think you'll ever make it to a real one in your lifetime, you might consider forking over the bucks for the **Aloha! Polynesian Luau** at Sea World. This is the best of the South Seas adventures, featuring traditional music, song and dance, and cuisine from the islands of Hawaii. A Polynesian luau is also offered at Disney's Polynesian Resort, including an all-you-can-eat feast and hula and fire dancers. But a better choice is the resort's **'Ohana** family-style dinner, with traditional storytelling, instrumental music, and Hawaiian songs. You'll get about the same caliber of entertainment, but tastier food at this particular feast. **Al Capone's Dinner and Show,** on the other hand, places visitors in the gangster-ridden streets of Chicago during the 1930s. Fill up at an Italian-American buffet while you watch a Broadway-style musical comedy. It's fun, but not all that professional. For higher-quality acting, pick up tickets to the **Mark Two Dinner Theater.** For more than 10 years, this professional-quality theater has been producing a yearly series of fully staged, live Broadway shows, performed by a local cast of professionals. The show is followed by a prime-rib dinner, but the show is the show here.

Boos... Skip the **Pirates Dinner Adventure.** The setting is fantastic—guests sit around a moat surrounding a giant pirate ship—but the show itself is a confusing mix of ill-acted scenes and stupid stunts. You'll want to leave long before the pirates begin their jet-ski race around the moat. **Hoop-Dee-Doo-Revue** is Disney's very popular country-western show. We don't get it: The hoedown-type, cornball jokes barely made the grade-schoolers in our audience smile. This show needs to grow up fast.

...and bravos... If you're going to spend one night on the town, go see the fantastic *La Nouba* **Cirque du Soleil** show. This over-the-top theatrical fantasy features extraordinary costumes, high-flying wire and trapeze acts (with truly amazing 360-degree spins, somersaults, and headstands on a 90-foot-long high wire...you'll hold your breath), gymnastics, and acrobatics. The story line is as surreal as the setting: "Once upon a time, a door opened and two worlds collided. Dreams clashed with reality. The mundane mixed with the marvelous...." Nothing mundane remains once the curtain opens on this production. Don't miss it…. Sunday morning at the theme park? Shame on you. Instead, reserve a table at the House of Blues' **Gospel Brunch.** Hallelujah for this show! First, you'll feast on a Southern-style, low-country buffet, including dishes like spicy shrimp, grits, catfish, and chicken, and the not-to-be-missed bread pudding drenched in silky bourbon sauce. The live music (provided by talented choruses from around the South) is loud and rambunctious; you'll be asked to put your hands together for Jesus and coaxed to your feet the minute the singing begins. The show is guaranteed to leave you feeling good for the rest of the day.

Playing Sherlock Holmes… Adults who love a mystery will enjoy the **MurderWatch Mystery Dinner Theater,** staged at the Grosvenor Resort in Disney World. Dine in a spacious Edwardian-style room and watch a talented cast perform. Subtle hints and clues dropped during the course of the evening, and a series of funny confessions, help guests solve the mystery. This somewhat sophisticated offering is one of Disney's best. **Sleuth's Mystery Show and Dinner** is Orlando's answer to whodunit dinners. It's a bit more lighthearted than the production at the Grosvenor, with plenty of audience participation. Unlimited beer and wine offerings tend to loosen up the crowd as the night's show moves on.

Piano licks and sing-alongs… Call it upscale karaoke: At **Blazing Pianos**, audience participation—and lots of it—is the goal. Three pianos play simultaneously in non-stop, zany fashion, while everyone in the joint is coerced into singing along. Don't be shy, and you'd better have no shame and don't expect to bring the kids. If you're feeling a bit subdued, it's best to stay away from the **Howl at the Moon Saloon,** too. Dueling grand pianos play favorite sing-along tunes and the audience is not allowed to just sit and listen. (Warning: This could be sheer torture for some.) Disney's sing-along venue is **Jellyrolls Piano Bar** at the BoardWalk entertainment district. It's designed to look like a giant warehouse full of mismatched chairs and tables, battered crates, and clutter. The featured musicians try to outdo each other, and the audience joins in. Loud, raucous, and sure to irritate if you're not in the mood. If

NIGHTLIFE & ENTERTAINMENT | THE LOWDOWN

you really like this kind of thing, you might want to check out the new **Pat O'Brien's** at Universal's CityWalk. This replica of the original Big Easy establishment prides itself on its dueling pianos; it's a magnet for tourists out on the town drinking fancy "flaming fountain" and "hurricane" drinks.

The big game... If you build it, they will come. Or so thinks Disney of its gigantic new **Wide World of Sports** complex—and they did come. The 200-acre facility includes fields, diamonds, courts, tracks, and stadiums, and can host more than 30 different sport events. Football, tennis, track, soccer, baseball, and more are featured, and all levels—amateur, youth, and professional—are represented. If you want to catch a game, pick up a schedule—something is going on here every day of the year. You can also see top-notch Orlando Magic basketball action at the downtown **Orlando Arena,** but tickets may be tough to come by. Sometimes fans can pick them up outside the arena the night of the game. Although many seem to do it, and the cops appear to look the other way, keep in mind that it *is* illegal. Baseball fans can catch double-A minor-league action at an Orlando Cubs game, played at **Tinker Field.** Built in 1914, this little park (capacity 5,000) has an old-time flavor that's a refreshing antidote to Disney-itis. Bring a picnic basket and a mitt for foul balls. In early spring, the Houston Astros baseball team holds spring training at the **Osceola County Stadium and Sports Complex** in Kissimmee. Minor-league baseball action goes on most of the year at this complex, as well. Also check the schedule for the **Florida Citrus Bowl,** where a number of professional sports events are hosted, including an occasional NFL game (usually an exhibition), Division 1 college football contests, and soccer matches. The Citrus Bowl is held here annually, and both World Cup and Olympic soccer action have taken place here.

Theater, opera, and dance... Sure, monster-truck rallies and wet T-shirt contests are popular down here, but if you look hard, you'll find some redeeming entertainment, too. The **Orlando Opera Company** has brought national and international performers to its stage for almost 30 years. Shows are performed at the **Bob Carr Auditorium** in downtown Orlando, drawing audiences from throughout central Florida. The **Orlando Broadway Series** is also performed at the Bob Carr Auditorium. The **Civic Theatre of Central Florida** presents Broadway, off-Broadway, and family classics on three stages. The theater is located in pretty Loch Haven Park, a quiet, tree-lined oasis that is also home to the Orlando Science Museum, the Orange County Historical Museum, and the Orlando Museum of Art (see Diversions). When it comes to dance, Orlandoans and visitors have one choice: the **Southern Ballet Theatre,** the only professional dance company in central Florida. SBT is both company and school, and its varied selection of scores tries to please traditionalists as well as those with more modern tastes. Performances are at the Bob Carr Auditorium.

Put your money down... There are lots of ways to spend your money in Orlando, but if you're feeling lucky, you may be able to win a little of it back. Spend a night at the dog races at the **Sanford Orlando Kennel Club** (November–May) or the **Seminole Greyhound Park** (May–November). These places can be depressing, though, especially if you get stuck sitting next to a group of Gamblers Anonymous candidates. Stay away from afternoon races; evenings draw a more fun-loving crowd. Kids are allowed at the races, but can't place bets. What's the fun in that? Best to hire a sitter, or, better yet, stay away altogether. You'll spend enough on this vacation, without giving it to the dogs.

216

The Index

Al Capone's Dinner and Show. This musical revue includes gangstas, dames, and coppers, and platefuls of Ma Capone's spaghetti. A little corny; your mother will like it.... *Tel 407/397–BEST. 4740 W. Hwy. 192, Kissimmee.*

(see p. 212)

Aloha! Polynesian Luau. This two-hour Polynesian dinner show at Sea World is one of the better ones, featuring an all-you-can-eat buffet and even a fire dancer or two!... *Tel 407/363–2200. 7007 Sea World Dr., Orlando.* **(see p. 212)**

Arabian Nights. If you want to take in a dinner show, this should be the one. Fifty horses and expert riders put on a colorful, amazing extravaganza that can give Las Vegas a run for it's money.... *Tel 407/239–9223. 6225 W. Hwy. 192, Kissimmee.* **(see p. 211)**

Art's. Premier cigar lounge and club in Orlando. Welcome to the age of decadence.... *Tel 888/770–ARTS. 1235 N. Orange Ave., Orlando.* **(see p. 204)**

Atlantic Ballroom. Dance to Big Band sounds at this 1930s-style retro lounge and ballroom. Martinis and twinkling lights set the stage.... *Tel 407/824–4321. Disney's BoardWalk Entertainment Complex, PO Box 10,000, Lake Buena Vista.* **(see p. 204)**

Baja Beach Club. College kids pack the bar and deck, and dance to disco. Outdoors, there's volleyball.... *Tel 407/239–9629. 8510 W. Palm Pkwy., Orlando.* **(see p. 203)**

Big Bang. A hangout for gays and lesbians in downtown Orlando, one of the few in the area.... *Tel 407/425–9277. 102 N. Orange Ave., Orlando.* **(see p. 210)**

NIGHTLIFE & ENTERTAINMENT | THE INDEX

Blazing Pianos. Raucous, multi-piano jam session that demands audience participation.... *Tel 407/363–3518. 8445 International Dr., Orlando.* **(see p. 213)**

Bob Carr Auditorium. Part of a taxpayer-funded complex that also boasts the Arena and an expo center, Bob Carr is Orlando's big-time stage for the performing arts. Broadway road casts perform fully staged shows in the **Orlando Broadway Series**. The **Orlando Opera Company** has brought national and international stars to the stage, including mezzo-soprano Cecilia Bartoli, while the **Southern Ballet Theatre** puts on shows like *The Nutcracker.... Broadway, tel 407/423–9999. Opera, tel 407/426–1700. Ballet, tel 407/426–1728. Bob Carr Auditorium, 1111 N. Orange Ave., Orlando.* **(see p. 214)**

Bob Marley—A Tribute to Freedom. Head here on a hot night for reggae and to pay homage to the man. Live music and lots of memorabilia.... *Tel 407/363–8000. Universal Studios CityWalk, 6000 Universal Blvd., Orlando.* **(see p. 205)**

Bongos Cuban Cafe. Gloria Estefan and hubby Emilio own this Latin-themed restaurant/nightclub. Festive and lively, especially after a couple of Mojitos.... *Tel 407/828–0999. Downtown Disney, Lake Buena Vista.* **(see p. 207)**

Camp Holiday. Holiday Inn Sunspree's supervised evening program for kids includes dinner, games, activities, variety shows, puppet shows, and kids' karaoke.... *Tel 407/239–4500. Holiday Inn Sunspree, 13351 State Rd. 535, Lake Buena Vista.* **(see p. 211)**

Campfire Program. Old-fashioned campout for kids held every night at the Fort Wilderness Campground, free to Disney resort guests.... *Tel 407/283–2788. Fort Wilderness Campground, 4510 N. Fort Wilderness Trail, Lake Buena Vista.* **(see p. 211)**

Cheyenne Saloon and Opera House. Live music and dancing at a Victorian-style Church Street Station showroom.... *Tel 407/422–2434. Church Street Station, 129 W. Church St., Orlando.* **(see p. 208)**

Church Street Station. The first on the block to offer one-stop entertainment. Located in downtown Orlando; features a variety of clubs housed in turn-of-the-century buildings.... *Tel 407/422–2434. 129 West Church St., Orlando.* **(see pp. 203, 204, 208)**

Cigarz. Pick up your primo stogies here, and puff away in the small smoking lounge.... *Tel 407/647–2427. 333 Park Ave. S., Winter Park.* **(see p. 205)**

Cirque du Soleil. Their *La Nouba* is one of the best shows in town. Extraordinary mix of costumes, music, high wire, trapeze, and acrobatics. Worth the steep $65 or so admission price.... *Tel 407/WDW–7600. Downtown Disney, Lake Buena Vista.* **(see p. 212)**

CityJazz. Universal's newest venue for jazz lovers, this place includes the Down Beat Jazz Hall of Fame, the Thelonious Monk Academy, and a concert hall. Look for big-name artists, and fine jazz players.... *Tel 407/363–8000. Universal Studios CityWalk, 1000 Universal Studios Plaza, Orlando.* **(see p. 205)**

CityWalk. Universal's newest entertainment complex boasts 30 acres of nightclubs, restaurants, and specialty shops. Check it out.... *Tel 407/363–8000. Universal CityWalk, 1000 Universal Studios Plaza, Orlando.***(see pp. 205, 207, 209, 214)**

Civic Theatre of Central Florida. Professional-quality Broadway, off-Broadway, and family classics are performed throughout the year.... *Tel 407/896–7365. 1001 E. Princeton St., Orlando.* **(see p. 215)**

The Club at Firestone. Magnet for affluent yuppies.... *Tel 407/ 426–0005. 578 N. Orange Ave., Orlando.* **(see p. 203)**

Comedy Warehouse. The cleanest comedy you'll ever hear, performed by Disney's house comedians.... *Tel 407/934– 7781. Pleasure Island, Lake Buena Vista.* **(see p. 209)**

Crew's Cup Lounge. This quiet and comfy lounge, tucked away in Disney's Yacht & Beach Club resort, is a cozy place to escape the madness.... *Tel 407/934–7639. Disney Yacht & Beach Club Resorts, Lake Buena Vista.* **(see p. 206)**

Cub's Den. Kids aged 4 to 12 are treated to dinner, movies, and an animal show. Open to Disney resort guests.... *Tel 407/ 824–3200. Wilderness Lodge, 901 Timberline Dr., Lake Buena Vista.* **(see p. 210)**

Devaney's Sports Pub. Popular sports bar.... *Tel 407/ 679–6600. Unigold Shopping Center, 7660 University Blvd., Orlando.* **(see p. 209)**

Downtown Disney. Disney's new entertainment complex adjacent to Pleasure Island. Home to the House of Blues, Cirque du Soleil, and a variety of restaurants and shops.... *Tel 407/828–3058. Downtown Disney, Lake Buena Vista.* **(see pp. 205, 207)**

8 Seconds. Ride 'em cowboys.... Oooo, doggie! This is one happening country-western scene—monster trucks, bulls, gambling, line dancing. Go on Saturday, when you can jump on the back of a 2,000-pound live bull and take a short ride.... *Tel 407/839–4800. 100 W. Livingston St., Orlando.* **(see p. 207)**

8Trax. Young tourists desperately trying to have fun, dancing to disco music.... *Tel 407/934–7781. Pleasure Island, Lake Buena Vista.* **(see p. 205)**

ESPN World. A huge sports-themed bar at Disney's BoardWalk entertainment district.... *Tel 407/939–6200. BoardWalk, 2101 N. Epcot Resorts Blvd., Lake Buena Vista.* **(see p. 208)**

Florida Citrus Bowl. Home to a number of sports events, including NFL games and Division 1 college football and soccer matches.... *Tel 407/423–2476. 1 Citrus Bowl Place, Orlando.* **(see p. 214)**

Gospel Brunch. Skip church and reserve a table at this fantastic House of Blues production. Great BBQ and low-country cooking mixes with talented troupes from around the country.... *Tel 407/934–2583. Downtown Disney, Lake Buena Vista.* **(see p. 213)**

Hard Rock Live Orlando. Large concert hall drawing top-name national and international artists.... *Tel 407/351–5483. Universal Studios CityWalk, 6000 Universal Blvd., Orlando.* **(see p. 203)**

Hoop-Dee-Doo Revue. This hoe-down, ho-hum dinner show is booked up months in advance. We don't understand why. A lot of money to spend for corn.... *Tel 407/939–3463. Disney's Fort Wilderness Resort, Lake Buena Vista.* **(see p. 212)**

House of Blues. A top-notch venue for all kinds of music—rock 'n' roll, jazz, R&B, country, swing, and lots of blues. Try to make one of their gospel brunches, or drop by anytime for their good Southern cuisine.... *Tel 407/934–BLUE. Downtown Disney West Side, E. Buena Vista Dr., Lake Buena Vista.* **(see pp. 202, 205, 213)**

Howl at the Moon Saloon. Here you'll find dueling pianos and a staff that refuses to let you sit there quietly.... *Tel 407/841–9118. 55 W. Church St., Orlando.* **(see p. 213)**

International Reggae Club. If you love island music, head to Bob Marley's at Universal CityWalk first. If you still haven't had enough after that, this no-frills Orlando club offers plenty of reggae tunes.... *Tel 407/425–2235. 1025 S. Orange Blossom Trail, Orlando.* **(see p. 205)**

JB's Sports Restaurant/All Star Club. This casual watering hole is a local favorite with sports fans.... *Tel 407/293–8881. 4880 S. Kirkman Rd., Orlando.* **(see p. 209)**

Jellyrolls Piano Bar. Two pianists battle it out while the audience cheers, claps, and sings along.... *Tel 407/939–6200. BoardWalk, 2101 N. Epcot Resorts Blvd., Lake Buena Vista.* **(see p. 213)**

Jimmy Buffett's Margaritaville. This Universal Studios CityWalk venue is a magnet for tourists. Bring your parrot shirt.... *Tel 407/363–8000. Universal Studios CityWalk, 1000 Universal Studios Plaza, Orlando.* **(see p. 203)**

Kate O'Brien's Irish Pub. Popular Irish bar with lively music, crowds, and happy hour specials. Orlandoans love it.... *Tel 407/649–7646. 46 West Central Blvd. Orlando.* **(see p. 207)**

King Henry's Feast. This two-hour dinner show features sword swallowers, jesters, fire blowers, and more. Young kids will love it.... *Tel 800/883–8181. 8984 International Dr., Orlando.* **(see p. 211)**

Kissimmee Sports Arena. If calf roping and steer wrestling are your style, come in on a Friday night, when genuine cowboys and cowgirls take part in a variety of rodeo competitions.... *Tel 407/933–0020. 958 S. Hoagland Blvd., Kissimmee.* **(see p. 208)**

Latin Quarter. This Universal Studios CityWalk venue is tops for Latin music, and the food's not bad either. Live music from 21 of the South American nations fills the bill.... *Tel 407/363–5922. Universal Studios CityWalk, Orlando.*
(see p. 207)

Laughing Kookaburra Good Time Bar. Shabby room but the music somehow keeps 'em dancing; free food helps, too.... *Tel 407/827–3722. Lake Buena Vista Palace Resort and Spa, 1900 Lake Buena Vista Dr., Orlando.* **(see p. 206)**

Mannequins Dance Palace. Pleasure Island's liveliest dance venue.... *Tel 407/934–7781. Pleasure Island, Lake Buena Vista.* **(see p. 204)**

Mark Two Dinner Theater. Live Broadway road show follows a buffet dinner. About as close to theater as you can get in Orlando.... *Tel 800/726–6275. 3376 Edgewater Dr., Orlando.* **(see p. 212)**

Medieval Times Dinner & Tournament. Finger-lickin' fun: Knights in shining armor compete on horseback as you tear apart chicken and ribs with your bare hands.... *Tel 800/229–8300. 4510 W. Hwy. 192, Kissimmee.*
(see p. 211)

Mickey's Tropical Revue. The big cheese does the hula at this Disney dinner show.... *Tel 407/934–7639. Polynesian Resort, Lake Buena Vista.* **(see p. 211)**

Motown Cafe. This restaurant/bar pays tribute to Motor City sounds. Live music is presented on two stages.... *Tel 407/224–2500. Universal Studios CityWalk, Orlando.*
(see p. 203)

Mouseketeer Clubhouse. A supervised night of entertainment and refreshments for small fry.... *Tel 407/824–1000, ext. 3038. Contemporary Resort, 4600 N. World Dr., Lake Buena Vista. Tel 407/934–2985. Grand Floridian Resort, 4401 Grand Floridian Way, Lake Buena Vista.* **(see p. 210)**

Mulvaney's Irish Pub. Considered by many to be the best Irish pub in Orlando. Lots of authentic music and crowds.... *Tel 407/872–3296. 27 W. Church St., Orlando.* **(see p. 207)**

MurderWatch Mystery Dinner Theater. No mystery to how this evening will unfold. Dinner, a murder, and you—along with the rest of the guests—try to solve the case.... *Tel 407/828–4444, ext. 24. Baskervilles restaurant, Grosvenor Resort, 1850 Hotel Plaza Blvd., Lake Buena Vista.* **(see p. 213)**

NBA City. Universal's answer for sports-obsessed fans, This restaurant/bar pays tribute to every aspect of roundball action.... *Tel 407/363–8000. Universal Studios CityWalk, Orlando.* **(see p. 209)**

Neverland Club. From 5pm to midnight, little ones are entertained with food, video games, movies, and animal shows.... *Tel 407/WDW–DINE. Polynesian Resort, 1600 Seven Seas Dr., Lake Buena Vista.* **(see p. 210)**

Official All-Star Cafe. One of a dozen new celebrity-owned sports bars/restaurants in Orlando. Lots of TVs and ongoing sports action. Skip it unless you're at the Wide World of Sports complex—it's the only place to eat at this Disney venue.... *Tel 800/WDW–DINE. PO Box 10000, Lake Buena Vista.* **(see p. 209)**

'Ohana. Disney's popular Polynesian dinner and show.... *Tel 407/WDW–DINE. Great Ceremonial House, Polynesian Resort, Walt Disney World, Lake Buena Vista.* **(see p. 212)**

Orchid Garden Ballroom. A live band plays oldies but goodies in this Church Street Station venue.... *Tel 407/422–2434. 120 W. Church St., Orlando.* **(see p. 203)**

Orlando Ale House & Raw Bar. A great place to watch your favorite game. Plenty of good munchies and friendly locals. Several locations throughout Orlando....*Tel 407/240–4080. 1667 Florida Mall Ave., Orlando.* **(see p. 209)**

Orlando Arena. Home to the Orlando Magic basketball team.... *Tel 407/649–2255. 1 Magic Place, Orlando.***(see p. 214)**

Orlando Broadway Series/Orlando Opera Company. See Bob Carr Auditorium.

Osceola County Stadium and Sports Complex. Home of Houston Astros baseball team's spring training.... *Tel 407/933–5400. 1000 Bill Beck Blvd., Kissimmee.* **(see p. 214)**

Pat O'Brien's. Replica of the dueling piano venue in the Big Easy. You have to be in the mood.... *Tel 407/363–8000. Universal Studios CityWalk, 1000 Universal Studios Plaza, Orlando.* **(see p. 214)**

Phineas Phogg's. High-energy music attracts young vacationers and occasionally a few locals. Talk is they plan to change the name and upgrade the atmosphere in near future.... *Tel 407/422–2434. Church Street Station, 129 W. Church St., Orlando.* **(see p. 204)**

Pinkie Lee's. The food is always good; the live jazz is hit-or-miss.... *Tel 407/872–7393. 380 W. Amelia St. (located in the parking lot adjacent to the Orlando Arena), Orlando.* **(see p. 206)**

Pirates Dinner Adventure. A colossal mess: pirates, mutinies, and Jet Skis. Save your money.... *Tel 800/866–AHOY. 6400 Carrier Dr., Orlando.* **(see p. 212)**

Pleasure Island. Disney's one-stop, one-price entertainment complex. You'll find a variety of clubs and hordes of tourists looking for fun in all the wrong places.... *Tel 407/939–7704. Downtown Disney, Walt Disney World Resort, Lake Buena Vista.* **(see p. 205)**

Pleasure Island Jazz Company. This cozy club on Pleasure Island is a regular stopover for top-notch jazz acts on tour.... *Tel 407/934–7781. Pleasure Island, Lake Buena Vista.* **(see p. 205)**

Pointe*Orlando. Yet another multi-level entertainment complex of shops, restaurants, attractions, and clubs. Most tourists can't pass it up.... *Tel 407/248–2838. International Dr., Orlando.* **(see p. 200)**

Rock 'n' Roll Beach Club. Disney trying to be hip. The decor is surfboards, billiards, and dart boards. Rock bands entice

NIGHTLIFE & ENTERTAINMENT | THE INDEX

tourists to move onto the dance floor.... *Tel 407/934–7781. Pleasure Island, Lake Buena Vista.* (see p. 203)

Rosie O'Grady's. Cute, corny entertainment, best appreciated by uncritical seniors.... *Tel 407/422–2434. 129 W. Church St., Orlando.* (see p. 200)

Sadie's Tavern. The top lesbian bar in the area.... *Tel 407/628–4562. 415 S. Orlando Ave., Winter Park.* (see p. 210)

SAK Comedy Lab. One of the best places for improv comedy. Hilarious enough stuff to make even Drew proud.... *Tel 407/648–0001. 380 W. Amelia Ave., Orlando.* (see p. 210)

SandCastle Club. Activities, entertainment, refreshments, all designed to keep little ones happy after hours. Open to kids aged 4 to 12.... *Tel 407/934–3750. Beach Club Resort, 1800 Epcot Resorts Blvd., Lake Buena Vista.* (see p. 210)

Sanford Orlando Kennel Club. Where you can watch the greyhounds chase the rabbits from November through May.... *Tel 407/831–1600. PO Box 520280, Longwood, 32752.* (see p. 215)

Sapphire Supper Club. The best spot in town for live music changes dramatically from night to night, depending on the act.... *Tel 407/246–1419. 54 N. Orange Ave., Orlando.* (see pp. 202, 205)

Scruffy Murphy's. This warm and wonderful Irish pub features dark woods and potent potables. Popular with locals.... *Tel 407/648–5460. 9 W. Washington, Orlando.* (see p. 207)

Seminole Greyhound Park. Dog racing, May through October.... *Tel 407/699–4510. 2000 Seminole Blvd., Casselberry.* (see p. 215)

Sleuth's Mystery Show and Dinner. Guests are called upon to solve a mystery from clues dropped by cast members.... *Tel 407/363–1985. 7508 Republic Dr., Orlando.* (see p. 213)

Sosa Family Cigars. Stogie chompers will want to check out this deluxe store featuring 350 square feet of cigar display.

There are nightly demos on the art of hand rolling, too.... *Tel 407/827–0114. Downtown Disney. Open daily, 10am–10pm..* **(see p. 207)**

Southern Ballet Theatre. See Bob Carr Auditorium.

Southern Nights. A local hangout for gays and lesbians in downtown Orlando.... *Tel 407/898–0424. 375 S. Bumby Ave., Orlando.* **(see p. 210)**

Tinker Field. Baseball fans can watch the double-A affiliate of the Chicago Cubs, the Orlando Cubs, play here from April through August.... *Tel 407/872–7593. 287 Tampa Ave. S., Tinker Field, Orlando.* **(see p. 214)**

Top of the Palace Lounge. Go for the view; and once you're here, why fight the crowds? This is the best place to stay and watch the Magic Kingdom's nightly fireworks show.... *Tel 407/827–3591. Wyndham Palace Resort & Spa, 1900 Buena Vista Drive, Lake Buena Vista.*

(see p. 206)

Wally's. Our choice for best dive bar. If you want to mix it up with a local crowd, belly up here.... *Tel 407/896–6975. 1001 N. Mills Ave., Orlando.* **(see p. 206)**

Wide World of Sports. Disney's new mega-sports complex, covering all the bases. Some 30 different sporting events can be hosted here at one time.... *Tel 407/363–6600. PO Box 10000, Lake Buena Vista.* **(see p. 214)**

Wildhorse Saloon. Country-western venue at Disney's Pleasure Island. Tourists crowd in; locals wouldn't be caught dead in here.... *Tel 407/934–7781. Pleasure Island, Lake Buena Vista.* **(see p. 208)**

Ybor's Martini Bar. Hip and upscale place to sip 'tinis and smoke stogies.... *Tel 407/843–5825. 41 W. Church St., Orlando.* **(see p. 204)**

Zuma Beach Club. High-energy music and a beer-drinking mixture of tourists and locals.... *Tel 407/648–8363. 46 N. Orange Ave., Orlando.* **(see p. 202)**

hotlines & other basics

Airport... Orlando is served by **Orlando International Airport** (MCO) (tel 407/825–2001). More than 44 scheduled airlines and 41 charters provide service to more than 100 cities worldwide. The airport is located about 15 miles from the major attractions and downtown Orlando.

Airport transportation to the city... If your Orlando package doesn't include transportation and you don't plan to rent a car, call your hotel to see if it provides shuttle service from the airport. If you strike out, contact the **Mears Transportation Group** (tel 407/423–5566, 800/759–5219), which has taxis or shuttles operating from the airport to all area hotels and attractions. They depart from the baggage-claim level of the airport 24 hours a day. After 1am, call from the courtesy phone and they'll come get you. Round-trip shuttle fares from the airport to International Drive, Lake Buena Vista, and downtown Orlando range from $23 to $27 per adult, $16 to $19 per child; cabs are $2.75 for the first mile, and $1.50 for each additional mile. From Universal area to downtown, the fare is around $18.

All-night pharmacies... If you're traveling with kids, it's a fact of life: Somebody will come down with something at the least convenient possible time. To pick up a bottle of grape-flavored cough syrup at 3am, try **Walgreen's** 24–hour pharmacy at 6201 International Drive (tel 407/345–8402), across from Wet 'n' Wild.

Baby-sitters... If you're staying at any Walt Disney World resort hotel (including the Wilderness Lodge and The Villas at the Disney Institute), you can take advantage of the child-care services offered: Child-care centers are also available at several of the resorts, in addition to in-room baby-sitting. The best known and most elaborate of these is the **Neverland Club** (tel 407/824–2170), operating out of Disney's Polynesian Resort. Even families who aren't staying at the Polynesian select this one, as it offers kids' buffet dinners and special activities for ages 4 to 12. (See "Where to dump the kids,?" p. 210.) **KinderCare Learning Centers** (tel 407/827–5437) are operated for the use of Disney employees, but they'll accept guest children aged 1 to 12, on a space-available basis, in the mornings and early afternoons. KinderCare also provides in-room baby-sitting (tel 407/846–2027). Or, ask your hotel concierge about in-room baby-sitting. A service called **All About Kids** (tel 407/812–9300, 800/728–6506; www.all-about-kids.com) provides 24–hour baby-sitting, using caregivers who are licensed, bonded, insured, and CPR-certified.

Buses... The city's **Lynx** bus system (tel 407/841–8240; www.golynx.com) provides economical transportation around Orlando. You'll know their vehicles by their wild paint jobs. Bus stops are marked with a "paw print" of a Lynx cat; fares are $1 for one stop; $1.10 for up to three transfers. The **I-Ride** trolleys (tel 407/248–9590; www.iridetrolly.com) serve International Drive, departing every 15 minutes from 7am until midnight. The 54 stops include Sea World on the south end and Belz Factory Outlet World on the north. Look for "I-Ride" on markers. The fare is 75 cents per ride (kids ride free); multi-day passes are available. **Lymmo** (407/841–8240) is a free downtown-only bus service, circulating through the main drags (including Orange Avenue) every five minutes. Lymmo operates from 6am to 10pm Monday to Thursday; 6am to midnight on Friday, 10am to midnight on Saturday, and 10am to 10pm on Sunday and holidays.

Car rentals... Even if you're staying at Walt Disney World, you might end up wishing upon a star for a car. If you're planning to park hop, you'll be feeling Grouchy and Sleepy during the long waits for Disney buses. Plus, if you have wheels, you're free to make grocery runs and find cheaper and/or better restaurants. Rates vary depending on the season, but be prepared to pay a sales tax, an airport tax, and a state surcharge on top of your rental fee; that $30 per day (or whatever) is just the beginning. Also, you'd better book at least two months in advance. And remember, this is the number one tourist destination in the world; we'd ask for something fuchsia and metallic to stand out in the sea of vehicles at the Chip 'n' Dale lot at Disney. All of the major rental car companies operate out of Orlando (mostly at or near the airport), including **Alamo** (tel 800/327–9633), **Avis** (tel 800/331–1212), **Budget** (tel 800/527–0700), **Dollar** (tel 800/800–4000), **Hertz** (tel 800/654–3131), and **National** (tel 800/227–7368).

Cash machines... The following banks offer cash advances against MasterCard or VISA: **Great Western Bank** (tel 407/645–2492) and **First Union National Bank of Florida** (tel 407/649–2265). To find the nearest ATM that will accept your **Cirrus** network card, call 800/424–7787; for the **Plus** system call 800/343–7587; for **Citibank** call 800/248–4286; and for **Diner's Club** call 800/248–4286. For foreign currency exchange and traveler's checks, contact **Thomas Cook Currency Services** (tel 407/839–1700) at 55 W. Church Street.

Climate... The key fact to remember is that central Florida has seasons—it's not always 75 and balmy. If you visit in late December, you might encounter 50-degree (10° C) days, although mid-60s to 70s are more common. And if you visit during summer, count on serious heat: Once June rolls around, 90 degrees (32° C) and up is the norm, right on through September. Afternoon thundershowers are common in spring and summer, but they usually blow over pretty quickly. Generally, the weather shapes up like this: October–May: mid-60s to mid-80s; June–September: upper 80s to mid-90s. Nights are a bit cooler, usually mild and pleasant. That's outdoors. Indoors, count on goose-bump-inducing air-conditioning, especially in grocery stores and movie theaters, though Floridians often crank up the heat when the temperature dips to 50. For a local weather update, call 407/851–7510.

Convention center... Orlando's **Orange County Convention Center** (tel 407/345–9800) is located in southwest Orlando in Plaza International. The center currently provides more than 1.1 million square feet of exhibit space. The center has its own food court and in-house telephone service, and it's located within 8 blocks of several thousand hotel rooms. Many more rooms are located within a 15-minute drive of the center.

Dentists... Nothing like a broken crown or throbbing molar to ruin your day. Fortunately, you can get round-the-clock help for dental emergencies, seven days a week, at **Dental Consultants of Orlando** (tel 407/351–2841). They're located at 7350 Sand Lake Commons Boulevard, next to Orlando Regional Sand Lake Hospital.

Discounted tickets... For discounted attractions tickets that don't require a day-long tour of a time-share property, visit the Orlando/Orange County Convention and Visitors Bureau's **Official Visitor Information Center** (tel 407/363–5872) at 8723 International Drive, Suite 201. It's located at the corner of I Drive and Austrian Row. The center also offers bilingual brochures and accommodations information, and its (unbiased) staff can answer virtually any question you might ask about Orlando. It's open 8am to 7pm daily, year-round, except on Christmas Day. While you're there, ask for your free **Orlando Magicard,** a piece of plastic that provides savings of 10 to 50 percent at 89 area businesses, including attractions, accommodations, and restaurants. To order a Magicard by phone (it comes with a complete visitor information kit), call 800/551–1081 or visit www.go 2orlando.com on the Internet. The Orlando CVB is also the source for OTIX!, half-price tickets for same-day performances at more than 90 of the city's cultural venues. Participating organizations include Cirque du Soleil, Orlando Civic Ballet, Orlando Gay Chorus, and SAK Comedy Lab.

Doctors... For minor problems that occur during a theme park visit (blisters, allergic reactions), visit the park's **First Aid Center;** these are noted on the park maps you pick up when you enter. If you have a serious emergency, go directly to a nearby hospital emergency room. **Orlando Regional Sand Lake Hospital** (tel 407/351–8500), at 9400 Turkey Lake Road, is a full-service hospital with a 24–hour emergency department. **Florida Hospital Central Care Medical Center** (407/239–7777), located near Florida Mall at 1239 S. Apopka-Vineland Road, provides walk-in medical services, including lab work and

X rays. Can't get to a hospital? **Dr. William Oakley, Jr.,** a general practicioner, makes house calls to area hotels and campgrounds from 8am to 8pm daily; call 407/238–2000.

Driving around... The speed limit on interstate highways is either 50 miles (80 kilometers) or 70 miles (112 kilometers) per hour, depending on the location. On local roads, it will range from 20 to 55 miles (32 to 88 kilometers) per hour. Florida law requires drivers and front-seat passengers, regardless of age, to wear a seat belt. Children under age three are required to ride in a child's safety seat. Children aged four and five must be in a safety seat or wear a seat belt. Most rental-car companies can provide you with a car seat. If you are going out drinking, take along a designated driver who will remain alcohol-free. Under Florida law, if you are caught driving with a blood-alcohol level of .08 or higher, or if you refuse to take breath, blood, or urine tests as requested by a police officer, your driver's license will be suspended immediately by the arresting officer. It can be a long walk home. Another word of caution: When driving, keep car doors locked.

Emergencies... Call 911 in an emergency for an ambulance, the fire department, or the police. Other helpful numbers: the **Orlando Fire Department,** 407/246–2141; the **Orlando Police Department,** 407/246–2414.

Festivals and special events... From rodeo to Boola Bowl, Orlando boasts a variety of annual events, about 140 in all. For details, dates, and ticket availability, contact the **Official Visitor Center** (tel 407/363–5872). Here's a sampling:

January: The **OurHouse.com Florida Citrus Bowl** (tel 800/297–2695) pits the second-rated teams of the Southeastern Conference against the Big Ten Conference. At Orlando's Citrus Bowl Stadium, E. Rio Grande Avenue. Afterward, everybody makes the scene at the **Boola Bowl Street Party,** the official post-game party of the Citrus Bowl, held at Church Street Station. The official game trophy is presented at the party. Tickets for the party are on sale before the event and at the Citrus Bowl during the game.

February: The **International Carillon Festival** (tel 941/676–1154) is held at Bok Tower Gardens. Daily recitals are held at 3pm. The three-day **Silver Spurs Rodeo** (tel 407/847–4052) kicks off twice a year, in February and October at Silver Springs Rodeo Arena. The biggest rodeo in the East, it draws the world's top rodeo athletes. Admission is $15.

March: From bluegrass to Creole to Texas swing, the music's the thing at the **Kissimmee Bluegrass Festival** (tel 813/935–1561), running for three days in early March at the Silver Spurs Rodeo Arena (see above). In mid-month, Winter Park celebrates the arts with a free **Sidewalk Festival** (tel 407/672–6390) in Central Park. This prestigious three-day event features the work of more than 250 artists who compete in nine categories. Music is provided by such jazz notables as Herbie Hancock, Nestor Torres, and Spyro Gyra.

April: Lake Eola, downtown, is the setting for **Spring Fiesta in the Park** (tel 407/246–2827), a regional arts-and-crafts festival along Robinson Street and Eola Drive. Profits are donated to the restoration and upkeep of the park and amphitheater. Free.

May: Children of the corn, unite, for the **Zellwood Sweet Corn Festival** (tel 407/886–0014), 25 miles from Orlando. Attendees consume more than 200,000 ears of corn. A corn-eating contest, carnival rides, and country music add to the old-fashioned fun.

June: The **Florida Film Festival** (tel 407/629–1088) showcases the work of Sunshine State filmmakers and screens more than 100 films from across the globe, for both juries and the public. Most events are held at the Enzian Theater, 1300 S. Orlando Avenue, Orlando.

July: Celebrate Independence Day with lots of flag-waving Orlandoans at the **Lake Eola Picnic in the Park**. Games, family activities, entertainment, and fireworks make it a festive event.

October: On **Halloween Horror Nights** (tel 407/363–8000), Universal Studios Florida turns into a happy haunting ground, with a spooky maze, haunted houses, and assorted monsters, mutants, and misfits. At Church Street Station (tel 407/422–2434, ext. 405), the **Halloween Street Party** features Central Florida's most popular costume contests, live music, and a Halloween party for kids.

November: The **Orlando Magic season opener** is the can't-miss event of the month. For tickets (yeah, right—almost every Magic game since the team's inception in 1989 has sold out) call Ticketmaster (tel 407/839–3900) or the Orlando Arena box office (tel 407/649–3200, see Nightlife and Entertainment).

December: The First Baptist Church of Orlando's **Singing Christmas Trees** (tel 407/425–2555) event is a beloved local tradition. Two 45-foot Christmas trees are decked with 204 "singing" ornaments, enhanced with spectacular lighting and holiday music (thanks to a pipe organ and full orchestra). And, of course, the theme parks are a-dazzle in holiday finery. **Mickey's Very Merry Christmas Party** (tel 407/824–4321) at the Magic Kingdom (early December) is always enchanting. The night is so magical, who knows? It may even "snow" on Main Street U.S.A.

Gay and lesbian resources... A good source of information on local clubs and events is **Gay and Lesbian Community Services** (tel 407/228–8272), located at 946 N. Mills. The recently refurbished **Parliament House Motor Inn** (tel 407/425–7571) at 410 N. Orange Blossom Trail offers gay-friendly lodgings.

Limousines... Orlando has several companies that'll whisk you away in style, including **Ace Luxury Transportation** (tel 800/258–1015), **Associated Transportation of Florida, Inc.** (tel 407/345–0020, 800/392–7759), and **Noris Limousines** (tel 407/240–4533, 888/240–4533), all offering 24–hour service.

Liquor laws... You must be 21 years old to buy alcohol in Orlando. Alcohol is sold from 9am to 2am in both supermarkets and liquor stores and served at bars and restaurants from 11am to 2am. There are no Sunday blue laws here.

Newspapers... The major daily newspaper is the *Orlando Sentinel*, published daily and Sundays. Weekly local papers include the *Orlando Times* (African-American interest); *Jam Entertainment News* (the downtown music scene); *Orlando Weekly* (arts/entertainment news); and *La Semana* (Spanish-language community newspaper).

Opening and closing times... At many amusements and attractions, hours stretch to accommodate heavy tourist flow. In general, stores are open from 9am to 9pm and bars are open from 11am to 2am. Restaurant hours vary, but many serve dinner until 10pm. Theme park hours vary with the season. To beat the crowds, arrive early. You'll sprint through those turnstiles and onto the hottest rides *before* the hordes arrive (typically around 10ish).

Parking... Unlike many tourist meccas, Orlando has plenty of parking. Most restaurants and shopping centers (including the outlet malls) have free lots. Theme parks and attractions have massive lots, but they fill up fast. The parks close when their parking lots are full (another reason to arrive early). The typical parking fee for these is $6, but Walt Disney World resort guests with cars do not have to pay for parking at theme park lots. Handicapped spaces are reserved near the park entrances; ask the gate attendant to direct you to these. You'll probably pay for parking at Church Street Station and downtown, but those accustomed to big-city rates will find Orlando parking a bargain—as little as $3 per day in many lots.

Radio stations... To get the theme from the It's a Small World ride out of your head, try one of these Orlando-area radio stations: **WOMX-FM 105.1** and **WMFG-FM 107.7** play "lite" rock favorites; **WUCF-FM 89.9** is a favorite of jazz fans; try **WHTQ-FM 96.5** for classic rock; **WMFE-FM 90.7** plays classical music; for country, dial into **WWKA-FM 92.3**; you can catch up on news and talk on **WTKS-FM 104.1**; and find out what the Magic are doing on the all-sports station **WQTM-AM 540**.

Smoking... Nearly all Orlando restaurants (including those at the theme parks) have designated smoking areas. At Walt Disney World and Universal Studios Florida, smoking policies are basically the same: Smoking is prohibited on all attractions, in all attraction waiting areas, and in all shops. Otherwise, guests are permitted to stroll around with butts in hand, so to speak.

Taxes... The state of Florida charges a 6 or 7 percent sales tax on all merchandise except "necessary" grocery items and medicine. (That means food items such as soda and ice cream are taxable.) The tax is added to the price marked on the merchandise. In addition to the sales tax, a 2- to 5-percent resort tax is added to hotel room rates.

Taxis... If you take a taxi, either use a metered cab or confirm the cost of the trip with the driver before beginning your trip. **Yellow Cab Company** (tel 407/422–4561) is Orlando's oldest, largest cab company, and offers metered rates.

Telephone... The area code for Orlando is 407. Pay phone calls cost 35 cents. (Note: You must dial the area code before making local calls.) For local telephone directory assistance, dial 411. For long-distance information, call 1/(area code)/555–1212. TDD users call 800/955–8771.

Time... Orlando is in the eastern time zone. For the correct time, call 407/646–3131.

Tipping... Gratuities are generally not included in restaurant or bar checks (unless you have a party of eight or more, when 15 percent is customarily added to the bill), but it pays to read the fine print, just in case. About 20 percent is typical at restaurants; taxi drivers get 15 percent; sky-caps and bellhops get $1 per bag for each time they carry it (or more, if it's huge).

Trains... AMTRAK offers direct service between Orlando and a number of cities, including New York, Washington, D.C., Philadelphia, Baltimore, and Los Angeles. Service from Chicago requires a change of trains in D.C. or New Orleans. For other cities and reservation information, call 800/USA–RAIL. The Orlando AMTRAK station is located one mile south of the city center at 1400 Sligh Boulevard (tel 407/843–7611). The Auto Train, an overnight express, allows passengers to avoid treacherous I-95 and carries passengers and their cars between Sanford, Florida (near Orlando), and Lorton, Virginia (outside of Washington, D.C.). Plan to be a little flexible on scheduling, and make sure they know if you have a mini-van or S.U.V. as space is limited.

Travelers with disabilities... Since much of Orlando's construction is fairly new, accessibility is generally good for travelers with special needs. Both Universal and Walt Disney World offer special **guidebooks** for disabled guests with tips on getting around. The two parks also provide complimentary **audiotapes and portable tape players** for vision-impaired guests, featuring guided tours of each park, as well as **TDD** (Telecommunications Device for the Deaf) and **studio scripts** for the hearing impaired (check with the Guest Services offices at Universal and Disney). At the rides, special entrances are available for nonambulatory guests, who may use them with their parties; guests can ride through many attractions without leaving their wheelchairs. In addition, the parks provide close-up parking for the disabled. Finally, at Universal, special discounts are offered to guests who may be physically unable to fully experience the studio attraction. (Discounts are awarded at the discretion of Guest Services personnel.)

TV stations... Virtually every hotel and resort has cable, so CNN won't be hard to track down (not to mention The Disney Channel). Local TV stations include **WOFL-TV 35,** the FOX affiliate; **WKMG-TV 6,** the CBS affiliate; **WESH-TV 2,** the NBC affiliate; **WFTV-9,** the ABC affiliate; and **WMFE-TV 24,** the local PBS station.

Visitor information... The Orlando/Orange County Convention and Visitors Bureau staffs an **Official Visi-**

tor Center at 8723 International Drive, suite 101 (tel 407/363–5872, 800/551–0181), that is open daily from 8am to 7pm. The Orlando CVB also has a website that allows Internet browsers to get up-to-the-minute info before leaving home, via **http://www.go2orlando.com.** Subscribers to America Online can access Orlando CVB information and Destination Florida info through the keyword **Visit Orlando.** To get your facts the old-fashioned way, you can call or write ahead. For information on Winter Park, contact the **Winter Park Chamber of Commerce** (tel 407/644–8281). For information on Kissimmee/St. Cloud, call the **Kissimmee/St. Cloud Convention and Visitors Bureau** (tel 407/847–5000, 800/327–9159).

238